Footprints of God

A Narrative Theology of Mission

CHARLES VAN ENGEN, NANCY THOMAS
AND ROBERT GALLAGHER
EDITORS

MARC

A division of World Vision
800 West Chestnut Avenue, Monrovia, California 91016-3198 USA

ISBN 1-887983-14-7

Published by MARC, a division of World Vision, 800 W. Chestnut Avenue, Monrovia, California 91016-3198, U.S.A.

Printed in the United States of America. Editor and typesetter: Joan Weber Laflamme. Cover design: J. Nils Lindstrom.

Contents

Foreword   ix
    GERALD H. ANDERSON

Preface   xi
    NANCY THOMAS

Introduction: Mission *of*, *in* and *on* the Way   xvii
    CHARLES VAN ENGEN

Part I
MISSION *OF* THE WAY

1   **Conversion process**   5
    James E. Loder in missiological perspective
    HAROLD R. THOMAS

2   **Karl Barth and a missiology of preaching**   19
    DAE RYEONG KIM

3   **Jakób Jocz**   32
    God's square peg
    STUART DAUERMANN

4   **David Seamands**   42
    A missiology of healing grace
    HITOMI KISHI GRAY

5   **E. Stanley Jones**   52
    Doing theology in a pluralistic context
    BOBBY BOSE

6   **Charles H. Kraft**   62
    Ethnotheology in mission
    LEVI T. DE CARVALHO

Part II
MISSION *IN* THE WAY

7   **Ernesto Cardenal**   79
     Poet and priest
         NANCY J. THOMAS

8   **A missiological perspective on suffering**   92
         YOUNG KEE LEE

9   **Jürgen Moltmann and a missiology of hope**   103
     Embracing the tensions
         MARY THIESSEN NATION

10   **Mother Teresa**   114
     To suffer with joy
         JUDE TIERSMA WATSON

11   **Who raises the child when there is no village?**   124
     Restoring Community in African Cities
         STANLEY MUTUNGA

12   **No longer aliens**   136
     A theology of mission from the U.S. Hispanic periphery
         DANIEL A. RODRIGUEZ

Part III
MISSION *ON* THE WAY

13   **Max Warren**   153
     The mission executive as missiologist
         IAN C. H. PRESCOTT

14   **David Lim**   164
     A transformation missiology for Asian contexts
         SANTOS YAO

15   **Charles Kraft's and Paul Hiebert's approaches
     to worldview**   174
     "Why don't you build a Christian shrine?"
         YOSHIYUKI BILLY NISHIOKA

16 **Feminism and missiology** 187
A Korean woman's perspective
BOKYOUNG PARK

17 **The forgotten factor** 199
*The Holy Spirit and mission in Protestant missiological
writings from 1945–95*
ROBERT L. GALLAGHER

18 **Missiology and the Internet** 215
Facing the faceless frontier
SHAWN B. REDFORD

Conclusion: Following the footprints of God 225
The contribution of narrative to mission theology
NANCY THOMAS

Foreword

GERALD H. ANDERSON

Christians are called to be Great Commission followers of Jesus, dedicated to his mission. That mission is to give witness—in word and deed—to the whole gospel in the whole world. In terms of Matthew 28:19–20, it means discipling, baptizing and teaching all that Jesus commanded, to everyone, everywhere.

Contrary to much public perception—or misperception—the global Christian movement is more vital and vigorous today than ever before in history, by almost any measure. This vitality is especially pronounced in the churches of the Southern hemisphere, but it is true also among many churches in the new missionary situation in North America. As a historian, I would say that the most exciting chapter in church history is the chapter presently being written. Pope John Paul II, in his 1991 encyclical *Redemptoris Missio (The Mission of the Redeemer)*, envisioned on the eve of the third millennium "the dawning of a new missionary age," with God "preparing a great springtime for Christianity."

The challenge today is to help pastors and churches understand what it means to be in mission in our secularized societies and in a new global context, to redefine and restate our ministry in terms of mission rather than maintenance of the church.

In the small Methodist church where I grew up in New Castle, Pennsylvania, a picture used to hang behind the pulpit. You could always see the picture as the minister was preaching (it was a good visual alternative in case the sermon wasn't helpful). It was William Holman Hunt's famous painting *The Light of the World*, which shows Jesus by night carrying a lantern and knocking at the door of a house. The traditional interpretation of this picture is taken from Jesus' own words, "Behold, I stand at the door and knock; if any one hears my voice and opens the door, I will come in to him and eat with him, and he with me" (Rev. 3:20, RSV). It is a great evangelistic text (although I never recall a pastor in my church mentioning the picture or the text). Today, thinking missiologically, I would interpret the painting somewhat differently: Christ is knocking on the door of the church and saying, "Come out! Come out and join me in reaching people who are struggling for meaning and survival in a world of sin and suffering and invite them to follow me."

Forty years ago I edited a book titled *The Theology of the Christian Mission*. In the foreword to that volume Lesslie Newbigin wrote, "Today the question of the theology of the Christian mission is a question that—whether recognized or not—knocks at the door of every congregation." Much has happened since then that needs to be taken into account, in both the context and the content of mission. But the question at the door of every congregation is still about mission theology, and it is more urgent today because churches face a rampant, radical relativism that challenges our congregations, our seminaries, and our theology, questioning the validity of Christian truth-claims and the mission of the church. What does it mean to be a church in mission in this situation, and what is the church's message?

This book—also about the theology of mission—deals with these issues. More specifically, it is designed to help Christians, especially pastors, as Charles Van Engen says, to think "theologically about mission and missiologically about theology." The genius of the book is that it uses biography and narratives of personal pilgrimage to shape and inform our missiology. Issues in mission theology are introduced and illustrated with the life and work of remarkable individuals—some well known, others not so well known—from many parts of the world. This puts flesh on the bones of theory and encourages an integrative process of missiological reflection.

Life in this world is like a desert wilderness where hordes of people are wandering around in confusion and deception, desperately trying to find the way out of their predicament. The "footprints of God" save us from being "lost." The footprints of God's mighty acts in salvation history indicate where we have come from and point to where we should be going—the kingdom of God. God sent Jesus Christ into the world to show us the Way. Christians are not lost people. As followers of Jesus, Christians are called to share the Good News that they have been found and saved by Jesus Christ, and to invite everyone to follow him. This book is about the Way of Jesus and the mission of people who follow him.

OVERSEAS MINISTRIES STUDY CENTER
NEW HAVEN, CONNECTICUT

Preface

NANCY THOMAS

Some people hike trails neatly carved on gentle slopes. Benches at measured intervals provide resting places, usually with a lovely view—waterfalls, rivers, distant mountains. These fine people bring their families, their dog, a picnic lunch—make a day of it. This provides good exercise in the open air and is relatively safe.

Others prefer uncharted wilderness. Equipped with machetes, snakebite kits and sheer determination, these hardy souls hack through the brush, creating the trail as they go. They get sweaty, tired, grouchy and, sometimes, lost. Paradoxically, they seem to have a lot of fun as they work together on the way. This type of wilderness hiking may take a long time. It is not safe. But the people willing to take the risk are the ones who discover new vistas and make new trails that others will follow.

I was a member of a group of doctoral students that began such a wilderness adventure. The site was not the Rockies or the Andes but came disguised as a simple seminar room on the campus of Fuller Theological Seminary. Under the inspiration of trail guide Charles Van Engen we gathered our experiences, expectations, questions, hopes and hassles, stuffed them along with our Bibles and a supply of strong coffee in our backpacks, and began looking for a place to enter the brush. We didn't know exactly where we were going or how we would get there, but we all had a sense that the adventure would be well worth the trouble. We were right.

Describing the terrain

The group was diverse—twenty-one men and four women whose countries of origin and places of ministry included Korea; the Philippines; India; the United States; Brazil; Australia; Japan; England; Malaysia; Kenya; the Netherlands; Nepal; Spain; Mexico; Canada; Bolivia; Papua,

New Guinea, Thailand; Russia; and the Jewish, Filipino, Japanese, Korean, African American and Hispanic communities of the greater Los Angeles area. All participants were doctoral students in the School of World Mission at Fuller Theological Seminary, working in the area of theology of mission. All of us were mission practitioners in our own right; together we represented over 335 years of service as missionaries, pastors, teachers, mission executives and church leaders.

During our first meeting Van Engen asked a series of questions that occupied us for two noisy weeks and set the tone of inquiry for the following fifteen months: "What is theology of mission? What is missiology? Who is a missiologist?" We began exploring issues of integration, the action/reflection balance, the "from above"/"from below" models, and the bringing together of text, ministry context, faith community and personal pilgrimage.

Van Engen then invited each of us to choose a person or issue related to our own doctoral program, investigate that person or issue using the integrative processes of theology of mission, and make a presentation to the group. One person would present each week, with time for interaction immediately following the presentation. This formed the pattern we followed through the ensuing school terms. Van Engen encouraged us not to critique the presentations but rather to interact with issues and ideas presented, each from the perspective of his or her own research and ministry context.

The range of topics presented was as broad as the group itself and covered areas normally considered part of the discipline (for example, church growth, worldview studies and pluralism), as well as areas outside the norm for missiology. It was interesting to note how many persons and issues not typically thought of as missiological were found to be important along the trail. For example, we dealt with theologians James Loder, Karl Barth and Jürgen Moltmann, with Mother Teresa (a missionary certainly, but a missiologist?), and with revolutionary Nicaraguan poet/priest Ernesto Cardenal. Nontraditional topics brought to the seminar included feminism, inner healing and the Internet. This highlighted the interdisciplinary nature of our enterprise.

We found we were learning not so much a set of new concepts, new information and new applications (although we did pick these up along the trail) as the process itself. We were growing in our ability to think and reflect missiologically.

Toward the end of our time together we were beginning to feel our stride. We had developed some new survival skills, could recognize many of the "plants" and "animals" along the trail, and were enjoying the benefits of sustained and invigorating exercise. At this point Van Engen suggested bringing our insights together into a sort of written trail guide that might encourage others wanting to grapple with wilderness issues of their own.

In other words, we began discussing the possibility of refining and gathering our presentations into a book on issues in mission theology. Van Engen invited Robert Gallagher and me to join him as general editors of this collection. Our group began extending our two-hour meetings into a third hour, inviting different writers from among the faculty to talk to us about writing and publishing in the field of missiology. Van Engen, C. Peter Wagner and Wilbert Shenk spoke from their personal experiences. I gave a seminar on cross-cultural principles of good writing, and we began the process of producing a book.

Writing the guidebook

Various steps in producing the book included writing the proposal, individual rewriting of initial class presentations, peer critique and extensive editing.

We decided our intended readers would be people concerned with connecting Bible, theology and ministry with the complexity and variety of contexts and issues facing Christians today. These readers would include pastors, students of missiology, missionaries, mission administrators and professors of mission. Our intention was to model the process of missiological reflection, showing the interaction of personal pilgrimage, Scripture, context and faith community. Our approach would be narrative, sharing our own stories, as well as showing how biography affected missiology in the lives of the people featured in our chapters. Using the guidelines of cross-cultural principles of good writing that I had presented to the group, we gave ourselves a few months to rewrite the chapters.

We then met once a week, considering one or two chapters in each session, keeping in mind our intended readers and the book's purpose. Discussions allowed chapter authors to move to a deeper understanding and sharper focusing of their chapters. These peer review sessions were among the most valuable parts of the process but were possible only with the foundation of the previous three terms of the seminar.

The editing team worked through three more school terms. Van Engen's address upon the occasion of his installation as Fuller Seminary's Arthur F. Glasser Professor of the Biblical Theology of Mission (re-presented in the introduction to this book) shaped our conceptualization of mission as "of, in and on the way." This conceptualization seemed to typify the mission theologizing process, and the book chapters flowed through the categories. "Of the Way" is the centering aspect, with Jesus Christ as the focus, motivation, means and goal of mission. "In the way" is the relational aspect, as mission occurs in specific contexts among real people. "On the way" is the directional aspect, as mission develops and moves forward to see the kingdom of God increasingly manifest.

Some observations from this end of the trail

The process we followed works. Initial questions we wrestled with in the seminar and the early presentations encouraged us to bring together our personal pilgrimages with the Scriptures and with the disciplines of missiology. Discussion, writing, reviewing, rewriting, editing and compiling stages encouraged the process. By these means, over time and in community, we grew in our ability to reflect missiologically and articulate results.

The best chapters have blood on their pages. Authors who grappled with real issues and willingly submitted their pain and insights to the community's scrutiny ultimately came up with strong contributions that will touch readers deeply. Personal investment, vulnerability, willingness to struggle and grow—these are ingredients of good missiological reflection and writing.

Community made the resulting reflection and articulation possible. Although we brought our personal issues and ministry contexts as individuals, we brought them to the group for interaction as the people of God. Partly because of this experience of missiological reflection in community, most of us would now ask, "Is there any other way?"

Culture plays a key role in the theologizing and writing process. Although all the non-Western writers have been influenced by Western education and Western academic writing styles, cultural differences are manifest throughout the book in the different approaches. Some community members exhibited a certain reticence in disclosing personal information. The group respected this reticence, even as we encouraged one another to bring issues of personal pilgrimage to bear on the theologizing process.

Finally, we must acknowledge the role Charles Van Engen played. Without his leadership, none of this would have happened. Yet his leadership was "from below," and "of, in and on the way," to use the seminar's terminology. He was a facilitator, an encourager, one who had hiked similar wilderness areas yet was on this particular trek alongside the rest of us, also for the first time.

Although seminar members have gone their separate ways, we've all realized this wilderness adventure has no ending. Nor would we want it to end. As we gained familiarity with the terrain, as we forged a trail, we discovered God's footprints. We saw that God had gone before us and been with us all along. As persons committed to God's mission as revealed in Scripture, as persons committed to serving among particular peoples in specific contexts, we will continue to seek God's footprints. As missiologists, we are learning to see those footprints in unexpected places. The hike will continue. God goes before.

We invite our readers to join us in following the footprints of God.

Mission *of, in* and *on* the Way

CHARLES VAN ENGEN

I was not yet 15. I was born in Mexico and raised of missionary parents as a Dutch Mexican-American. At that time there were few good secondary schools in our part of Mexico, so my parents decided to send me to a Christian high school in North Carolina, USA. Thus we found ourselves in Mexico City. I was to ride with people I barely knew, travel a week to a school I had never seen, and live in an area of the United States where I had never been.

I will not forget the morning when my parents said goodbye to me. Standing beside the old brown carry-all van in which I was to ride, with a family of strangers waiting for me to get in, my father gave me a hug—then shook my hand and looked into my eyes.

I had been the family troublemaker, the middle child who grew up restless, rebellious, ornery, mischievous—the problem child. In desperation, maybe in hope and with prayer, since I was such a rascal, my father shook my hand, saying, "I have taught you all I can. Now it is up to you."

My pilgrimage *of, in* and *on* the Way had begun. Thirty-four years have passed since that day—and I am still on a journey of faith. There were times in college when I walked far from the lordship and presence of the One who is the Way. There have been moments when I have walked in the way, beside people in the United States, in Mexico, in the Netherlands, whose patient joy in the midst of pain and suffering have dramatically changed me—including 80,000 Guatemalan refugees I and others were asked to keep alive for several years. And the forty-week doctoral seminar from which this book flows has been for me another

---

The substance of this chapter was originally delivered at Charles Van Engen's installation in the Arthur F. Glasser Chair of Biblical Theology of Mission in the School of World Mission, Fuller Theological Seminary, May 15, 1996.

step *on* the way in my pilgrimage of seeking to understand more deeply what is involved in our participating in the mission of Jesus. I have learned so very much from the participants of this seminar whose chapters follow.

The book you are about to read involves a deep search together on the part of a group of committed Christians for appropriate ways to reflect and act in Christ's mission—ways that will positively contribute to mobilizing the church in participating in Jesus' mission of transforming people and structures in God's world. This book flows from our search to understand what is theology of mission, from our desire to learn how to think theologically about mission and how to reflect missiologically about theology.

Theology of mission was established as a discipline in 1961 by Gerald Anderson with the publication of *The Theology of the Christian Mission*, which Anderson edited.[1] Since this book seeks to illustrate what theology of mission is, and how it does its reflection, it seems appropriate that I offer the reader a brief description of the discipline and reflect on how it relates to the persons and issues presented in the chapters that follow. I define biblical theology of mission as a multidisciplinary field that reads the Bible with missiological eyes and, based on that reading, continually reexamines, reevaluates and redirects the church's participation in God's mission in God's world.

The thesis of this introduction provides the organizational framework for this book. It is that biblical theology of mission (1) must be centered in Jesus Christ—mission *of the Way*; (2) happens among the peoples and cultures of our world—mission *in the way*; and (3) moves forward over time in the faith-pilgrimage of God's people, as they anticipate Christ's present and coming kingdom—mission *on the way*.

I will locate my reflection in the Gospel of Luke, chapter 9. Earlier, in Luke 4, Jesus draws from Isaiah to define his messianic mission as preaching the Good News to the poor, declaring freedom for the prisoners, and proclaiming the year of the Lord's favor. Following this, in Luke 9, Jesus describes the mission of his disciples: mission *of* the Way, *in* the way, and *on* the way.

The gospel story is mission *of* the Way

Our mission is centered in Jesus Christ, who is the Way. The most important issue in Luke 9 is the matter of who Jesus is. As the chapter opens, Jesus sends out the Twelve and they cause such an uproar that

Herod thinks Jesus is John the Baptist come back to life. "Who is this?" Herod asks. Upon their return, Jesus asks the disciples who the crowds say he is, and Peter confesses, "The Messiah of God." Later Jesus is transfigured and the divine voice says, "This is my Son, my chosen; listen to him!" Then in 10:1 Jesus sends the Seventy[2] on the Gentile mission.[3] The point is unmistakable. The mission of the disciples derives from Jesus' mission. Jesus is the Way.[4]

Our mission is none other, neither more nor less, than participation in Jesus' mission. To say it negatively, when it is not Christ's mission, it may be colonial expansion, church extension, proselytism or social services—but it is not mission. Our mission is biblical mission only when it is centered in Jesus Christ. Our mission is *of* the Way.

Arthur Glasser has said, "The gospel has at its heart the affirmation that Jesus Christ alone is Lord and that he offers to enter the lives of all who come to him in repentance and faith" (Glasser 1984, 726).[5]

So missiology needs theology.[6] The missiologist needs theology's tools of the biblical languages and biblical studies, understanding of ancient biblical cultures, and history of the church's reading of Scripture down through the centuries. Theology can help missiologists avoid the pitfalls and theological dead-ends that the church has learned to recognize.[7] This is what David Bosch called "critical hermeneutics" (1991, 23–24).

In a similar way missiology needs Christian psychology, sociology and anthropology to help the missiologist better understand what happens personally, socially and culturally when persons confess their faith and dedicate their lives to the lordship of Jesus Christ. Precisely what is going on in the transformation of the psycho-emotional and relational reality of those who come to faith in Jesus Christ? What is happening psychologically when a missionary crosses cultures, learns a new language, internalizes entirely new ways of thinking, and expresses faith in new categories?

In September 1995 I was at Tokyo Christian University. After a morning chapel a young Japanese woman came up to tell me her story. Two years before she had wanted to become a Christian, but her parents would not let her convert. So she made arrangements for an international study leave in Australia, where she promptly began attending church and accepted Jesus Christ. With tears in her eyes and pain in her voice she told me how it had been several months now since she had returned to Japan, and her parents were adamantly opposed to her being a Christian. "They are afraid I'll never marry," she told me. But then, her eyes glistening, she said to me, "But I have met Jesus and I know he is God—my Savior—he loves me and I love him. I would not trade that for the world! I want to serve Jesus and evangelize Japan—including my parents." This young woman understood that her mission is mission *of* the Way—her mission flows from her discipleship in following Jesus, the Way.

The gospel story is mission *in* the way

Our mission happens among the peoples and cultures of our world. The gospel story is mission in the street. When we join Jesus as his disciples, he takes us by the hand and leads us to the cities and into the valleys among the people, in compassionate search for their transformation.

In Luke 9:6 Luke points out that the *crowds* are following Jesus, seeking to hear his teaching and receive his healing. In verse 15 Jesus and his disciples feed the people. Later, although Peter wants to stay up on the mountain of transfiguration, Jesus descends to encounter again the "crowd" (verses 37, 38)—and to heal a man's only child. This incarnational identification with the poor, sick, powerless and oppressed is the heart of Jesus' mission. Disciples of Jesus choose to exist for the sake of the world.[8]

Orlando Costas spoke of our meeting "Christ outside the gate." Only as we walk in the here and now of suffering humanity can we truly be encountered by Jesus Christ. John Mackay spoke of the difference of perspective between the Balcony and the Road:

> By the Balcony, I do not mean the gallery of a church or theater. I mean that little platform in wood or stone that protrudes from the upper window of a Spanish home. There the family may gather of an evening to gaze spectator-wise upon the street beneath, or at the sunset or the stars beyond. The Balcony thus conceived is a classical standpoint, and so the symbol of the perfect spectator, for whom life and the universe are permanent objects of study and contemplation. . . . By the Road I mean the place where life is intensely lived, where thought has its birth in conflict and concern, where choices are made and decisions are carried out. It is the place of action, of pilgrimage . . . where concern is never absent from the wayfarer's heart (Mackay 1943, 27–30).

A few years ago a member of my church received a letter from Sue, an American missionary in Daba, Kenya. Sue and her husband had been visiting a town in Kenya, and Sue wrote:

About 10:00 P.M. we were ready to head home when Jare, the father of the 4–month-old treated earlier for pneumonia, came up trembling. He said, "I think my little girl is dying. Can you come?" I walked with Jare toward his home. He said, "She was rolling her eyes back in her head and not respond-ing when I left—I don't know if she'll be alive when we get there." I asked if I could pray with him as we walked through the darkness under the brilliant stars toward his home. I prayed for a miracle of healing in Jesus' name. There was silence. I felt convicted to say more as I wondered what it meant to Jare to have me pray in Jesus' name. I explained to him that the Bible teaches that anything we ask of the Father in Jesus' name will be heard, and that prayer is honored be-cause of Jesus. We were nearing the hut and we could hear coughing, so she was still alive. As we walked in we were sur-prised to see her looking pretty good; [she was] awake, alert and with just slightly labored breathing. The mother started right in explaining that the little girl had been bad, but had dramatically improved over the last 15 minutes or so. Jare was thrilled and I began an immediate prayer, praising God for revealing the power of Jesus. I explained about our prayer to the mother. Both she and Jare were silent . . . and so more seeds are planted.[9]

This is mission *in* the way.

Theology needs missiology in order to find its grounding *in* the way. To do theology in a detached, supposedly "objective" manner (from the Balcony) is to contribute to the death of the church.[10] As Johannes Blauw said, "There is no other church than the church sent into the world, and there is no other mission than that of the church of Christ" (1962, 121).

If the local congregation of disciples of Jesus is in fact what Lesslie Newbigin has termed "the hermeneutic of the gospel" (1989, 232) for the world, then theological reflection must first and foremost be missionally directed, and contextually located. Ministry formation needs to be formation *in and for mission*. In Karl Barth's words, it means "being for the world" (1958, 762–63).

Without mission, theological education may be a professional finish-ing school or an entryway to graduate school, or a department of reli-gious studies, but it is *not* formation for the manifold ministries of Christ and his church among people in the world.

Biblical theology of mission reminds us that Christians in psychology, sociology and anthropology should seek not merely *humanization* but rather conversion to a *new* humanity in Jesus Christ. Christian psychology needs missiology to remember that its ultimate purpose must be essentially missiological, seeking conversion and transformation by the power of the Holy Spirit in the womb of the church, offered to the world. Biblical theology of mission is unapologetically *contextual*.

The gospel story is mission *on* the way

Mission moves forward over time in the faith-pilgrimage of God's people as they anticipate Christ's present and coming kingdom. When we join Jesus our Lord *in* the way, we discover that we are in the presence of the King, we are now part of his rule, which is *on* the way to the present and coming kingdom of God.

Mission on the way is at the heart of Luke 9. This chapter is narrative theology at its best, set in the context of a journey on the way to Jerusalem. Chapter 9 begins with Jesus sending the Twelve to preach the gospel of the kingdom and heal. Later Jesus sets out for Jerusalem by way of a town in Samaria. Then, in verse 57, they are walking along the road and Jesus says, "Follow me. . . . No one who puts a hand to the plow and looks back is fit for of the kingdom of God" (9:59, 62). The kingdom of God is mentioned five times in this chapter.

You see, Jesus was *on the way* not only to Jerusalem but to the Cross, Resurrection, Ascension and Second Coming. In Acts the journey will continue through Jesus' disciples, who will go on to Asia, Rome and throughout the then-known world. Following Acts, the church would extend the knowledge of the King until today the church covers the entire globe, speaks more languages, represents more cultures, and has more resources than anyone ever imagined.

This kingdom perspective offers at least four major contributions to missiology. First, the kingdom of God concept broadens missiological reflection beyond a predominantly individualized and vertical understanding of salvation to a holistic view of the interaction of church and world.

Second, kingdom-of-God missiology breaks the impasse between evangelism and social action that has plagued evangelicals.

Third, kingdom-of-God missiology creates the possibility of new conversation among evangelicals, representatives of the conciliar movement, Roman Catholics, Orthodox, Pentecostals and Charismatics.

Fourth, the viewpoint of the kingdom of God has profound social and political implications that challenge all governments, all forms of racism, all social structures that would seek to deify themselves.

Missiology needs biblical theology of mission to keep it from becoming mission studies, or a technical skills center, or a location for interfaith dialogue, or a meeting place for global churchly conversation. Arthur Glasser says, "There is but one acid test that should be applied to all activities that claim to represent obedience in mission. Do they or do they not produce disciples of Jesus Christ?" (1974, 8). Here Glasser was echoing Donald McGavran's conviction, on which McGavran founded Fuller Theological Seminary's School of World Mission. McGavran understood mission "as an enterprise devoted to proclaiming the good news of Jesus Christ, and to persuading men and women to become his disciples and responsible members of his church" (1990, 23–24). McGavran (1989) believed this was the basis on which ministry formation should be evaluated.

Biblical theology of mission is a servant to missiology, theology and the social sciences as each and all of them are profoundly affected by the question of *purpose*—that is, by the reality of the kingdom of God. As 1 Peter 2 points out, kingdom mission is pilgrim mission. Johannes Verkuyl says,

> Missiology may never become a substitute for action and participation. . . . If study does not lead to participation, whether at home or abroad, missiology has lost her humble calling. . . . Any good missiology is also a *missiologia viatorum*—"pilgrim missiology" (1978, 6, 18).

This means that the church exists for mission "in the power of the Spirit," using Jürgen Moltmann's (1977) phrase. It means that everything the church does must intentionally be directed in mission toward the world, *on the way* to the present and coming kingdom.

Mission studies should always seek to contribute to crossing barriers in missional action among people with a view to their coming to faith in Jesus Christ. In mission theology we must avoid becoming overly "church-centric," academy-focused or professionally oriented. As disciples of Jesus, we walk with him *in* the way, *on* the way to the present and coming kingdom of God.

A number of significant challenges face us in biblical theology of mission *on the way*. Space allows me to list only some of them. Into the next century biblical theology of mission will involve at least the following:

Reaffirming the church's motivation for mission, which is declining in the West and is rising in Asia, Africa and Latin America.

Reexamining the relation of Bible and mission as churches in many cultures read the same Bible and serve the same Lord.

Rethinking the church's role in nation-building, as life seems to get cheaper and more precarious all over the world, especially in cities.

Reevaluating the way Christians in the world church partner together for world evangelization.

Reconceptualizing Christian response to the resurgence of world religions and folk religious movements.

Renewing the invaluable and essential contribution that women have made in missiological action, reflection and theory.

Reshaping the forms, processes and methods by which we prepare and equip women and men for ministry and mission, both in their own culture and cross-culturally as world Christians.

Refocusing the ministry of church members and local congregations toward mission in God's world.[11]

Conclusion

I am still *on the way*, seeking to discover more completely how my relationship with Jesus Christ transforms my walk among the people for whom Jesus gave his life. I am beginning to learn that my own—and every missiologist's—personal faith-pilgrimage profoundly influences our perspective of, and participation in, the mission of the Messiah. This is a road to Emmaus (Luke 24:13–35), which involves a deep walk of discovery, an "inward-outward" journey (using Henri Nouwen's term), a pilgrimage of discipleship that calls the church to participate in Jesus' mission.

The reader will, I believe, be affected, transformed, encouraged and guided by the narratives that follow, stories of reflection that involve mission *of*, *in* and *on* the way.

When my father shook my hand and said, "Now it is up to you," he was telling me something very profound. As disciples of Jesus our pilgrimage in mission is "up to us" to walk with, learn from, act out and reflect on, the mission of Jesus who is himself the Way. Dad had, in fact, taught me "all he could"—and all he taught me has informed my journey of discovery, my pilgrimage in Christ Jesus, whose mission as portrayed in Luke 9 is mission *of*, *in* and *on* the way. What I have learned is that Jesus has not finished teaching me all that *he* can!

Biblical theology of mission, then, needs to be biblically informed, contextually appropriate and kingdom-directed missional action. The intimate connection of reflection with action is essential for missiology.

And action-reflection together must be critiqued, encompassed and directed by the already/not-yet kingdom of God.

In the chapters that follow the reader will find a marvelous collection of windows through which to see more clearly how Jesus' mission works through the lives of the disciples of Jesus. Each chapter involves a personal narrative that is also a glimpse of the whole world. Each story offers a unique perspective on how mission is *of* the Way, *in* the way and *on* the way.

The story of God's dealings with humankind is not finished. In a profound sense the missionary acts of the Holy Spirit through the church to the world are still going on—until Jesus Christ comes again. Biblical theology of mission can help us explore more deeply the wonderful mystery, in the words of the apostle Paul, "that through the gospel the Gentiles are heirs together with Israel, members together of one body, and sharers together in the promise in Christ Jesus" (Eph. 3:6, NIV).

The narrative continues in this interim time between Christ's ascension and his return. The gospel story calls for biblical theology of mission to be centered in Jesus Christ (mission *of* the Way), to happen among the peoples and cultures of our world (mission *in* the way), and to move forward over time as God's people continue to anticipate Christ's present and coming kingdom (mission *on* the way). This is the story of *God's* mission—and the chapters that follow intend to show how we may continue to be part of that story!

Notes

[1] Gerald H. Anderson, ed., *The Theology of the Christian Mission* (New York: McGraw-Hill, 1961). In *A Concise Dictionary of the Christian World Mission* Gerald Anderson defined theology of mission as an enterprise that is "concerned with the basic presuppositions and underlying principles that determine, from the standpoint of the Christian faith, the motives, message, methods, strategy and goals of the Christian world mission" (Neill, Anderson and Goodwin 1971, 594).

[2] I follow Arthur Glasser here in opting for 70 rather than 72 as the number sent. The number 70 is reminiscent of the number of elders who served Moses (Num. 6:11, 16, 17); the number of the Sanhedrin who served Jewry in the New Testament times; and now the number of those who serve Jesus the Messiah.

[3] The entire chapter has to do with mission, beginning with Jesus' sending the Twelve on their first missionary journey. Then chapter 10 begins with Jesus' sending the Seventy. As the Twelve are sent to the towns and villages of Galilee at the end of Jesus' Galilean ministry, so the Seventy are sent ahead of Jesus to "every town and place where he was about to go" (10:1), This marks the beginning of the Gentile mission by the disciples of Jesus, a matter to which Jesus

alludes when he says in 10:13–14, "Woe to you, Chorazin! Woe to you, Bethsaida [towns in Galilee]! For if the deeds of power done in you had been done in Tyre and Sidon [Gentile towns in Phoenicia, north of Galilee], they would have repented long ago. . . . But at the judgment it will be more tolerable for Tyre and Sidon than for you."

⁴ John would later record Jesus' words, "I am the way, and the truth and the life" (John 14:6). And in Acts, the disciples would come to be known as those who belonged to "the Way" (Acts 9:2; 19:9, 23; 24:14).

⁵ In another place Glasser says, "In recent years evangelicals have become increasingly concerned to become more comprehensively biblical in their understanding and performance of the Christian mission. . . . They are determined as never before to keep his redemptive work central, for by his substitutionary death and bodily resurrection he alone provides access for sinful human beings into the presence and fellowship of God" (Glasser 1985, 9).

⁶ "The entire theme of ministry in the New Testament is bound to the person of Jesus Christ as the decisive eschatological event of God's reconciling Word," says Carl Braaten of the Lutheran School of Theology in Chicago. "Christ alone is the unity in, with, and under the pluriformity of ministries that arose in primitive Christianity. Ministry is Christocentric in all the New Testament writings. . . . If there is any authority in the church, that authority can be none other than Jesus Christ, as the authority is mediated through those whom he commissioned to be his ambassadors" (1985, 123–24).

Biblical theology of mission is *theology* because fundamentally it involves reflection about God. It seeks to understand God's mission, God's intentions and purposes in the Word, and God's use of human instruments.

Twenty-five years ago Gerald Anderson defined theology of mission as an enterprise that is "concerned with the basic presuppositions and underlying principles which determine, from the standpoint of the Christian faith, the motives, message, methods, strategy and goals of the Christian world mission" (Neill, Anderson and Goodwin 1971, 594). Within this larger enterprise biblical theology of mission looks to Scripture for the basis on which to question, define, guide and evaluate the missionary enterprise. This is what David Bosch called "critical hermeneutics" (1991, 23–24).

⁷ Missiologists need to stay close to Jesus their Lord, both personally and spiritually—as well as intellectually and theoretically. The Bible is quite clear in its warnings about true and false prophets (as for example in Num. 11:24–30; 12:6–8; Deut. 13:1–5; 18:14–22; 23:4–5; 1 Sam. 3:7, 21; 10:5–7; Ezek. 13:1–9; and in Paul's injunctions about not accepting a "different gospel" other than the one of the grace of Jesus Christ, Gal. 1:6; and also in 2 Pet. 2:15; Jude 1. Amid multiple cultures around the world the missiologist must be concerned about *truth*, not merely tolerance. Without a center in Jesus Christ, multiculturalism and globalism become balkanization, isolation and meaningless plurality. Only in Jesus the Lord may the church today and tomorrow find its true mission and purpose.

⁸ So Jesus is recorded by Matthew as saying, "Truly I tell you, just as you did it to one of the least of these who are members of my family, you did it to me" (Matt. 25:40).

⁹ Letter from Roger and Sue Scheenstra to Jill Fredricks, Easter Sunday, 1996.

¹⁰In the words of John Stott, "The church cannot be understood rightly except in a perspective which is at once missionary and eschatological" (1971, 17).

¹¹Another way to list these issues:

Motivation for Mission. Lately, there has been a dramatic decrease in the amount of money and energy that congregations in North America devote to world evangelization. Paul McKaughan, of the Evangelical Fellowship of Mission Agencies (EFMA), has stated, "I feel that without massive reordering of the U.S. missionary enterprise and a dynamic movement of the Spirit of God renewing His church in the U.S., the structures and industry which we represent will in the not too distant future, appear analogous to an abandoned ship buried by the tides on a sandy seashore with only their weather-beaten ribs as visible testimony to far better and more useful days." This means that we need renewal in terms of spirituality and mission as well,

Bible and Mission. Hermeneutics will continue to call for our attention, especially now that this involves a world church representing hundreds of cultures, reading together the Bible, each with different glasses—but all seeking to follow the same Jesus.

The Church's Role in Nation-Building. How can the church stand unequivocally for the sanctity of human life? This calls for careful biblical rethinking concerning the "powers," be they politics and economics, the unseen world of the demonic, or tribalism, ethnocentrism or racism. This matter is especially urgent in the cities of our world.

The World Church. Over 60 percent of world Christianity is now to be found in Africa, Asia and Latin America; there are now as many full-time cross-cultural missionaries being sent from there as from Europe and North America. How do we partner with Christians from many contexts, learning from their unique perspectives and participating *together* in Jesus' mission?

Other Religions. Everywhere in the world the church is now one faith in a marketplace of multiple religious affiliations. Biblical theology of mission will need to wrestle more deeply than it has with its response to other religions.

Women in Mission. The beginning of mission-sending in North America and the origins of many churches in the Two-Thirds World were intimately tied to the missionary vision and commitment of women. In North America much of this was lost after the 1930s. Biblical theology of mission could be immeasurably enriched through the contribution of women.

The Mission of the Local Congregation. In this postmodern world the church must begin to think globally and act locally. The mission of the local congregation in every place needs to be clarified. We must see the local church as itself a primary agent of mission.

References

Barth, Karl. 1958. *Church Dogmatics.* Vol. 4.3.2. Edinburgh: T & T Clark.

———. 1965. *The German Church Conflict: Ecumenical Studies in History.* Richmond, Va.: John Knox.

Berkhof, Hendrikus. 1985. *Introduction to the Study of Dogmatics*. Grand Rapids, Mich.: Eerdmans.

Blauw, Johannes. 1962. *The Missionary Nature of the Church*. Grand Rapids, Mich.: Eerdmans.

Bosch, David. 1991. *Transforming Mission: Paradigm Shifts in Theology of Mission*. Maryknoll, N.Y.: Orbis Books.

Braaten, Carl. 1985. *The Apostolic Imperative: The Nature and Aim of the Church's Mission and Ministry*. Minneapolis: Augsburg.

Costas. Orlando. 1988. *Christ Outside the Gate*. Maryknoll, N.Y.: Orbis Books.

Glasser, Arthur. 1984. "Missiology." In *Evangelical Dictionary of Theology*, edited by Walter A. Elwell, 726. Grand Rapids, Mich.: Baker.

———. 1985. "Foreword to the American Edition." *The Mission of the Church in the World*, edited by Roger Hedlund. Grand Rapids, Mich.: Baker.

———. 1989. "Kingdom and Mission." Pasadena, Calif.: Fuller Theological Seminary.

———. 1974. "What Is 'Mission' Today? Two Views." In *Mission Trends No. 1*, edited by Gerald H. Anderson and Thomas F. Stransky. Grand Rapids, Mich.: Eerdmans.

Mackay, John. 1943. *A Preface to Christian Theology*. New York: Macmillan.

McGavran, Donald. 1988. *Effective Evangelism: A Theological Mandate*. Phillipsburgh, N.J.: Presbyterian and Reformed.

———. 1989. "Are Seminaries Shortchanging Evangelism?" *Missions Tomorrow* (Spring/Summer), 22–26. (This article is excerpted from McGavran 1988.)

———. 1990 <1970>. *Understanding Church Growth*. Grand Rapids, Mich.: Eerdmans.

Moltmann, Jürgen. 1977. *The Church in the Power of the Spirit*. New York: Harper & Row.

Neill, Stephen, Gerald H. Anderson, and John Goodwin, eds. 1971. *A Concise Dictionary of the Christian World Mission*. London: Lutterworth.

Newbigin, Lesslie. 1989. *The Gospel in a Pluralist Society*. Grand Rapids, Mich.: Eerdmans.

Stott, John. 1971. *One People*. Downers Grove, Ill.: InterVarsity Press.

Van Engen, Charles. 1991. *God's Missionary People*. Grand Rapids, Mich.: Baker.

MISSION *OF* THE WAY

It is proper that this volume begin with a section that views Christian mission as centered in Jesus Christ, who is the Way. The church's mission is participation in Jesus' mission and is biblical only when focused on him. In other words, mission flows from our discipleship in following Jesus and his mission. Biblical theology of mission needs to be biblically informed and centered in Jesus Christ. The chapters in this section highlight mission as centering in Jesus Christ and are examples of mission *of* the Way.

Hal Thomas begins with a story focusing on the power of God transforming an Aymara family. Through a demonstration of God's healing power to the grandmother, the whole family changed allegiance from their ancient gods to the living God. Thomas, a missionary to the Aymara of Bolivia, uses James Loder's "transforming moment" as a model for missiological research in conversion. Loder's theory allows us to explain in theological and psychological terms the transformational work of Christ.

Dae Ryeong Kim's chapter centers on Karl Barth's ideas of Christian mission. As a Korean missionary to Russia, Kim shows Barth as a pastor who believes that effective preaching is missionary communication, both to the nations and to nominal Christians in the West. The German theologian views the church as a mission community and theology as a servant to the evangelistic proclamation of the gospel. Barth is very aware of the need for the Bible to be relevant to the present generation. Kim suggests that this is accomplished as the missionary preacher becomes one with the people.

The life of Jakób Jocz is sketched against the turbulent years of pre-Nazi Europe by Beverly Hills messianic rabbi Stuart Dauermann. Jocz's calling from God to evangelize his fellow Jew is frustratingly diverted to Anglican parish work in England and then in Canada, where his energies turn to writing. His life is portrayed as a lack of mission focus, since he often spoke about the Jewish people rather than about the Messiah to the Jews. Dauermann holds up Jocz's life as a warning to missionaries and mission agencies, calling them to pay heed to God's unique call upon each of his servants.

David Seamands's writings, centering on Christ and the cross, have brought healing grace to Hitomi Kishi Gray. This Japanese national, who is currently serving international students in Los Angeles, recognizes that God seeks intimacy with us in our brokenness. Seamands offers a way in

Christ to become whole. In the process of receiving God's healing grace through Christ, the pilgrim becomes God's missionary agent to minister healing to others. This transformation leads to mission *of* the Way.

Bobby Bose, a Bengali from India, writes from a deep sense of struggle to proclaim Christ in a pluralistic setting. He discovers a model in the methods and theology of E. Stanley Jones. As a United Methodist missionary evangelist to India and the world, Jones developed a "round table" methodology, hosting interreligious conferences for sharing the integration of personal faith and experience. His focus on the living person of Jesus Christ led to his emphasis on Reality, rather than on religion. Bose sees Jones's methodology of the interrelation of biblical text, Christian experience and the church, all focused on Christ, as an appropriate approach to religious pluralism.

How to communicate effectively the gospel of Christ to the Terena people of Brazil? Out of frustration, Levi DeCarvalho turned to the writings of Chuck Kraft for answers and found anthropology combined with theological insight. The Brazilian missionary attempts to understand the worldview of the Terena community and the individualistic missionary, and to bridge the gap between the two. By combining the anthropology of the people with Christian theology, De Carvalho is attempting to produce a Christian ethnotheology that enhances the opportunity for the Terena to pledge full allegiance to Christ.

Robert L. Gallagher

Conversion process

James E. Loder in missiological perspective

Harold R. Thomas

I listened as Pedro told me the story of his conversion. Pedro lived on the high Andean plains of Bolivia, between Lake Titicaca and the city of La Paz, a member of a three-generation family. His was a traditional Aymara peasant community, with its blend of beliefs and customs, rooted in pre-Columbian origins, and shaped through nearly five centuries of Spanish conquest and systematic exploitation.

"One day," Pedro recounted, "my grandmother became ill, and no one, not even the curers, could heal her. She had been sick for three months when, one market day, she walked to the town of Tambillo. A friend saw her there and gave her a book, saying it contained many things about salvation and could help her. My grandmother took the book, thinking it was about natural medicine. Upon returning to our community, she showed the book to a person who could read. When she learned that it was a Bible of the evangelicals, she determined to find the evangelicals. She returned to Tambillo and found the evangelicals' chapel. The congregation welcomed her, listened to her story, cried with her, and made plans to visit us that week.

Harold R. Thomas served with the Friends Church in Bolivia (INELA) from 1972 to 1989 among the Aymara people. His work included pastoral training, rural and urban church planting, and social development projects. Thomas's research focuses on the changing evangelical Aymara perception of conversion, as nearly half of this major Andean social group has now moved to the city of La Paz. Thomas and his wife, Nancy, are co-directors of a new graduate school of missiology for Latin Americans, as part of the Bolivian Evangelical University in the city of Santa Cruz.

"It was one of the happiest day of my life when at sixteen I, with my brothers and sisters, parents, and grandparents, knelt before God in our home. I experienced profound change.

"When the rest of the community saw that we now belonged to Christ, they became angry. But my grandmother was without pain and becoming stronger. Each day confirmed to us that God cares for us and has power. Each day led us to greater confidence and commitment. We no longer call to the mountains or the winds. We no longer offer the sacrifices for the house and crops. We have changed this part of our way of life."

As I listened to Pedro's story, I asked myself, How can I go about understanding why more than 400,000 Aymara people, like Pedro's family, have become evangelical Christians? I wanted to understand as much as I could from their perspective.

As a missiologist I approach Christian conversion as that part of mission which emphasizes "reconciling people to God . . . and gathering them into the Church through repentance and faith in Jesus Christ by the work of the Holy Spirit."[1] This definition implies three dimensions of conversion: new relationship implied by "gathering," new understanding of truth implied by "repentance and faith," and divine interaction implied by "the work of the Holy Spirit."

I was using worldview theory and corresponding ethnographic interview methodology to identify cultural themes evident in conversion narratives among Aymara evangelicals. This approach let me focus on Aymara experience and perception. But it did not give me a sufficient theoretical framework from which to conceptualize the specific phenomena of conversion or to interpret its themes.

In the course of my literature review, I discovered James E. Loder's *The Transforming Moment* (1989), and recognized two pieces I was missing. Loder provides a model of creative cognitive process that allowed me to view the conversion process according to five interactive components. He also provides a model of the nature of human being that builds from the same foundations as worldview theory and facilitates theological and missiological reflection.

James E. Loder in personal perspective

James E. Loder is professor of the philosophy of Christian education at Princeton Theological Seminary. He graduated from Carleton College, Princeton Theological Seminary (B.D.), and Harvard University (Ph.D.).

His special research interests have been developmental psychology, the relation and interaction between science and theology, and an examination of experiential encounter with God.

Loder's three major works are Religious Pathology and Christian Faith (1966), *The Transforming Moment* (1989), and *The Knight's Move: The Relational Logic of the Spirit in Theology and Science* (1992), written with physicist W. Jim Neidhardt. In this chapter I will concentrate on Loder's foundational ideas in *The Transforming Moment*.

Loder has focused his research on authentic Christian experience. In the context of increasing emphasis in Western society, both Christian and non-Christian, on spirituality, he calls for understanding and good judgment.

His developmental focus, as he considers issues of cognition, convictional experiences, and transformation, compares to that of James W. Fowler's stages of faith (1981; 1991). But while Fowler examines characteristic expressions of faith at each developmental stage, Loder emphasizes the tensions of stage transition.

Loder's theological focus is specifically Christological, as he considers issues of the nature of human being. It is through the universal experience of threatened void and nonexistence that God meets us in covenant through God's own broken body and shed blood. In Christ's resurrection we too are raised and are enabled to begin to understand and organize our world from God's perspective.

The Transforming Moment

The title of Loder's book requires explanation. Within the context of the dynamic process of creative insight is the moment of knowing. This moment is sudden and "blow-like" (Loder 1989, 225; following page references are also to this book). It involves an intuitive leap that is prior to, more foundational and more significant than knowing in rational, logical and objective ways. It is in such events of knowing that the kingdom of God manifests itself as Christ himself joins together eternity, empirical time and our response of faith. Such moments result in transformation.

These moments of insight are what Loder terms "convictional experiences" (222). Convictional experiences reorganize perception itself, going beyond normal processes of creative insight. Thus Loder does not use "transformation" to refer to positive change in behavior, as in its popular usage, even though such surface change inevitably results (229).

To examine convictional experiences is to examine conversion as points in an ongoing process. Loder uses the terms *metanoia, convictional experiences* and *transformational moments* as "signs of the presence of the Kingdom of God," which occur within the context of "the ongoing transformation of human life under divine initiative" (19). He prefers the New Testament *metanoia* to the English "conversion." And he uses its sense of "changing one's mind," not primarily as remorse and "turning from" wrong, but positively as "turning to" the kingdom of God present in and mediated by Christ (225).

Two personal experiences

Loder recounts two personal experiences of encounter with God. On September 2, 1970, Loder stopped on a throughway in New York to give aid to a woman with a flat tire (9–13). As he knelt in front of the right front fender to set the jack, a second car struck from behind. Pushing desperately with his feet and hands to keep his head and shoulders ahead of the bumper, he kept himself from being crushed until the car hit his own parked vehicle and stopped. His wife, with desperate strength, lifted the car sufficiently to free him. He had lost his thumb, broken several ribs, suffered cuts and bruises from head to foot, and should have been dying. In spite of this, he felt God's life graciously pouring into him, and he stood to walk to the stretcher. A steady surge of life and love continued to course through him as he was rushed to the hospital. Once in the operating room, he led a startled surgical team in singing a few bars of "Fairest Lord Jesus" before they began the procedures to save his life. The experience forced him to refocus his life and has been a major force behind his research.

A second event occurred sixteen years before the accident, during his first term of seminary in 1954. His father had been diagnosed with brain cancer and had died within nine months. This was for Loder a time of increasing emptiness and depression. Finally, in a moment of frustration and anger, he shouted, "If you're there, *do* something!" He recounts, "A warm life, like gentle electricity, that started at the bottom of my feet and rushed through my entire body [filled] me with such strength and vitality that it almost threw me out of bed. I leaped up singing what no good philosophy major should sing, 'Blessed assurance, Jesus is Mine!' . . . I was delighted . . . in the magnificent Presence of the One who enabled me once again to compose a meaningful 'world'" (88–89). Examination of the experience of genuine encounter with God is at the foundation of Loder's research.

Loder in theoretical perspective

Loder's model of creative insight

At the heart of Loder's model of transformational process is the priority of knowing as "event" over knowing as progressive steps of logical induction or deduction. He summarizes:

> Knowing—generally and convictionally—is first, foremost, and fundamentally an event. At the center of an event is a nonrational intrusion of a convincing insight. It is constructed by the imagination and constitutes a leap that may be found in any seemingly closed sequential movement from proposition to proposition. A similar sort of leap is found at the crux of every convicting event. This is the central common feature that makes every convictional event an act of knowing and every act of knowing an event (33).

This point of knowing as event becomes the philosophical foundation for his model of transformation. I present his model in graphic form as a spiraling process (Figure 1–1).

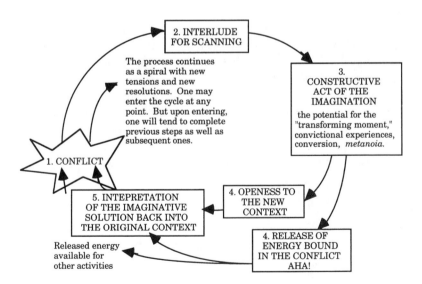

Figure 1—1: Loder's transformational process
(see Loder 1989, 35—44)

A knowing event follows a discernible pattern and logic. First, it is initiated with some sort of conflict. The more intense and personal the tension, the more significant the knowing event will be.

The second step involves the person beginning to seek solutions, entering a period of temporary bafflement. To initiate what Loder terms the "interlude for scanning," the person's attention must be diverted from the problem itself; for example, one might look out the window for an instant to remember a telephone number. It may continue for a considerable time while the person is occupied with other things but continues to hold the unresolved problem in mind.

The third step in the knowing event is the "constructive act of the imagination." This is Loder's moment of insight that suggests imaginative resolution of the conflict. "It is by this central act that the elements of the ruptured situation are *transformed*, and a new perception, perspective, or world view is bestowed on the knower" (38). Loder comments that "this striking discontinuity at the critical juncture of the knowing event suggests intentionally cooperative intervention from a realm of reality beyond consciousness itself " (41).[2] This is the moment that both transforms and leads to transformation.

The fourth step of the knowing event is the person's response to release from conflict. The insight—the "aha!" moment of understanding—brings relief and releases energy along with a rush of new associations and implications.

The final step of the knowing event is integration of the imaginative solution into the original conflict. Such integration works backward as a way to explain and understand the conflict in terms of the potential solution. It also works forward in two ways to bring closure to the person: it must resolve the conflict to an acceptable degree, and it must be acceptable to the larger social group to which the individual belongs. It is in the human impulse to share the solution that Loder's personal cognitive model engages social context. This affirms the importance of Christian community to the conversion process.

Loder's model of human being

Loder places the model of creative cognitive process in its wider context of human being. He identifies four dimensions of human beings—"environment, selfhood, the possibility of not being, and the possibility of new being" (69). Figure 1–2 presents my expression of Loder's model.

The first dimension of human being is environment. Loder terms this the "lived world," a recognition that perception of reality is created subjectively. Our worlds compose us through the society and culture of which we are a part. In turn, we compose our own worlds, corresponding to our age and maturity, by means of imagination, symbols and an inner drive toward coherence and meaning. The realities we construct and inhabit may first appear to be objective and stable. But, as Loder sums it up, their true nature is fragile and flexible (69, 71–75).

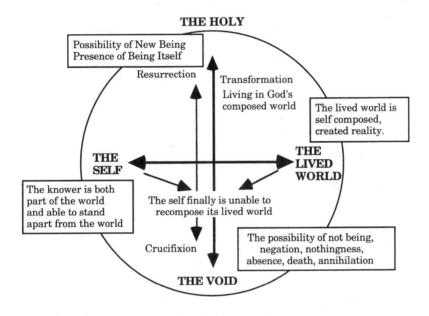

Figure 1—2: Loder's four dimensions of being

The second dimension of our being is the self. It is the dimension of the knower, who is a part of both inner and outer worlds, yet able to stand apart and reflect on them. This is the location of the process of creative insight. The self cannot be reduced to equivalence with its body, yet it has a body. Nor can it be reduced to equivalence with its social group, cultural formation or physical environment, though it reflects all of these. The self is able to stand apart and reflect on itself, raising issues of the relationship of mind and brain. It is also able to relate to itself, raising issues of self-identity and conscience. Finally, it is spirit in that it can transcend itself and reflect on its own source, raising the ultimate issues of being itself (69, 75–80).

The third dimension is the void, the possibility of not being. This threat is stronger than either environment or self. The void is implicit at birth in the gasping that breaks through the threat of suffocation. It is explicit in the inevitable experience of death. All experiences of nothingness—conflict, absence, loneliness—press toward the void and the intense need to recompose the lived world. The experience of void is part of human being and foundational for the process of transformational knowing. The self with no reference point outside itself becomes vulnerable to the void. It seeks desperately and with decreasing success to recompose its world through activity and effort. The threat of void drives us toward despair as we recognize we can bring no permanent meaning to a world grounded in ourselves. We are forced to the void (69, 80–85).

The fourth dimension is the possibility of new being. This is the dimension of the Presence of Being Itself, the Holy. It is the Holy that encompasses us, that gives a reference point outside ourselves. It is the Holy that not only surrounds us but encompasses the void as well. It is the Holy that ultimately forces us to the void, where we find that Being Itself has already entered in the crucifixion and death of Jesus. Bringing our incompleteness and brokenness to the brokenness of God in Christ also brings us to Christ's resurrection and wholeness. Encounter, recognition and worship of the Holy One undoes nothingness and redeems the whole sequence of transformational knowing. The self becomes grounded in the reality of its Source, and its formerly self-composed world becomes God's composed world (70, 85–91).[3]

We thus may see convictional experiences as invitations to a relationship that is already initiated by God. They are assurances that death and meaninglessness are not ultimate reality but are actually calls to the resurrected life of Christ. They are invitations to live in freedom beyond the boundaries we have built up against the void. "Convictional knowing describes the structural and dynamic link between knowing about Christianity and becoming Christian" (122).

Loder in the context of conversion and worldview investigation

As a psychologist studying conversion, Loder participates in research that began with the founding of psychology itself. William James in 1901 and 1902 articulated the interest of the times in understanding religious conversion from perspectives of the new science when he delivered the Gifford lectures, entitled *Varieties of Religious Experience.*

Lewis R. Rambo represents a similarly comprehensive synthesis of the state of conversion research nearly a century later. His approach is far wider than James's; it integrates the disciplines of psychology, sociology, anthropology and history. Rambo presents a seven-part model of conversion process. Loder's focus on creative cognitive process in social context is less comprehensive, although in many ways parallel to Rambo's cross-disciplinary synthesis of conversion studies. The strength of Loder's model is its perspective on personal psychological process in the context of social interaction. It has the advantage of offering compatibilities with worldview perspective.

As a theologian and philosopher examining genuine encounter with God, Loder again participates in a research interest that comes from the beginning of conversion studies. William James had suggested that the law of inferring causes from effects might well point to an objective unseen world that impinged purposefully on the material world (James 1958, 386–87). Rudolf Otto, in 1923, presented foundations for investigating this unseen dimension in *The Idea of the Holy*. Otto specifically moved beyond James's empirical limitations of examining objective presence through inference from the subjective mechanisms of cognition. Rather, Otto suggested "faculties of knowledge and potentialities of thought in the spirit itself " (Otto 1950, 11). He introduced a vocabulary to describe the "numinous" encounter commonly reported in religious experience. Loder builds on Otto's concepts as he defines the ontological dimension of the Holy as the wider unseen context in which human being exists.

Critical to my own research interest, Loder's two major models, with their distinction and interaction between "self " and "other," build on the same theoretical foundations of perception as worldview theory. Anthropologists Robert Redfield, Michael Kearney and Charles Kraft emphasize culture as a projection organized by the way a society categorizes its perception of reality, and interprets/evaluates causality, time/event, space/material and person/group. Loder provides perspectives of the cognitive workings of the process and the nature of projective reality (Kearney 1984, 106, 120; Kraft 1989, 202; Kraft 1996, 58–65).

Loder's perspectives applied to Pedro's conversion narrative

The conflict that initiated conversion for Pedro and his extended household was the grandmother's failing health. The social context rather than personal experience predominates in the narrative. For the Aymaras, sickness is a major preoccupation, and it defines significant cultural themes. At the more encompassing worldview level of relation between "self and other," Aymaras perceive the outside world as hostile. Sickness is part of this hostility. In the more limited area of human relationships as part of the "other," the Aymaras's greatest level of trust is within the extended family. But even this ideal level of trust may fracture with deceit and betrayal. Social and personal survival are major preoccupations for most Aymara families.

The crisis of the grandmother's sickness triggered a search for possible solutions. The Aymaras have a wealth of traditional herbal knowledge and procedures for caring for sick persons, and the grandmother's initial perception of the book her friend gave her was quite reasonable. Pedro mentioned that they also paid the traditional curers for help, using more and more of the family's limited resources. There are repeated and expanding cultural themes here of daily survival, natural medicine and traditional curers. Central worldview perspectives focused on economics and causation, and integrated the possibility of natural and supernatural agency. All of these became issues in "the interlude for scanning."

The process leading to the point of "the constructive act of the imagination" began in the interlude for scanning. Pedro's narrative focuses not just on economic hardship and causation but also brings attention back to cultural ideals. He notes the gift of the Bible given in the context where kinship and reciprocal relations are of highest importance. He describes how the evangelical believers in Tambillo welcomed his grandmother in appropriately respectful ways. Evident here are the cultural values of the Aymara person, the *jaki*.

Pedro highlights the point of "the constructive act of the imagination" by referring to himself in the context of his family as the family members received their new friends and later knelt together before God in their own home. This meant an act of confession and worship from the perspective of both their traditional Aymara and Roman Catholic background. Pedro's next remark shows something profound had occurred, something that indicated intrusion of the fourth dimension of the Holy: "It was one of the happiest days of my life." The new "nonrational intrusion of a convincing insight," as indicated by his following comments, resulted in new allegiance. Pedro's perception is that he personally, in the context of the family, met God there.

Pedro's narrative immediately moves to recount what had happened in the family. He recognizes personal changes, but he immediately describes how the family consolidated the conversion decision. His grandmother became stronger every day until she was well again. His family members received daily confirmation that the God they had perceived as remote and uninterested was actually compassionate and near to them. God's power was greater than the other powers they had called on for help. There is a sense that, even as he looks back, Pedro is still in the process of understanding the implications of that moment of convincing insight, of encounter with God.

Finally, Pedro touches on how his family integrated the solution of their conflict over his grandmother's sickness. The family's center of allegiance changed decisively from the mountains and natural forces around which their life had previously revolved. No longer did they offer traditional sacrifices that served to maintain equilibrium and harmony in the community. This kind of allegiance they now gave to God, who ruled over all these powers.

But integration of their new understanding into the community was a point of new conflict. The larger community became angry. From its perspective, such a change of allegiance upset the balance that maintained health, safety and productive fields. This new allegiance challenged some of the deepest presuppositions of the traditional way of life. But even as the other kinships of the community reacted against Pedro's family, they themselves felt tension in recognizing that the grandmother had become well.[4] Many in their families were also sick and faced the same desperation Pedro's family had experienced. What had happened fit their worldview perceptions of causation yet at the same time threatened traditions. Here we are confronting tensions that affirm and challenge the traditional way of life, provoking hostility. At the same time, the power of the experience of convincing insight has infused remarkable determination in new converts, especially as extended families and kinships together decide to follow Christ.

Loder in missiological perspective

Loder is not intentionally a missiologist. His primary focus is on the nature of convictional experiences that God initiates rather than the intentional crossing of barriers from church to non-church or faith to non-faith. But Loder opens the possibility of missiological application in his concern for renewal in the church.

For example, although he doesn't write from the perspective of the mission of the church—most of his references to the organized church are guidelines and cautions in facilitating the transformational process—he does consider the social context and the koinonia to be of highest significance (1989, 193–96). And again, although he doesn't develop his theology according to the mission of God, one of his stated purposes in writing is to show how his insights will enable "people to indwell the transforming moment, let it unfold its content, and let it move the person into an unfolding of Christ's transformational work in personal life and world history" (185). His theologizing is to result in action. For Loder, the present kingdom of God and participation from God's perspective in the world God loves are major evidence of transformation.

Following are some suggestions of the importance of Loder's work to missiology. First, Loder deliberately takes a Christocentric approach. He doesn't develop this in terms of mission, but he does emphasize working from the perspective of the Holy and letting this become the controlling paradigm of the other three dimensions of self, composed world and void. The dimension of the Holy is the reality of the resurrected Christ. Loder emphasizes seeing and acting in the world from the transforming perspective of Christ—a thoroughly missiological perspective.

Loder is working from an interdisciplinary perspective and presents a model that synthesizes cognition and developmental perspectives with theology. The process of creative thinking and discovery (conflict, scanning, insight, release, integration) is also seen to be the process by which the Holy encounters us. What is true in the relationship between the composed world, the self and the void is also the context of encounter with the higher reality of God's composed world, which contains all lesser composed worlds and exposes their inadequacy. Loder's perspective and methodology is useful to missiology.

Loder's focus is on God who is there, who sovereignly reveals himself, and who encompasses all subjective reality. The emphasis of Harvie Conn and Charles Van Engen on covenant reflects the same concern (see Conn 1984, 211–60; Van Engen 1996, 71–89). Loder's model of the interaction of subjective ego, composed reality, and God's reality gives a rationale for the missiological perspective of contextualization.

Loder offers serious consideration of kingdom moments of God's inbreaking into human experience. Missiology is on the edge of the sciences and theology as it deals with this kind of "unresearchable" interaction. The dynamics of spiritual power is becoming a major area of missiological research, and Loder provides a substantial contribution to such research.

Finally, Loder brings together four essential components as he theologizes. He begins from the context of actual experiences of convictional knowing, including his own. He draws on insights from an interdisciplinary perspective, especially reflecting his own specialty in developmental psychology. He brings these insights to Scripture in order to interpret experiences of convictional knowing from the perspective of the kingdom of God. And he recognizes and writes from his own Presbyterian Reformed perspective.

Loder offers process models and theological perspectives that are potentially significant to missiology. And he provides models that facilitate investigation of conversion from worldview perspective.

Notes

[1] The complete definition I am using here comes from Charles Van Engen (1996, 26). "Mission is the people of God intentionally crossing barriers from church to non-church, faith to non-faith to proclaim by word and deed the coming of the Kingdom of God in Jesus Christ, through the Church's participation in God's mission of reconciling people to God, to themselves, to each other, and to the world, and gathering them into the Church through repentance and faith in Jesus Christ by the work of the Holy Spirit with a view to the transformation of the world as a sign of the coming of the Kingdom in Jesus Christ."

[2] This view of intentionality from a source outside of the person is also related to Karl Jung's concept of synchronicity. Loder's concept of Spirit and the Holy develops his point here.

[3] Loder draws and adapts the various points of this logical process of negation and double negation from various sources, but especially from Kierkegaard, Levi-Strauss and Jung. He terms this "transformational logic," which he sees as part of the nature of reality itself, not an imposition of a logical model of existence or an incidental or insignificant pattern. Transformational logic is "anchored in the very marrow of existence as convictional experiences tell the convicted soul" (65). He relates the process and logic of transformation in the creative act to the logic of the transformation of transformation itself in the fourth dimension through analogy. Basing his analysis on 1 Corinthians 2:11, Loder notes that just as a person's spirit is the only one who comprehends his or her thoughts, the Holy Spirit is the only one who comprehends God's thoughts. This analogical relationship between the human spirit and the Holy Spirit is the key to convictional knowing (93).

[4] The sociological study of Cordova (1990), which identifies physical healing as one of the major identified factors in the conversion decisions of Aymara evangelicals in La Paz, is unable to investigate seriously such issues and instead identifies social protest as the major overall factor for the rise of the movement. While this has a significant level of structural validity, it does not illumine the inner dynamics of conversion.

References

Conn, Harvie M. 1984. *Eternal Word and Changing Worlds: Theology, Anthropology, and Mission in Trialogue*. Phillipsburg, N.J.: P. & R. Publishing.

Cordova, Julio. 1990. "Confesiones Fundamentalistas en El Alto: Disidencia Religiosa y Sectores Urbano Populares." La Paz, Bolivia: La Conferencia Episcopal de Bolivia.

Ellens, J. Harold. 1984. "The Psychodynamics of Christian Conversion." *Journal of Psychology and Christianity* 3(4): 29–36.

Fowler, James W. 1981. *Stages of Faith: The Psychology of Human Development and the Quest for Meaning*. San Francisco: Harper & Row.

———— 1991. *Weaving the New Creation*. San Francisco: HarperCollins Publishers.

James, William. 1958. *The Varieties of Religious Experience: A Study in Human Nature*. New York: The New American Library of World Literature. (Original: The Gifford Lectures on Natural Religion, delivered at Edinburgh in 1901–1902).

Kearney, Michael. 1984. *World View*. Novato, Calif.: Chandler & Sharp Publishers.

Kraft, Charles H. 1989. *Christianity with Power: Your Worldview and Your Experience of the Supernatural*. Ann Arbor, Mich.: Servant Publications.

————. 1992. "Allegiance, Truth and Power Encounters in Christian Witness." In *Pentecost, Mission and Ecumenism: Essays on Intercultural Theology*, ed. Jan A. B. Jongeneel, 215–30. New York: Peter Lang.

————. 1996. *Anthropology for Christian Witness*. Maryknoll, N.Y.: Orbis Books.

Loder, James E. 1966. *Religious Pathology and Christian Faith*. Philadelphia: Westminster Press.

————. 1989. *The Transforming Moment*. 2d edition. Colorado Springs, Colo.: Helmers & Howard.

Loder, James E., and James W. Fowler. 1982. "Conversations on Fowler's Stages of Faith and Loder's The Transforming Moment." *Religious Education* 77(2):133–48.

Loder, James E., and Mark Laaser. 1973. "Authenticating Christian Experience: A Research Request." *The Princeton Seminary Bulletin* 66(1):120–24.

Loder, James E., and W. Jim Neidhardt. 1992. *The Knight's Move: The Relational Logic of the Spirit in Theology and Science*. Colorado Springs, Colo.: Helmers & Howard.

Otto, Rudolf. 1950 <1923>. *The Idea of the Holy: An Inquiry into the Non-rational Factor in the Idea of the Divine and Its Relation to the Rational*. 2d ed. New York: Oxford University Press.

Rambo, Lewis R. 1993. *Understanding Religious Conversion*. New Haven, Conn.: Yale University Press.

Van Engen, Charles. 1996. *Mission-on-the-Way: Issues in Mission Theology*. Grand Rapids, Mich.: Baker Books.

Wyckoff, D. Campbell, and George Brown Jr., comps. 1995. *Religious Education: 1960–1993: An Annotated Bibliography*. Westport, Conn.: Greenwood Press.

2

Karl Barth and a missiology of preaching

Dae Ryeong Kim

Our life is like the journey of a wanderer through the
    night;
and each one, advancing slowly, knows: deep sorrow
    is his plight (Barth 1961a, 14).

Karl Barth was quoting from a well-known Swiss song as he made his
opening remarks to the inmates in a Swiss prison. He continued his sermon, saying,

Each one! Sorrow is your plight, and so it is mine. We suffer
here within the walls of this house, and so do the people of
this city, even of the whole world. Behind the sorrow of each
individual there lies the sorrow of a world in disorder. . . .
There also lies the sorrow of man as he is: not good . . . but
living in misery (ibid.).

The preacher and the audience were from two different worlds; what
a contrast of spiritual, educational and social backgrounds! The preacher

Dae Ryeong Kim is a candidate for the Ph.D. in the School of World Mission,
Fuller Theological Seminary. He is a minister with the Presbyterian Church of
Korea, on the faculty at the Presbyterian Theological Academy in Moscow, and
a recognized writer in the field of missiology. He has been published in Korean.
Kim serves as a pioneering editor who is devoted to scholarly missiological pub-
lication and is working on a project to implement seminary education in the
fields of domestic missiology and theology of cultural plurality in the non-
Western context.

was professor of theology at Basel University; the audience, inmates in the city prison. But with a few words Barth was able to enter the situation of the congregation and speak to the prisoners' needs.

Barth earned the reputation of being a preaching theologian, one who translated the profundity and complexity of the gospel into the simplicity of preaching. He was a theologian by title, a pastor by heart and a missionary preacher by ministry.

Ironically, when I came to seminary in the United States, I had resolved I would never read Barth again. During my seminary years in Korea, Barth had strongly influenced my theological thinking. But my subsequent church-planting experience in Russia had left me disappointed with an abstract theology that seemed irrelevant to the needs of real people. I became aware of the tension between theology and proclamation.

I also became aware that effective preaching is not just biblical exposition but missionary communication, and, while there must be a deep understanding of the Bible, there also must be simplicity in communication. With the motivation to seek a missiological understanding of preaching, I came to Fuller, saying goodbye to Karl Barth along the way. I wanted no more sophisticated theological language understood only by seminarians, but rather a theology that would serve the evangelistic proclamation of the gospel.

But in a class of mission theology I discovered Barth's *Credo* was a required text. The professor, Charles Van Engen, even told us, "Karl Barth was a missiologist of his day." Karl Barth—a missiologist? I was puzzled. Yet reading Barth from a missiological perspective and encountering him as an evangelistic preacher have given me fresh insight as I seek to understand missionary proclamation.

Brief biography

Karl Barth was born and raised in the tradition of the Swiss Reformation. His father, Fritz Barth, was teaching at the Evangelical School of Preachers in Basel when Karl was born on May 10, 1886. Three years later Fritz Barth was called to Berne to become professor of church history and New Testament exegesis (Come 1963, 24). It was natural, then, that Karl Barth developed a strong interest in theological study.

At the age of eighteen Barth began his theological studies under the direction of his father, who passed on to his son a thorough grounding in Reformed theology. Although his father stood for a more orthodox position against developing liberalism, in 1906 Barth himself came under the powerful influence of liberal theologian Adolf Harnack. Liberal theology dominated his thinking for the next ten years (Come 1963, 25; cf. Bromiley 1969, 27–28).

Upon the completion of his studies in 1909, Barth spent two years as an apprentice pastor in Geneva. In 1911 he moved to Safenwil in north-central Switzerland and became a pastor. He was twenty-five years old. Geoffrey Bromiley remarks that at that time Barth had little message to preach except the Christianized culture expressed in Harnack's *What Is Christianity?* (1969, 27–28).

During his ten years as pastor in this country village Barth went through the agonies of heart, mind and soul that finally led to a change in his theological position. Bromiley observes, "Experience in the pastorate quickly produced a sense of incongruity between commission and performance. Liberal platitudes answered neither the demands of his calling nor actual problems in his parish" (ibid., 29). During these ten years we see Barth giving his attention to preaching—to the problem of the content of the message that, Sunday after Sunday, is the heavy responsibility of the one commissioned to enter the Christian pulpit (Casalis 1963, 43).

Barth taught theology in Gotting Munster and Bonn, Germany, between 1921 and 1935. While there he challenged Harnack, contending that Harnack's scientific theology is only a preliminary to the true task of theology, which is identical to that of preaching. With the rise of Adolf Hitler, Barth emerged as one of the church leaders to oppose the Nazi movement.

Deprived of his chair at Bonn, Barth returned to Switzerland and, from 1935 to his retirement in 1962, taught theology at Basel. He frequently conducted worship at the main prison in the city, preaching with simplicity the gospel of freedom to a large congregation of inmates (Casalis 1963, 89). A collection of his sermons, *Deliverance to the Captives* (1961a), gives moving testimony to Barth's calling to preach to this particular group.

Barth's mission theology

Barth's mission theology lays the foundation for his missiology of preaching. Barth holds that the Christian church is by nature a missionary community with an evangelistic mandate to the world. In an exposition of Matthew 28:19, he declares that "sending or sending out to the nations to attest the gospel is the very root of the existence and therefore the whole ministry of the community" (1962a, 874).

For Barth, the church community is a body of Christians who are essentially witnesses. The church community is comprised of the company of those who hear God's word of atonement in order to represent it to others. The Christian community as a confessing church "will necessarily be a missionary Church, that is, it will not exist only for 'Christians,' and therefore, so to speak, only for its own sake, but in existing for Christians, it will at the same time exist for the 'heathen,' it will exist for the sake of the world reconciled in Christ to God" (1962b, 145). The church community does not live in a vacuum, but rather, "in every age and situation it stands in definite relation to the world around, i.e., non-Christians" (ibid., 850).

Barth sees the missionary calling of the church expressed in two situations: in what was known as "foreign missions," and, in a more general sense, in mission to the unreached, including nominal members of Christian churches.

Concerning the first, Barth recognizes the vocation of the Christian community to take the gospel message to the nations. He asserts that unless the church is an active subject in foreign missions, it is not the Christian community (ibid., 874–75).

A unique aspect of Barth's mission theology is the way he addresses the nominal segment of "Christian" society as a mission field. Mission, for Barth, includes both going to a foreign culture with the Christian gospel and expressing God's missionary intentions within a secular culture. At the heart of mission theology lies the evangelistic mandate to the world—to those who are still outside the kingdom, wherever they may be.

Barth describes why a nominal Christian society is a mission field:

> Those countless nominal Christians are undoubtedly the immediate neighbors of the community as the assembly of serious Christians. Do not even the latter continually find that they themselves are nominal Christians and urgently need to receive the Gospel afresh? The concern of evangelisation is precisely to sound out the gospel on this shifting frontier between true and merely nominal Christians (ibid.).

Barth indicates that evangelism in a context of nominality may require the reorientation of church ministry:

> It is obvious that the worship, preaching and teaching of the community, which the world also hears in some sense, or at least may hear, in its form as the Christian world, must always

have the character of evangelisation of a call to those who are within in theory but not in practice (ibid., 873).

Barth's missiological understanding of preaching

Barth's homiletics reflects his mission theology. He does not attempt to distinguish missionary preaching from preaching in a Christian church service, as it is generally understood. All preaching is a call to repentance and faith. All preaching bears the task of missionary proclamation to the world.

A theology of proclamation

A fundamental aspect of Barth's theological understanding of mission can be described as a theology of proclamation. For Barth, theology results when both the preacher and the church reflect about their proper message. The church, then, is a witnessing people, charged with responsibility for proclaiming the Good News of the kingdom of God to the world (Casalis 1963, 47). The function of theology is to serve church proclamation for missionary outreach.

As Barth defines it, proclamation is human speech in and by which God *speaks* like a king through the mouth of his herald; it is meant to be *heard* and *accepted* as speech in and by which God speaks; and it is the message of divine pardon, therefore, the eternal gospel (1980, 52). Proclamation is a missionary communication of God's divine grace.

Barth views ministers as priests *(Geistliche)* who mediate between God and humanity by hearing both the questions of the people and the answers of God. Hence, "not until our preaching arises from need will our work become a *mission*. Mission alone can legitimize preaching" (1957, 128).

Barth's response to the problem of preaching

Arnold Come observes that it was the practical problem of preaching that Barth faced which formed his theology:

> Barth's whole unique theological formulation had its origin
> and rise from the specific problem of the sermon. He tells us
> that the theology he had been taught appeared less relevant as
> he was confronted each week with the needs of the people on
> the one hand, and Bible on the other, and the task of bringing

the two together in the sermon. Out of this torment came his
commentary on Paul's Epistle to the Romans, and a new theological era was born (Come 1963, 14–15).

For Barth, theology has not only its origin but also its goal in the
problem of preaching. Formulation of Christian faith into doctrinal statements cannot be an end in itself. Theology does not replace the Bible or
the revelatory event in which God speaks God's own words to people
(ibid., 15).

From his own ministry experience Barth expresses the minister's problem, that is, the sermon theology alone does not address:

> I sought to find my way between the problem of human life
> on the one hand and the content of the Bible on the other. As
> a minister I wanted to speak to the people in the infinite con-
> tradiction of their life but to speak the no less infinite mes-
> sage of the Bible, which was as much of a riddle as life. Often
> enough these two magnitudes, life and the Bible, have risen
> before me (and still rise) like Scylla and Charybdis (1957,
> 100–101).

The problem of preaching is that of the relation between life and text
(Barth 1991, 113). How can a preacher get close to the life of the receptors and, at the same time, get equally close to the biblical text? According to Barth, the two must be intimately related in preaching.

Barth's principle of contextual hermeneutics requires meditation on
both the historical context of the biblical text and the life situation of the
audience. As Barth explains it, "When preparing their sermons, preachers have to meditate on the texts both as genuine people of their day but
also in such a way that the text can really become a Way to their contemporaries. . . . Each word that is to be proclaimed to the listeners must
become a word that is specifically and decisively addressed to our own
present" (ibid., 114).

Exposition, not exegesis

Barth is well aware of communication barriers between the pulpit and
pew, and between the church and the world. His missiology of preaching
seeks to overcome those barriers through exposition that brings the biblical text alive in a contemporary situation: "Preaching is exposition, not
exegesis. It follows the text but moves on from it to the preacher's own
heart and to the congregation" (ibid., 81).

Barth suggests that originality in preaching contributes to making biblical exposition relevant to a contemporary audience. What constitutes original preaching is the courage to say to others what is real and vital for the messenger.

> Exegesis and meditation must become speech to others: Address my own speech. I myself am now called upon to be a witness who will remain biblical but will not be stuck fast in exegesis. . . . From the very sentence, preaching must be addressed to the people with central communication out of the text (ibid., 82).

Originality in preaching springs from the example of the Incarnation. As Barth puts it, "The man who speaks is a real man of flesh and blood, with a personality and a history and a background of his own, whom God has laid hold of in the actual situation in which he is placed" (ibid.). "We are to preach as the people we are: in a history, on the way that the Bible takes with us. For this reason we should give honest information and reports about our own situation. . . . Christian truth is constantly won afresh in history. You must preach as the one you are today" (ibid., 83).

Barth's focus on exposition integrates the profundity of the gospel with the simplicity of preaching. He expected good preaching to be plain and simple. He admonished his students to guard against any display of doctrinal erudition. Rather, preachers should see biblical truths as they unfold in actual experience. Christian truth is always fresh when set in the context of daily life (1963, 52).

According to Barth, exposition in preaching cannot be merely a matter of thought. The messenger must pay attention to phrases and sentences. "The sermon demands an orderly language which is appropriate from the standpoint of content as well as expression. Form and content are not to be separated in preaching. The right form is part of right content" (1991, 120).

A focus on the receptors

"In a sermon exposition must relate to application as subject does to predicate." Thus Barth reminds us that exposition of the biblical text should apply to the situation of our audience. "The people I wish to address must be in my mind's eye as I prepare my sermon" (ibid., 112). What the preacher knows about the receptors will suggest "unexpected ideas and associations which will be with him as he studies his text and will provide the elements of actuality, the application of his text to the contemporary situation" (1963, 74). Preaching is addressed not to humanity in the abstract but to the living, breathing person of today, whether within the church or still outside it (ibid.). The context of a sermon is "the concrete situation of the audience's earthly condition with all its life problem." As Barth puts it, "The people we address are people with all kinds of anxieties and needs. It is in this concrete situation . . . that the call of Jesus Christ comes to them as people of the present age. Neither preacher nor congregation must be viewed as an abstract entity" (1991, 112–13).

To focus on the receptors, the preacher must humbly recognize that he or she "belongs" to the congregation, as one with the people of God. Barth says, "The preacher must never feel superior to the congregation, but see that he is set within it as one who must also simply hear the Word of God again and again." He goes on to emphasize, "Recognition of this situation of the preacher is the prerequisite for the proper application of the Word" (ibid., 113).

Barth warns against the danger of the preacher addressing the congregation from a standpoint outside the congregation, instead of becoming one with it. The preacher has no right to feel "set on high" because of knowledge of theology. Rather, the preacher should consciously strive to stay on the level of the people (1963, 75).

In focusing on the receptor, Barth says a preacher should adapt the message to the congregation; to do this, love, an incarnational lifestyle and a concern for relevance are necessary. The preacher needs to love the congregation—with a genuine love that expresses itself in an incarnational lifestyle. His or her constant thought will be: "These are my people and I long to share with them what God has given to me" (ibid., 52–53).

The preacher needs to live the life of the congregation, knowing the same struggles, hearing the questions, walking alongside. A preacher does not have to be the sage of the people but will continually be concerned with their questions and struggles. Preaching in Barth's missiological sense is more than speech communication—it involves a life message.[1] The validity of the preacher's message will most clearly be seen in the way that preacher lives (Barth 1963, 53).

Finally, in adapting the message to the lives of the people, the preacher must have a vital concern for relevance.[2] What demands does the contemporary situation make on the preacher and the congregation? Together they share a historical experience, and the words of the preacher must be relevant to immediate preoccupation of the hearers. A preacher is not a hermit dwelling apart (Barth 1991, 54).

For Barth, the preacher's task is "to cause the testimony presented in the text to be heard; his preaching is good if it brings to life in this present age the testimony of the prophets and apostles" (1963, 64–65). The preacher's work is, then, to make exposition of the Bible relevant for those in need of divine grace. "Purely historical material is relevant only insofar as it forms part of the testimony. In preaching, it is necessary to follow the direction of the text and relate it to our own times" (ibid.).

Barth and his unity of reflection and action

In Karl Barth's missiology of preaching we find a balance of reflection and action. As Charles Van Engen declares, missiology continuously attempts to interface reflection and action. It is critical reflection that takes place in the praxis of mission. It occurs in the concrete missionary situation, as part of the church's missionary obedience to and participation in God's mission (Van Engen 1996, 17–18).

Barth has a theme that parallels Van Engen's reflection and action—explication and application. For Barth, reflection on the Word of God does not take place in a void. It takes place at the transitional point between *explication* (observation) and *application* (assimilation), between the understanding and practice of Scripture (1956, 766–67). He argues: "Preaching is not to be explication alone. It may not be limited to expounding with no regard for the hearers. . . . Every sermon must also take the form of application. An exposition, no matter how true to the text, will die away ineffectually in a vacuum, if there is no possibility of a responsive echo from those who hear it" (1991, 111).

The following excerpt from one of Barth's sermons illustrates how he united exposition and application. The text reads, "By grace you have been saved!"; his audience is inmates in a Swiss prison:

> We are all great sinners. Please understand me: I include myself. I stand ready to confess being the greatest sinner among you all. . . . Sinners are people who in the judgment of God, and perhaps of their own consciences, missed and lost their way. . . . We are such sinners, and we are prisoners. Believe me, there is a captivity much worse than the captivity in this house. There are walls much thicker and doors much heavier than those closed upon you. All of us, the people without and you within, are prisoners of our own obstinacy, of our many greeds, of our various anxieties. . . . We are all sufferers. . . . We spend our life in the midst of a whole world of sin and captivity and suffering. . . .

> But now listen. Into the depth of our predicament the word
> is spoken from high: *By Grace you have been saved!* To be saved
> does not just mean to be a little encouraged, a little com-
> forted, a little relieved. It means to be pulled out like a log
> from a burning fire. You have been saved! We are not told:
> you may be saved sometimes, or a little bit. No, you *have been*
> saved, totally and for all times. You? Yes, we! Not just any
> other people, more pious and better than we are, no, we, each
> one of us (1961a, 37).

Barth points out that an evangelistic sermon needs to produce a response in the hearts of the audience:

> To address men evangelically, however, is decisively to present
> to them the great likeness of the declaration and explanation
> of the gospel in such a way that they come to see its crucial
> application to them, that so far as any human word can do so
> it pricks their hearts (Ac. 2:37), that it brings them to realise
> that the reference is to them (1962a, 852–53).

Conclusions and applications

Karl Barth's ministry was multifaceted. He was a professor of theology
by title, a pastor by personal identification and a missionary preacher by
his hidden ministry. In all of this Barth's theology had one clear goal—
missionary proclamation of the gospel for the redemption of the lost. In
this respect he was a classic mission theologian of proclamation.

Barth helps us recognize missionary preaching as the intracultural
communication of the gospel, especially preaching that occurs within
secularized "Christian" culture. For Barth, the evangelistic task of missionary preaching is not achieved by geographical advance but by penetration of the hearts of people so that conversion results, the conversion of those outside the church and those inside the church in name
alone.

This understanding of missionary preaching has strong implications
in contemporary world mission. In the New Testament era, missionary
preaching involved proclamation of the gospel to an audience outside
the Christian faith. In modern church history, missionary preaching has
been associated with geographical advancement. But recently, a growing
number of missionaries find themselves serving in a nominally Christian
society. Russia is such an example.

Since the 1991 collapse of the Communist regime in the Soviet Union, great numbers of missionaries have arrived in Russia to assist in the great task of reevangelizing the nation. Yet many in Russia are asking, "Why should missionaries preach to Christians in Russia?" Mounting tension between missions (including those from Korea) and the Russian host churches (especially the Russian Orthodox Church) stems from this unresolved question.

Russia is not eighteenth-century Africa—Russia has a thousand years of Christian history. The seventy years of "the Babylonian exile" under communism did not blot out the rich Christian heritage deeply embedded in Russian culture. Russia today is as a mosaic of European and Asian cultures, of a rich Christian heritage and unreached people groups, and of devoted Christians and those who have become nominal.

One readily sees a parallel between Barth's Germany and contemporary Russia. In both countries Christianity had been the state religion—in Germany, the Lutheran Church, and in Russia, the Orthodox Church. Statistically, most of the population were registered as Christian. And both countries suffered through periods of totalitarian government—Nazism in Germany, communism in Russia.

Yet this type of nominalism, originating from the existence of a state church, has no parallels in the Korean experience, which I represent. Barth can help us understand the central issues for missionary preaching in such a situation.

Barth reminds us that the heart of missionary preaching is to preach as one who is sent to the audience. To be sent as a preacher means more than physical presence. It means entering into the situation of the audience in heart and mind, in prayer and Bible exposition, in spoken language and life message. It means rereading the Bible in the situation of the people so the message is relevant to them in their need of divine grace.

I have had the experience of preaching on the same text to two audiences, one in Korea and the other in Russia. The audience in Russia responded with much more enthusiasm than the group in Korea. Why? In Russia I entered deeply into the situation of my audience, preaching as one sent by God to them. I reflected deeply on their life questions framed in this particular time in their history, and I attempted to reread the Bible from this perspective. Considering the barrier of cross-cultural communication and the fact that most of my audience came from backgrounds of nominality, their tearful and joyful response emphasizes the importance of a missiological understanding of preaching.

I believe in missionary preaching. I believe every true preacher is a missionary preacher, sent and commissioned by God primarily to proclaim divine grace to those still outside God's fold. Experiences like my time in Russia, along with my research and reflection, have convinced me that the characteristics of missiological preaching apply in both intracultural and cross-cultural pulpit communication. This is precisely what Barth teaches in his missiology of preaching.

Notes

¹ Mission anthropologist Charles Kraft is the proponent of "life message" in his communication theory (see Kraft 1991).

² In two definitions of preaching, Barth focuses on the relevance of the message. First, he defines preaching as "the Word of God which he himself speaks, claiming for the purpose the exposition of a biblical text in free human words that are relevant to contemporaries by those who are called to do this in the church that is obedient to its commission" (1991, 53). In his second definition of preaching, Barth claims "preaching is the attempt enjoined upon the church to serve God's own Word, through one who is called thereto, by expounding a biblical text in human words and making it relevant to contemporaries in intimation of what they have to hear from God himself" (ibid.).

References

Barth, Karl. 1957 <1928>. *The Word of God and the Word of Man.* New York: Harper Torchbooks.

———. 1961a. *Deliverance to the Captives.* New York: Harper & Brothers.

———. 1961b. *The Doctrine of Creation.* Vol. 3, Part 4 of *Church Dogmatics,* trans. G. W. Bromiley and T. F. Torrance. Edinburgh: T. &. T. Clark. (Original: *Die Kirchkliche Dogmatik,* III: *Die Lehre von der Schöpfung,* 3 zweite Hälfte.)

———. 1962a. *The Doctrine of Reconciliation.* Vol. 4, Part 3b of *Church Dogmatics,* trans. G. W. Bromiley and T. F. Torrance. Edinburgh: T. &. T. Clark. (Original: *Die Kirchliche Dogmatik,* IV: *Die Lehre von der Versöhung,* 3 zweite Hälfte.)

———. 1962b. *Credo.* New York: Charles Scribner's Sons.

———. 1963. *The Preaching of the Gospel.* Philadelphia: Westminster Press. (Original: *La Proclamation de l'Evangile.*)

———. 1980. *The Doctrine of the Word of God.* Vol. 1, Part 1 of *Church Dogmatics,* trans. G. W. Bromiley and T. F. Torrance. Edinburgh: T. & T. Clark. (Original: *Die Kirchliche Dogmatik* 1: *Die Lehre vom Worte Gottes,* 1, 1932.)

———. 1991. *Homiletics,* trans. G. W. Bromiley and D. E. Daniels, Louisville, Ky.: John Knox Press. (Original: *Homiletik,* 1966.)

Bromiley, G. W. 1969. "Karl Barth." In *Creative Minds in Contemporary Theology,* ed. P. E. Hughes. Grand Rapids: Eerdmans.

Casalis, Georges. 1963. *Portrait of Karl Barth*, trans. Robert McAfee Brown. Garden City, N.Y.: Doubleday.

Come, Arnold B. 1963. *An Introduction to Barth's Dogmatics for Preachers*. Philadelphia: Westminster Press.

Kraft, Charles H. *Communication Theory for Christian Witness*. Maryknoll, N.Y.: Orbis Books.

Van Engen, Charles. 1996. "Specialization/Integration in Mission Education." In *Missiological Education for the Twenty-First Century: The Book, the Circle, and the Sandals*, ed. J. Dudley Woodberry, Charles Van Engen and Edgar J. Elliston. Maryknoll, N.Y.: Orbis Books.

3

Jakób Jocz

God's square peg

STUART DAUERMANN

God shapes his servants to embody the Word they proclaim. But other forces are also at work, shaping or misshaping God's servants for their divinely appointed tasks. People are sometimes twisted out of the form God intended for them through the actions of misguided church and mission leaders, and this process can transform some of God's fittest servants into misfits. Jakób Jocz was such a servant.

In this chapter I examine the life and ministry of Jakób Jocz (1906–83), one of God's choicest square pegs, and like myself, a Jew called by God to serve the Messiah among his people. I will trace how church and mission leaders squeezed him into roles that were a mismatch for his gifts, his heart and God's missionary call on his life. I will conclude with some lessons his story teaches us.

Shaped before birth

Our story begins in Lithuania at the dawn of the twentieth century.[1] Johanan Don, like Tevye of *Fiddler on the Roof*, was a poor milk-peddler

Stuart Dauermann has been involved in contextualized ministry to the Jewish people since the 1960s. Currently serving as rabbi of Ahavat Zion Messianic Synagogue in Beverly Hills, California, his doctoral research involves developing a new paradigm for understanding Messianic Jewish leadership rooted in the biblical priesthood and in Jewish community leadership models. Dauermann serves as president of Hashivenu, Inc., a foundation for the Maturation of Messianic Judaism. Under those auspices he directs Messianic T.O.R.A.H. (Teaching Our Rituals and Heritage) Institute throughout the Messianic Jewish community. He lives in Altadena, California, with his wife, Naomi, and three children.

who lived in a *shtetl*, a village. One night his 14–year-old daughter, Hannah, severely wrenched her back when the village fool attacked and frightened her. Johanan took her to the only medical treatment facility he could afford, the Lutheran Medical Mission in the nearby city of Vilna, where a certain Dr. Fröhwein treated Hannah without charge.

While Hannah was being tended to, her father picked up from the waiting-room table a small black book with the Hebrew title *B'rith Chadasha (The New Testament)*. Coming out of his office and seeing Johanan engrossed in his reading, the doctor encouraged him to take the book home. By candlelight, that night and many nights to follow, Johanan devoured the holy words. In the fullness of time God's seed bore the fruit of salvation in Johanan's heart. Shortly afterward, to the shame and disgust of his wife, Sarah, Johanan was baptized in a local Protestant church.

Pogroms rampant in the area made it unsafe for Jews living in outlying villages, so the Don family moved from the *shtetl* of Zolse to Vilna. Soon afterward, Johanan died, and Sarah, needing to make ends meet, took in a boarder. Bazyli Jocz was a cabinetmaker by trade, but by passion a student at the prestigious Vilna Yeshiva (School of Rabbinic Studies), the Harvard of Orthodox Judaism. While studying the Book of Isaiah there, Bazyli raised unconventional questions about the prophet's portrait of the Messiah, bringing down upon his head the wrath of his teachers. Burning to find answers, young Bazyli turned to the same Dr. Fröhwein, widely known in the Jewish community as "a Jew of a different kind." The doctor opened the Scriptures with Bazyli, revealing to him who it was of whom the prophet wrote. So it was that Bazyli embraced Yeshua as the fulfillment of 5,000 years of Jewish revelation and hope.

By now a friendship had developed between Bazyli and Hannah, the landlady's daughter. Believing it wrong to keep his new faith a secret from Hannah, one day, as they walked in the park, Bazyli told Hannah of his discovery. How astounded he was when she told him that her father had believed as well and had told her to never forget Yeshua. Soon she too declared her faith. A short time later Bazyli and Hannah were married, and in 1906 they had a son, whom they named Jakób.

Notice how Jewish was the cradle in which the couple placed their first son. Jakób's father, Bazyli, had been a student at the Vilna Yeshiva, steeped and skilled in the law and lore revered by Eastern European Jewry. Jakób's mother was raised in a *shtetl*. The first word the child spoke was Yiddish.

These were hard times for Lithuania and Russia. Throughout Jakób's youth unrest, dislocations, wars, skirmishes and anti-Semitism were his

---

constant companions. Amid the chaos there was little opportunity for formal education. But Jakób was a fast learner and a gifted linguist. By his late teens he had become fluent in Polish, German, Russian and English, in addition to his native Yiddish. It was also during these years that his father led him to faith in Jesus.

Preparing for a life of ministry

Shortly after World War I, Bazyli became an evangelist under the auspices of the Church's Mission to Jews (CMJ—Anglican). After a brief sojourn traveling in Europe, Jakób returned home and, following in his father's footsteps, also became a volunteer with the mission. He then began seven years of formal theological training, first at the mission Bible school in Warsaw, then in a Methodist seminary in Germany, and eventually in England at St. Aidan's College, where he was ordained by the Church of England, first as a deacon, then as a priest. During these years he met Joan Cecelia Gapp, an Anglican mission volunteer, whom he married in August 1935.

Jakób's world was changing. He had spent seven years in Christian theological training, his thinking shaped by other worlds and other contexts. He was thinking new thoughts in new ways, and most often speaking not his mother tongue but the strange cadences of the foreigner. And, from the Jewish point of view, he had married one of the daughters of Canaan.[2]

Harvest before the Holocaust

Jakób returned to Warsaw with his wife, Joan, assigned to the CMJ ministry in Poland. In view of the Holocaust to come, it is fascinating and poignant to read of Jocz's fruitful ministry during this period. In one of his missionary reports, he writes:

> One of our greatest experiences was the three meetings at Chelm [a small city of 29,000, nearly half of them Jews]. . . . After having persuaded the Lutheran pastor of the place that mission work to the Jews is a good cause, he gave us his church, although reluctantly, doubting very much if any Jew would appear at such a meeting. He said: "I know their opinions, surely nobody will come." On Saturday, an hour before the

meeting, crowds filled the courtyard. Very soon, before we started, the church was filled and a bigger crowd was sent home than the one which was inside. When we began to address them, we saw that we had before us a crowd of good-looking and well-behaved young men and women, who did not come out of curiosity, but who really sought for something which could fill their lives. ... It was indeed a very inspiring meeting: sometimes we forgot that we had Jews before us. The stillness and the attentive faces made us almost believe that we were speaking to Christian people. Before the close of the meeting, the Pastor came and later expressed amazement at a sight which before he would have never thought possible (Jocz 1937, 88).

Preaching the gospel to Jews in Poland, even before the Holocaust, was a daunting task, in large part because of Jewish attitudes misshapen for centuries in kilns of pervasive and cruel anti-Semitism. Nevertheless, the ministry of Jocz and his team was deeply successful. God was doing something through these Yiddish-speaking evangelists, snatching brands from fires of anti-Semitism soon to be heated to unprecedented intensity at Auschwitz and beyond.

A danger not to be ignored

My Jewish eyes detect a danger sign in Jocz's account (see above). I note how he caters to the attitudes of his mission readers, how he remarks that *these* Jews were good-looking and well-behaved. Does that mean other Jews generally were not? I note how he states that "sometimes we forgot that we had Jews before us. The stillness and the attentive faces made us almost believe that we were speaking to Christian people." He refers to the Jewish people as "them," and positions himself in contrast to the Jewish community as a representative of a largely Gentile Christian "us." It is clear, both here and throughout his life, that Jocz had a passionate concern for the Jewish people. It is also clear that this "square peg" was already being whittled down to fit the "round hole" of Gentile Christian forms.

Jocz's years of service in Poland were rich and fruitful. In addition to itinerant evangelism in Polish villages and cities, he edited the Yiddish missionary journal *Der Weg* and helped to lead the approximately 75–member congregation at the Anglican Mission in Warsaw.

Snatched from the fire

Jocz was destined to be one of only three or four Jewish believers in six Warsaw congregations to survive the Holocaust. That he did so was surely miraculous. His wife, Joan, was pregnant with their first child and was spending the summer in England awaiting the birth. In England CMJ was sponsoring a conference that was in danger of collapse because the keynote speaker had taken ill. Jocz was recruited from Warsaw to fill the spot. Having done so, he sought to return to Warsaw only to find the borders had been closed. The carnage had begun. Had he remained in Poland, it is certain he would have perished together with his congregation, most of his family, and three-and-one-half million other Polish Jews.

In England, understandably distraught, he had time to reflect on the previous four years of effective ministry to crowds, individuals and his congregation. Now all lay in ruins. News from Poland was scarce and alarming, and CMJ assigned him to a never-ending cycle of deputation meetings, where he was obliged to recount again and again vignettes of life in Poland, life as it had been but would never be again.

Keeping on

Jocz turned his grief in two directions: to his books and to his pen. He began work toward the Ph.D. at Edinburgh, where he had been offered a research fellowship. His dissertation, *The Jewish People and Jesus Christ: A Study in the Controversy Between Church and Synagogue*, was completed in 1945 and published in 1949. In the work he sought "to investigate the deeper reasons that have led, first to the separation of the Jews from Jesus Christ, and later their complete estrangement" (1949, 2). He explored the tensions between the church and synagogue, which he viewed to be rooted in Christ's personal claims, which the synagogue could not accept, and the diametrically opposite anthropologies of the two faith communities: Christianity predicated on the necessity of personal surrender, and Judaism predicated on the efficacy of self-effort. In the process he surveyed the history of the relationship between church and synagogue. Especially strong and gripping is his chronicle of historical and theological anti-Semitism. He placed responsibility for Jewish estrangement from Christ at the feet of the church.

The plight of the Jewish people was to be the theme of most of his writing in the immediate postwar period, as he sought to stir the Christian public to compassion and missionary action. Indeed, the Jewish people and the missionary responsibility of the church toward them was to prove a constant theme throughout his writing career.

What Jocz was not able to do during this postwar period was to minister to Jews firsthand, and this was most certainly both a grave personal frustration and an incalculable waste of his talents and calling. Elizabeth Louise Myers writes:

> The mission structures which might have enabled Jocz to spearhead a significant outreach to London's Jewish community were simply not in place. CMJ, discouraged and disheartened by the loss of its most successful mission stations—not to mention the people to whom the work of those stations had been directed—was slow to respond to the needs of the Jews on its own doorstep. And so Jocz found himself at the helm of the struggling little chapel on Downshire Hill, its congregation decimated and its windows still shattered from the German bombs that had been dropped around it (1989, 35).

In this new assignment Jocz labored faithfully but suffered multiple barbs: the anti-Semitism on the part of parishioners vexed to be saddled with a heavily accented Jewish priest, the frustration of not being able to minister to his own people in this hour of overwhelming need, and a job assignment for which he was overqualified. Myers puts it this way: "He did long for a parish which could serve as an effective center for neighborhood evangelism of the Jewish people of London; and although the Bishop made extensive inquiries on his behalf, nothing came of it" (ibid., 37).

We must pause to note again what was happening to this "square peg" God had fashioned. Instead of being placed in a situation where his gifts could best be utilized and the needs of spiritually devastated Jewish people addressed, the mission and church structures to which Jocz was accountable denied him that placement in favor of a situation where, in part, his very presence was an occasion for resentment and outrage.

Jocz continued writing and looking for a more suitable situation. These were for him years of great frustration. Irene Lipson, wife of a respected Jewish Christian whom Jocz won to faith, remarked in a 1997 phone interview that Jocz "was frustrated at CMJ because he couldn't achieve his full potential." During those years, says Lipson, CMJ was "so very Anglican and so very English. They still regarded Jewish believers as 'the natives.'"

Indeed, it was through the influence of Eric Lipson, Irene's husband, a Jew from a well-known British rabbinical family, that Jocz's own Jewishness assumed sharper focus. In his childhood home in Poland his parents "had made little fuss of their Jewishness; indeed, grandmother Sarah was always very reluctant to visit them [Jocz's family] for fear of what *trayf* (unclean food) she might find next on the table! But now, approaching his fiftieth birthday, Jocz began to appreciate anew the Jewish festivals and traditions" (Myers 1989, 19).

O Canada

In 1956 Jocz accepted a position directing the Nathanael Institute, a Jewish mission in Toronto, Canada, hoping he would find there the kind of stimulation and usefulness he had known in Poland and that had eluded him in England. He was to be disappointed yet again. The mission was in a deteriorating neighborhood, the center of Jewish settlement had moved from the area, and the congregation attached to the mission was moribund and struggling financially.

By now, Jocz had two post-graduate degrees, having recently been awarded the D.Litt. from Edinburgh, in addition to the Ph.D. Restless for stimulation and aching with frustration, he was grateful in 1957 when the opportunity arose for him to lecture at Wycliffe College (Anglican). In 1960 he accepted a position there as chair of systematic theology.

During his remaining years Jocz ministered widely through his writing, teaching and extensive speaking schedule. During the Canadian years he published five major books: *A Theology of Election* (1958), *A Spiritual History of Israel* (1961), *Christians and Jews: Encounter and Mission* (1966), *The Covenant: A Theology of Human Destiny (1968)*, and *The Jewish People and Jesus Christ After Auschwitz* (1981).

His books show the breadth of his reading and knowledge; Jocz put his knowledge of many languages to good use. His continuing loyalty and love for the Jewish people are clear. It is fitting that both his first and last major works deal with the narrative encounter of Jewish people with Jesus Christ, for these two realities and their interaction with one another were the primary preoccupations of Jocz's life. His writing seems clearest and most focused when he writes out of these passions.

I am struck by how foreign to Jewish life and thought and how very difficult his theological writing is to read. The master linguist had clearly mastered yet another language, that of high-level theological discourse. It seems to me that he wrote for a very small audience, chiefly other Christian systematic theologians.

The Scene of the Crime

The more I examine the evidence, the more convinced I am that the life of Jakób Jocz was a missionary tragedy. This man who was created, gifted and called by God to be an effective missionary to his people was forced by a combination of historical circumstance and mission and church policies to be a person whose life increasingly was one of talking *about* the Jews to others rather than *to* the Jews about Yeshua.

Jocz's life was a tragedy in three areas: his parents' experience, his theological training and his missionary assignments.

His parents' experience was a missionary tragedy. Both had substantial Jewish backgrounds and a deep basis for commonality with other Jews. But we read that his father, a former student at the Vilna Yeshiva, was baptized in a local church that he began attending, thus becoming an outcast and stranger to his people. How much better it would have been had there been a Jewish context in which to grow as a Christian. Later in life Jocz's parents made little fuss about their Jewishness and were just as apt to serve unkosher food as anything else. Where did these behaviors come from? Why did they abandon kosher living? It seems clear that the theological and social climate of the Warsaw Mission of CMJ and of its school undermined their continuity with and loyalty to the Jewish way of life. This is certainly a tragedy—for Jakób's parents, for the cause of Jewish mission and for Jakób himself.[3]

Jocz's theological training was a missionary tragedy. Regardless of the spiritual benefit he may have received, this training made him a stranger to the Jewish people. As Joseph's years in Egypt made him unrecognizable to his brothers, so Jocz's years of Christian theological training made him increasingly a conceptual stranger to his people. He spoke a different language, identified with a different narrative and troubled himself with different questions than those his Jewish people knew or cared about.

Finally, his mission assignments were a missionary tragedy. After 1939, he was never placed in a position where he could have effective ministry to Eastern European Jews. Can there be any excuse for such neglect? I can only assume that the mission cared more for its financial stability than for Jewish refugees. Why else did it saddle Jocz with so much deputation? Irene Lipson is correct in characterizing the postwar CMJ as "so very Anglican and so very English," and so very patronizing to Jewish staff and refugees, whom it regarded as "the natives." For CMJ to fail to place Jocz in situations where he could be an effective missionary, fail to mount a concerted effort to reach the thousands of displaced Jewish refugees on its very doorstep, and assign Jocz to positions where he was so under-utilized was surely criminal.

While it is true that Jocz knew much effectiveness in deputation, in speaking engagements, and in theological writing and education, this effectiveness is a tribute to his own brilliance and adaptability and to how effectively he was whittled down from being God's "square peg" that he might better fit church and mission "round holes." He was a great man, a great theologian and a great teacher. But I believe the kingdom of God and the God of the kingdom were cheated out of a great missionary.

Conclusion

Some might say mission agencies and church structures are means God uses to shape God's servants for God's purposes. That is certainly true. Others would say we must never forget the sovereignty of God, who works in mysterious ways to accomplish all things according to his will. That would be true as well. But it is just as true that there are times when institutional leaders use God's servants for ends that have more to do with cultural arrogance and organizational agendas than the call of God.

In my own career I parted company with an effective mission agency largely because I knew God was not calling me to be a "square peg" in its "round hole." I know now that had I continued trying to accommodate myself to such demands, I would have betrayed God's call on my life. Trying to fit in where one doesn't belong results in friction and breakage. In the end, no one benefits. And in the process a certain barrenness replaces the fruit-bearing that God intended.

The more aware I become of God's call on my life, the more selective I can be concerning assignments I will accept and formational experiences I will choose. As one of God's "square pegs," I want to be in the places he has designed for me and to finish well the course laid out for me.[4] After what we have learned from Jocz's life, can any of us as wise servants of God afford to do less?

Notes

[1] For biographical data on Jocz I am indebted to two excellent sources: Glasser 1994 and Myers 1989.

[2] My own father was, like Jocz, born in Eastern Europe before the World War I. When he married my mother, an Italian Gentile, his Orthodox mother

began talking suicide. Although she became an Orthodox convert to Judaism, after my father's death my mother told me she'd never really felt accepted by his family. I share this to demonstrate how strong Jewish feelings were at this time concerning marriage outside the group. In a way, little had changed since the time of Rebekkah, who dreaded that her son Jacob might marry an outsider (see Gen. 27:46).

[3] One of the passions of my life is to motivate, educate, train and assist Messianic Jews in reacculturating as Jews and reconnecting with their Jewishness, a rich legacy only a fool would discard. Accordingly, I have founded Messianic T.O.R.A.H. Institute, dedicated to Teaching Our Rituals And Heritage. Messianic Jews should be encouraged and helped to think and live as who they are— *Jews who serve the Messiah.*

[4] "Finishing well" is one of the themes stressed by Dr. J. Robert (Bobby) Clinton in the Leadership concentration at Fuller Theological Seminary's School of World Mission. This biographical study on Jocz owes much to Clinton's lessons in how God shapes leaders for God's purposes.

References

Glasser, Arthur F. 1994. "Jakób Jocz 1906–1983: 'To the Jew First': First Principle in Mission." In *Mission Legacies: Biographical Studies of Leaders of the Modern Missionary Movement,* ed. Gerald Anderson, Robert T. Coote, Norman A. Horner, James M. Phillips, 525–31. Maryknoll, N.Y.: Orbis Books.

Jocz, Jakób. 1937. "The Gospel in the Little Towns of Poland." *Jewish Missionary Intelligence* 28, no. 8: 88–90.

——— 1949. *The Jewish People and Jesus Christ: A Study in the Controversy Between Church and Synagogue.* London: SPCK.

——— 1958. *A Theology of Election: Israel and the Church.* London: SPCK.

——— 1961. *The Spiritual History of Israel.* London: Eyre and Spottiswoode.

——— 1966. *Christians and Jews: Encounter and Mission.* London: SPCK.

——— 1968. *The Covenant: A Theology of Human Destiny.* Grand Rapids, Mich.: Eerdmans.

——— 1981. *The Jewish People and Jesus Christ After Auschwitz.* Grand Rapids, Mich.: Baker Book House.

Lipson, Irene. 1997. Telephone interview with Stuart Dauermann, March 17.

Myers, Elizabeth Louise. 1989. "The Literary Legacy of Jacob Jocz." Master's thesis, Fuller Theological Seminary, Pasadena, California.

4

David Seamands

A missiology of healing grace

Hitomi Kishi Gray

How can we face God when we are broken? How does God care for our broken hearts? How can we participate in God's mission in the world when we are broken people? How can we communicate God's healing love across cultural boundaries? I have asked these and other questions as I have faced my own brokenness and my sense of call to mission.

Through the writings of David Seamands, I am finding some answers. Seamands, a missionary to India for sixteen years,[1] has researched and written in the area of inner healing. While he does not write with specifically missiological intentions, I see much in Seamands that I can apply to both preparing for and doing mission.

David Seamands introduced me to the God who intimately communes with us in our brokenness.[2] Our relationship with God is not just a matter of salvation from eternal death but also of our everyday walk. God is a God who embraces our hurting selves with love and transforms our relationships with God, ourselves and others. God calls us in and out of our brokenness to participate in God's mission of bringing wholeness to a hurting world.

Hitomi Kishi Gray, a native of Japan, currently serves in Mosaic, a local church in Los Angeles, with her husband, Andy. They develop small-group ministry among international students, mostly from South and East Asia. Many of the students hear the gospel for the first time and are nurtured into relationship with God through the community. After competing in swimming for more than 10 years, Gray now enjoys fishing, backpacking, kayaking, sitting in hot springs, journaling and chatting in coffee shops. She received the Ph.D. from the School of World Mission, Fuller Theological Seminary, in June 1999.

In this chapter I will not present the "how tos" of inner healing, nor will I present a psychological analysis of human brokenness and inner healing. Rather, I will interact as a missiologist with David Seamands's theological understanding of this God who seeks intimacy with us in our brokenness.

But first, let me tell my own story.

My journey

I have been searching for intimacy with God and for a true sense of who I am. When I was in high school, God clearly called me into service. But during my college years in Japan, I started to question my faith. Growing up as a pastor's daughter, I had an intellectual understanding of God. I had memorized many Scripture verses, and I knew how to do church work. But God did not seem real to me. God belonged in the church I attended on Sundays, but I didn't know how to face God with the complexities of my life. I sought and found community with my friends at school, many of whom had nothing to do with my faith. I gradually stopped praying. I concluded that I could live a good life without God and find my own answers to life's complicated questions.

One part of me, however, did not want to disappoint my parents, who had devoted their lives to the church. I knew their faith in God was real, and that kept me going to church every week.

I reached a crisis point after I graduated from college. All of a sudden I felt very lost. I didn't know where I was going or what I wanted to do for the rest of my life. I realized how fragile was the self I thought I had found during my college days. At the same time that I lost close interaction with my college friends, I also lost my strong sense of self. It seemed no one understood the emptiness I was experiencing.

One day God spoke to me in a profound way. I was walking home from church through a rice paddy when I heard a voice within me saying, "The Lord is my Shepherd, I shall not be in want"—one of my favorite memory verses. The next moment I was in tears. I knew God had spoken to reassure me of his presence. God was my Shepherd, guiding my life. I had nothing to worry about.

"God, I am yours," I responded. "Take my life." God became real to me again. God heard my cry for security. In an instant I knew everything I had learned from childhood about God, Jesus, the Cross and the Resurrection was true. God's healing grace flooded me, and I deeply felt God's love. I had met God face to face.

My walk with the Lord has grown in amazing ways since that encounter. Our relationship has become the solid center of my life. I have shared my relationship with God with other believers as we encourage each other to grow deeper with the Lord and with each other. My call to ministry has been renewed, and I think more about God's mission to reach out in intimacy to hurting people.

The year after my encounter with God, I attended a Bible college in Australia. While in Australia I became involved with university outreach to international students. I have continued this ministry during my time in Los Angeles, working especially with Japanese students. I have observed that many of these students struggle as I had, partly because Japanese social expectations seem to prevent them from facing personal brokenness. Those who become Christians often say intimacy with God has helped them find personal healing and discover who they are.

David Seamands writes on the healing work of God, a God who is intimately involved in our journey of growth. This theology of healing grace takes us deeper into face-to-face communion with the Healer in the context of our communities. God's work in our lives allows us to participate in the mission of extending God's healing and wholeness to others, even across cultural barriers.

Seamands's theology of healing grace

Seamands says, "The main task in counseling and inner healing is to remove the barriers to forgiveness so that people can receive grace—the gift of God's love freely offered to the undeserving and the unworthy. . . . I discovered that the experience of grace is the most therapeutic factor in emotional and spiritual healing" (1988, 7). During his years as a missionary in India, Seamands faced issues of brokenness in himself and in his interpersonal relationships. These prodded him in his search for a healing intimacy with God. The development and articulation of his ministry have come in the years since India, and his books have become standard texts in the field of inner healing.[3]

The theological foundation for Seamands's ministry of inner healing can be expressed in the words *healing grace*. I will look at four areas of Seamands's theology of healing grace: God's desire to extend healing grace to all people, the fact of human brokenness, the possibility of transformation into wholeness and the place of the church in the process. I will apply Seamands's theology of healing grace to God's mission in the world.

God's desire to heal

Seamands defines grace as God's love in action on behalf of human beings, freely giving forgiveness, acceptance and favor. He shows a God who seeks intimacy with people and is willing to take the initiative. God's healing grace is motivated by God's love and is expressed in spite of sin, guilt and the broken relationships of those who would receive God's grace. Seamands shows God reaching to humanity through Christ, who identified with human brokenness, and through the work of the Holy Spirit.

Seamands does not separate God's grace from the life, death and resurrection of Christ. God's grace is "essentially the redeeming activity of God in Christ" (1988, 109). Seamands points out that the life of Christ "was a nonstop demonstration of the fact that [God] offered the gift of salvation to everyone, without any regard for their worthiness" (ibid., 110). He goes on to write that "this love is manifested as grace, offered us in the life and death of Christ" (ibid., 115). Although people can reject God's love, they cannot stop God from loving them through Christ.

Seamands explains face-to-face intimacy with Christ to be a living reality with "an empathetic and understanding God" (1985, 55). God identifies with human beings. Because Christ experienced being human, "he is touched with the feelings, the feelings that arise in you from that hurt. He feels the problems that touch you. He wants to heal. He wants you to know that He is not angry with you about your feelings. He understands" (1981, 64).

Seamands identifies the Cross as the greatest expression of God's grace: "In His full identification with our humanity, and especially on that cross, He took unto Himself the entire range of our feelings and He bore the feeling of our infirmities, that we would not have to bear them alone" (ibid., 69; see also 1995, 58–59).

Seamands uses the image of a priest to help us understand how God identifies with us through Christ:

> Therefore, when he made his sacrifices, he was also sacrificing for himself to cover all his imperfection, as well as presenting an offering for his people. However, because he had infirmities, he could understand the infirmities of his people and deal more gently with them. He could be more understanding as a priest. For he too was subjected to the inner infirmities which predispose all of us to temptation and sin (1981, 57).

Seamands also sees God's healing grace as coming through the work of the Holy Spirit. He identifies two major roles of the Holy Spirit in the ministry of inner healing. The first is to assure persons that God is really with them in their pain: "Grace needs to be fully realized. . . . For this to happen, grace needs to penetrate and permeate the heart" (1988, 118). The Holy Spirit touches persons on the level of their feelings.

The second work of the Holy Spirit in the ministry of inner healing is an active participation in that healing. In the Greek word *paraklete*, the role of the Holy Spirit is defined as "the one called to come alongside us." In Romans 8:26, the word *help* has the medical connotation of a nurse who assists in the healing process (1981, 20). Seamands goes on to say that "the Holy Spirit becomes our partner and helper, who works along with us in a mutual participation, for our healing. . . . It is a beautiful and sensitive picture of the knowing, understanding, caring God who is now participating with us in our healing" (ibid., 67; 1985, 55).

Although Seamands does not write missiologically, his picture of a God who takes the initiative and reaches out in grace to hurting people is the picture of a missionary God. It is part of God's character to reach out to humanity. God's healing grace transcends time, race and culture, and becomes part of the motivation for mission.

The problem of human brokenness

Seamands identifies four perceptual areas in the lives of human beings that help or hinder in living a life of grace: God, self, others and the reality that people carry with them, often unconsciously, and that help determine quality of life and relationships (1985, 39–40; 1988, 47–53). Since we live in an imperfect world, mistaken concepts of reality can hinder grace. By faith, people believe in God, yet they often fail to allow God's grace to reach in and fill the brokenness. Believing grace in their heads, they do not feel it or live it out in their relationships (1988, 39).

Seamands points out that the heart of the problem is sin: "According to the Bible, sin is both the root of what we've described as the problem of the heart–fallen, diseased, and powerless to change itself" (1988, 56), a malignant disease that hinders persons from a close relationship with God.

Human brokenness is expressed in various ways: a sense of unworthiness; feelings of anxiety, inadequacy and inferiority; shame; hate; anger; a growing individualism; an unhealthy activism; legalism; perfectionism; repressed memories; depression; low self-esteem; and fear. This brokenness, resulting from an inadequate view of God, self and others, puts up barriers to the grace God wants to bestow. People say, "I know God

understands my pain and loves me in my weakness, but I can't feel it."
Seamands identifies with this inner conflict between "what they think
about God and what they feel about God" (1985, 95). Right doctrines
about God that do not penetrate to the feeling level do not automatically
"clear up a person's concepts of God and enable him to believe in God
and trust Him" (1985, 97).

Missiology would place Seamands's focus on personal concepts of self,
others, God and reality in the larger context of worldview studies.[4] It
would explore how a person's perceptions of reality relate to the larger
perceptions held by the surrounding society in general. In addition to
the healing of persons, should we seek the healing of cultures? Can a
broken person become whole in a culture in which worldview perceptions are not in accord with biblical truth? What is the intersection of
person and culture in inner healing?

Missiology would also explore cultural expressions of brokenness.
While the fact of brokenness may be universal, are its expressions culturally determined, at least in part? How would this affect the presentation
of God's Good News of wholeness in specific contexts?

The journey toward wholeness

Seamands defines sanctification as "essentially a humanizing process"
(1982, 50). As God touches people with healing grace, they begin to
walk in relationship with God on a journey of becoming holy and whole.
In order to take this journey, people need to discover how to apply grace
to their specific brokenness and unhealed relationships. They need first
to be in touch with themselves, and then allow God to touch the brokenness with God's grace. "As a Christian, you can be a realist. This means
you don't need to be afraid to face the worst, the ugliest, the most painful. You don't have to be afraid to express your feelings of grief, sorrow,
hurt, loneliness, struggle, even depression" (1981, 181).

The healing grace of God reveals Jesus as Savior, Healer and Wonderful Counselor, the One who brings people to emotional, spiritual and
relational wholeness (1995, 13). For example, the factual nature of past
memories does not change, yet God can change their meaning and impact on a person's life (1981, 232; 1995, 88). By healing grace, people
can compassionately live with themselves and learn not to judge other
people harshly when those people exhibit confusing and contradictory
behavior. God's plan is, through salvation and sanctification, to transform God's children "into the likeness of Christ" (2 Cor. 3:18), so they
can enjoy "both earthly and eternal fellowship with God and other people"
(1988, 93). God longs to bring persons toward wholeness at the personal

and corporate levels, "so that we will be better equipped to do ministry both within and outside of the Church according to His will" (ibid., 184).

Seamands's emphasis on relational wholeness is missiologically significant. Most of the world's cultures are community oriented, and relationships are of central importance. Individuals are not isolated, as is so often the case in the West, but are always seen as part of communities. A missiology of inner healing would emphasize these corporate and relational aspects.

Seamands's observation that as persons become healed and whole they are thus enabled for ministry is also missiologically significant. Persons who would be missionaries are often as much in need of healing grace as are the people to whom they desire to minister. Should this emphasis become part of missionary training? Should a wise mission administration have a focus on the healing and wholeness of its staff as part of its ongoing oversight?

The place of the church in healing grace

Since the Fall, human beings have feared being open and uncovered, not only with God but also with others and even with themselves (see Gen. 3:8–10.) Facing pain with honesty, bringing about lasting change, and deepening one's relationship with God almost always require the help of another person. Seamands says that "it is in this constructive personal relationship in the present that we fully come to know ourselves for real" (ibid., 180; 1995, 146). He points out that "supportive Christians need to surround struggling and suffering persons with an atmosphere of understanding and love" (1981, 56).

Members of the body of Christ can minister to one another other out of "the very place where they hurt the most" (1988, 182). Personal pain is not wasted. A person's own painful experience allows God's strength to be made perfect (2 Cor. 12:9–10) (1981, 240).

According to Seamands, a central purpose of trusting each other and bearing each other's burdens is to "pave the way for receiving God's grace" (1988, 89). Body life becomes the channel of grace. As a person is accepted by the body of believers, that person senses God's healing grace and experiences transformation in relationships with God, self and others. Divine healing grace restores and enriches community in the church and enables the church to reach out in healthy ways to others.

Again, the communal nature of inner healing is missiologically significant, especially in contexts of the majority world that are community oriented. Perhaps it will be in this area that majority world churches will have much to teach their sisters and brothers in the West.

Inner healing in specific contexts

Cultural contexts must be taken into consideration as God's people minister to others of various backgrounds. Each culture, society, church or family has its unique context that enhances or hinders the experience of God's healing grace. Each culture experiences brokenness in a different way. And God's wholeness will be expressed in unique ways in each context.

Naoto is a Japanese student studying at a university in Los Angeles. I met him through the Japanese Bible study we both attended. When Naoto started coming to the study, he had no desire to become a Christian. One of his roommates was leading the Bible study, so Naoto just went to be with us. He had lost his Christian mother in a car accident in Japan before coming to the United States. Although we did not talk about that in any deep way in the group, he began to open up some of his pain to the study leader.

The Bible study provided community for all of us. We ate together often, helped one another when there was a need, celebrated birthdays, traveled and did many other things together, as so often happens in a Japanese community. Everyone, both Christians and nonbelievers, felt accepted and loved.

One summer was very difficult for Naoto as he struggled with his mother's death and his own sense of inadequacy. He decided to commit suicide. But as he approached the window from which he was going to jump, Naoto was reminded of the verse he heard in the Bible study that says nothing is impossible with God. He couldn't move his feet. In a moment he was persuaded to give his heart to God. This was his last option. Through the Bible studies and through relationships with Christians, Naoto had been prepared to encounter God and to accept his grace.

Since that time God's love has embraced Naoto's sorrow and anger, and he is beginning to make sense of the painful past. Naoto himself is becoming a loving person and learning to reach out to others.

It is sad to think that in his moment of crisis, there was no one Naoto felt he could speak with. Talking about personal matters does not usually happen in a Japanese community. One shares mostly in one-on-one relationships, especially with a leader figure or a person who is not part of the group. Cultural sensitivity is required in order to facilitate relationships in which a person can open up safely.

Furthermore, the shame-based Japanese culture defines how a Japanese person is in touch with pain and determines the level of trust needed before that person can open up to others. It affects the sense of need or the willingness to externalize pain. It takes time for the Christian community to grow into mutual trust so people confide openly in one another. However, growing in a face-to-face relationship with God can be encouraged in culturally appropriate ways, through which the church matures in loving relationships with God, self, others and the world.

I rejoice because the Healer who completely understands human brokenness intervened to deliver Naoto from destroying the precious gift of life. Naoto has found his true self and has discovered he is unconditionally loved by Jesus. He continues to grow in Christ through the community of believers. He was baptized in a few years ago, with his sister and a friend who had also trusted their lives to Jesus.

Conclusion

David Seamands's theology of healing grace helps us understand God's work of restoring wounded souls and broken communities as God builds face-to-face relationships with people. God's healing grace reaches out to all people regardless of their ethnic or cultural backgrounds. It leads to transformation on both individual and relational levels. It responds to a God-given yearning to be loved through intimate communion with the Creator and with other people in community. It encourages the church to become a fellowship of grace bearers, so that God's purposes in the world prevail.

As I continue my involvement in the ministry of building healing communities, I want to walk the journey of being transformed by God's healing grace. I want to study the cultural context in which I minister and understand its effect on people. In community with others, I want to become a vessel through which God loves, restores and empowers people, leading them from brokenness to intimacy, wholeness and mission.

Notes

[1] David A. Seamands was born to missionary parents in India, graduated from Drew Theological Seminary (M.Div.), and Hartford Seminary Foundation (M.A.), and served as a Methodist missionary to India for sixteen years. Later he served as pastor of the United Methodist Church in Wilmore, Kentucky, for 22 years and currently is professor emeritus at Asbury Theological Seminary in Wilmore, Kentucky, and lives with his wife, Helen, in Nokomis, Florida.

[2] In this chapter I refer to brokenness in a general sense, encompassing emotional, relational or spiritual pain. It is not my purpose here to give a complete

definition of brokenness or to discuss the contexts in which people experience brokenness.

[3] What we call the ministry of inner healing has been practiced in the church for centuries under the rubric of spiritual direction. Recently, inner healing is being practiced in a number of different traditions influenced by the Pentecostal movement. Under influence of the charismatic renewal, mainline churches have pioneered the methods of inner healing that are most in use today (Flynn 1993, 22). Despite the wide range of diversity, Flynn proposes the definition of inner healing as "a method of prayer by which Jesus Christ is invited to address the hurts of the past and heal us of their negative results" (ibid.). Different from *grief work* or a *recovery program*, inner healing is seen as more Jesus-centered and more dependent on the power of God to enter the heart and change lives. Inner healing is about intimacy with God at the depth of the self and God's transformational work in relationships with God, self and others.

[4] See, for example, the chapters by Billy Nishioka and Levi De Carvalho in this volume.

References

Flynn, Michael, and Doug Gregg. 1993. *Inner Healing: A Handbook for Helping Yourself and Others*. Downers Grove, Ill.: InterVarsity Press.

Seamands, David. 1981. *Healing for Damaged Emotions*. Wheaton, Ill.: Victor Books.

——— 1982. *Putting away Childish Things*. Wheaton, Ill.: Victor Books.

——— 1985. *Healing of Memories*. Wheaton, Ill.: Victor Books.

——— 1988. *Healing Grace*. Wheaton, Ill.: Victor Books.

——— 1995. *If Only*. Wheaton, Ill.: Victor Books.

5

E. Stanley Jones

Doing theology in a pluralistic context

BOBBY BOSE

I was born and raised in a Christian family in Calcutta, India. We were Bengali Christians living in a vast cosmopolitan sea of ethnic and religious groups from all over India, as well as ethnic minorities such as Armenians, Chinese and Parsis. I attended a Catholic school, but my schoolmates were Hindu, Muslim, Jewish and Christian. My Hindu friends would challenge me, saying, "Your name [Bose] is Bengali. You can't be a Christian!" My Muslim friends would say, "Your Bible is all corrupt. Jesus is not the Son of God. The real story comes from Islam!" I remember wanting to move away, to find a place where all the people were Christians, but my parents told me there was no such place.

At the age of sixteen God called me to ministry. I began handing out literature in trains and markets and preaching in home groups where Christians would invite non-Christians. After college graduation I decided to study the Bible in London, and I entered another pluralistic context. During the summer months a church in London gave me a position working with Asians. I found myself ministering to many different kinds of people from many religious backgrounds. Once a friend invited me to his house to preach to some of his friends. I encountered a spirit-

---

Bobby Bose was born and raised in the pluralistic context of Calcutta, India. He has ministered through evangelism, discipling and training in Calcutta, London and the Los Angeles area. Bose has taught theology at Calcutta Bible College/ Carey Center and currently teaches missiology at Union Biblical Seminary, Pune, India. His Ph.D. research focuses on theology in a religiously pluralistic society. He and his wife, Margie, have one daughter.

ist, a Jehovah's Witness, and a Muslim, all three asking questions, disagreeing with each other, and all disagreeing with me.

The more I worked in this context, the more I struggled, wondering how to be open to all people so I could befriend them and witness to them, yet at the same time hold firmly to my faith in Jesus as the only way to the Father. How could I proclaim the exclusive claims of Christianity and at the same time be genuinely inclusive in my approach to people? How could I communicate the absolute claims of Christ and the Christian faith in the midst of other competing truth-claims? How should the gospel story interact with the many stories of a pluralist context?

My interest in mission in pluralistic contexts heightened, and I discovered that E. Stanley Jones had something to teach me. I had read some of Jones's works while living in India, but now I reflected anew on his methods of doing theology in a pluralistic setting.

E. Stanley Jones, a United Methodist missionary in India for more than 66 years, has been an influential and beloved proponent of Christianity. Biographer Richard W. Taylor writes:

> Missionary, evangelist, India, America, trusted, interpreter, pacifist–these are the major dimensions of the Jones legacy. Perhaps the most admirable aspect of the legacy is that Jones was able to keep all these dimensions together–each enriching the others. And he was remarkably creative in interrelating these dimensions. He had an awesomely synthetic mind, and the ability to gather people around him who had fresh and timely ideas to contribute. There are not many missionaries like that any more. Times have changed. But there is still much that we can learn from him (1982, 102–7).

My interest in E. Stanley Jones revolves around the ways he carried out his ministry and developed his theology in a pluralistic context. Of the many things we can learn from him, I focus here on his "round table" ministry.

Biographical background

E. Stanley Jones was born on January 3, 1884, in Clarksville, Maryland, USA.[1] He studied at Asbury College and went as a missionary to India in 1907 at the age of 23 under the Board of the Methodist Episcopal Church. In 1911 he married Mabel Lossing, a missionary colleague stationed with him in Lucknow. He served in India until his death at Bareilly in northern India on January 25, 1973.

During his lifetime Jones had the opportunity to minister in many parts of the world and to many peoples, but he saw himself primarily as an evangelist. In 1928 the General Conference of the Methodist Episcopal Church (US) elected him as a bishop, but he resigned the morning before his consecration, feeling his call was to continue as a missionary evangelist. In 1930 he was appointed "evangelist-at-large for India and the world" (Taylor 1982, 102). He clearly felt called not only as an evangelist to India but to the rest of the world. Three of his many publications especially bear witness to this calling: The *Christ of the Indian Road* (1925), *The Christ of Every Road* (1931) and *The Christ of the American Road* (1946). In his autobiography he writes:

> Before I reached India, I had unconsciously stumbled on an important principle and procedure. My inner voice had said, "It's India"—not "It's Indians." India was to be the center of my endeavors, but Indians and non-Indians were my field. I would not be a professional missionary to Indians, but a personal missionary to everybody. I had begun to win people to Christ before I reached India, and they were non-Indians. The all important fact began to take possession of me: All men are one, their needs are one; all men need conversion regardless of label. So I wouldn't talk to Westerners or Easterners, to Hindus or Muslims; I would talk to people in the same basic human need, anywhere, everywhere. That was a seed attitude which would blossom into a world evangelism instead of a severely Indian evangelism. Later, I found the Indians liked this attitude: "We do not mind your coming to us, providing you go to other people. For we don't like to feel we are in sole need of conversion." My reply: "You are not in sole need of conversion. Man as man needs conversion, not man as Hindu or Muslim or whatnot." I had stumbled into the universal before I reached India—the specific (Jones 1968, 77–78).

I suggest this inclusive attitude toward people and human need was a key ingredient in Jones's fruitful ministry in a pluralist context. At any rate, as William M. Pickard puts it, "[Jones's] entire message and method were hammered out in a religiously plural society and are particularly appropriate for the kind of pluralistic world we face today" (1994, 28).

"Round table" methodology

E. Stanley Jones's *Christ at the Round Table* (1928) is seminal not only for understanding his method of evangelism but also his method of doing theology in religiously pluralistic contexts.

From the outset Jones discerned that Indians had long been thinking deeply about the supernatural and its relation to human beings; India's philosophy had not suffered "from underthought but from overstrain" (1928, 9). On the other hand, Jones pointed out that those who are Christian in name may not be Christian in reality; though the Crusaders conquered Jerusalem, they didn't find Christ there as they "lost him through the very spirit and methods by which they sought to serve him" (ibid., 11).

In looking at attitudes toward other faiths and cultures Jones pointed out that the pendulum swings from criticism and lack of appreciation to total unqualified approval of all faiths. For him, a Christian attitude must lie between the two extremes and "evaluation must not be merely intellectual" but "must be deeply experimental" (ibid., 17).

Around 1915 Jones began hosting "round table conferences," typically inviting about fifteen people of different religious and cultural backgrounds and five or six Christians. Hindus, Muslims, skeptics (that is, those influenced by secular atheism), and Christians gathered to speak and to listen to one another. Pickard notes, "Representatives of all religions were invited to sit down as equals around a table and to share their faith. And it is interesting that many non-Christians not only participated in and supported such conferences, but joined in sponsoring them. There was no confrontation or tension. Everyone felt comfortable. The atmosphere was one of mutual and friendly sharing" (1994, 38).

In summing up his round-table ministry, Jones described the opening procedure for each conference:

> As we sit around in a circle we suggest to them that we take a new approach to religion–new when we think of the ordinary approaches in common use. We suggest that we have had the controversial, the comparative, and the dogmatic approaches to religion. There is another approach possible. Let us come at it by the method more closely akin to the scientific method–a method so gripping to the mind of the world today. This method has three outstanding things in it: Experimentation, Verification, and Sharing of Results. . . .

We are all religious men, some more and some less, and we have all been experimenting with this matter of religion over a number of years. We have tried it as a working hypothesis of life. As we face the problems of life–its joys and its sorrows, its perplexities and its pains, the demands of duty, the moral struggle with sin and evil, the upward call to higher life, the desire to help our fellow men and to be of use, the craving for God, for redemption—what has religion brought to us? What has it brought to us of light, or moral dynamic for personal and social life, of inward peace and harmony, of redemption from sin and from the power of this world, of God? What have we and what are we verifying as true in experience? Will you share with us the results of your verification? (1928, 21).

Jones considered sharing personal experience the espousal of the scientific method. The focus on subjective experience, to his way of thinking, was putting faith to the test of life. Jones's evangelistic focus in his pluralistic context was not on religion, but on reality, and, in particular, on Reality centered in the person of Jesus Christ (Pickard 1994, 35).

Pickard rightly observes that, first and foremost, "Stanley Jones' evangelism focused on Jesus, not on beliefs about Jesus" (ibid., 32).

Stanley Jones held firmly to the basic biblical and evangelical beliefs of the Christian faith all his life. He believed in the inspiration and authority of the Bible, the Incarnation, the virgin birth and deity of Jesus, the Trinity, the atoning death of Jesus on the cross, the resurrection, Christ's second coming, the fallenness of humanity, salvation by the grace of God alone through faith in Jesus Christ, and the church as the body of those joined to, and under the Lordship of, Jesus Christ. These beliefs were the bedrock of all his preaching and teaching. Yet, they were not the center. The center was Jesus Himself, the "Word become Flesh," the person, Jesus Christ, risen and living today (Pickard 1994, 33).

Pickard goes on to show that Jones's focus on the living person of Jesus Christ led him to his emphasis not on religion or on pitting Christianity against other religions but on Reality. "He put Reality over against unreality and proclaimed that living in harmony with Reality meant abundant life, whereas living in accord with unreality meant destruction and death, both for the individual and for society" (ibid., 35).

The purpose of the round-table conferences for Jones "was to face the question of how religion was working, what it was doing for us, and how we could find deeper reality" (Jones 1928, 16). He wanted to give people a chance to express how their religious beliefs affected their personal experiences, and, as part of the conference, Christians would have equal time to share the work of Jesus Christ on a personal level. The focus was personal narrative, not argument.

Although he gave equal time to religious communities involved in the round-table discussions, Jones did not consider all religions to be equal. He did, however, see human need as universal. According to Jones, "The fundamental need of the human heart is redemption. Life is not what it ought to be. The 'ought to be' stands over against 'is' and will not let us rest. . . . And as long as men want to be better—not merely wiser or happier or more comfortable, but better—religion will remain" (ibid., 50).

Pickard claims that the part of the Christian in the round-table conferences was "to make Jesus Christ known in a rational, intelligent, and compelling way as a real person living today, winsome, loving, not only demanding as the embodiment of God's rule, but redeeming as the power of God's enabling the human race to meet God's demands" (1994, 41). The relational and human presence aspects of the witness were as important as the verbal aspects.

Although no efforts were made to persuade by argument, and preaching or seeking to make converts was actually "forbidden" in the conferences, the Christian witness was profoundly effective. Jones testifies that "there was not a single situation that I can remember where before the close of the Round Table Conference Christ was not in moral and spiritual command of the situation" (1928, 50).

> There was no drawing of contrasts between the different disclosures of the adherents of the various faiths, no pointing out of superiorities by a clever summing up—we left the statements to speak for themselves, to be their own witness by their own worth-whileness. Nevertheless—and I do not overstate which I say it, for no one could escape the impression—at the close everything else had been pushed to the edges as irrelevant and Christ controlled the situation. As men listened to what those who were in touch with him were quietly saying, they instinctively felt that here was something redemptively at work at the heart of life, redeeming men from themselves and from sin, putting worth and meaning into life, giving an unquenchable hope to men, lighting up the inward depths of life, bringing them into fellowship with God

in beautiful intimacy and furnishing a dynamic for human
service. The living freshness of it struck us all. Here was life
catching its rhythm and bursting into song. Here was God,
not an absent Deity or an abstraction, but God tender, available, opening the sources of divine love to the healing of human need and entering into fellowship with the human in an
intimacy too close for words to express (ibid., 50–51).

Jones had a profound faith that the person of Jesus Christ, as manifest in
the lives of Christ's followers, could stand on Christ's own merits in any
context and draw people to himself.

Years later, in his spiritual autobiography, *A Song of Ascents*, Jones
mentions the importance of Jesus not merely as the founder of our faith
but as the foundation of our faith. He refers to Bultmann's view that if
Jesus never lived, it would make no difference to his theology, because
Bultmann would still have Jesus' teaching. Jones's response to that was,
"Well, it would make a vital difference to me, for my theology is based
not merely on the teachings of Christ but on the Person himself" (1968,
96). Here Jones is highlighting the importance of the objective reality of
the person of Jesus Christ as revealed in the Bible—the narrative of his
life, death and resurrection.

Jones states, "When I began my work in India, I felt I had absolute
uniqueness in Jesus, but I had a series of shocks. For everything I brought
up, the non-Christian intellectuals brought up a parallel." But he goes on
to say, "Then the dawning came—and what a dawning! I saw that everything they brought up was the Word become word, and what the gospel
presented was the Word become flesh" (ibid., 96–97). He elaborates,

This Word become word and this Word become flesh—here
is the profound and decisive difference between the Christian faith and all others. It separates them not in degree but
in kind. All other faiths are philosophies or moralisms—man's
search upward. The gospel is God's search downward. . . .

Therefore, the method of comparative religions, studying
which idea is in which religion, is beside the point. It is comparing incomparable things—the Word become word and the
Word become flesh. Therefore it is all beside the point and
hence pointless. . . .

Philosophies point to truths; Jesus said, "I am the Truth."
Moralisms point to the Way; Jesus said, "I am the Way." Religions point to the Life; Jesus said, "I am the Life" (ibid.).

Jones also talks about two kinds of reality—"objective reality and subjective reality, the reality of history and the reality of experience. Each of these kinds of reality can bring a high degree of certainty. . . . But not the highest degree. The highest degree of certainty would come where the two kinds of reality—the objective and the subjective—would come together, dovetail, speak the same thing, and thus corroborate each other" (ibid., 102). Referring again to Bultmann's theology, Jones says, "Then so much worse for your theology, for it leaves you with his teaching, but not with his Person; leaves you with the Word become word, a philosophy, a moralism, but not the Word become flesh; leaves you with good views but not good news; leaves you with a set of principles and teachings about life, but no illustration of those principles and teachings—it is all verbal, not vital" (ibid.).

Jones also points out that subjective reality should not be based on only one individual's experience, but "must be corroborated by the collective experience on a wide scale, a world scale" (ibid., 104).

> Through the centuries the Christians have fastened on three infallibilities: The infallible Bible, the infallible Christian experience, the infallible church. But none of these taken alone produces the infallibility . . . .
>
> Where, then, is the place of authority in the Christian faith? It is at the junction of these three coming together and all three saying the same thing. The objective reality (the infallible Bible) becomes the subjective reality (the infallible Christian experience) and is corrected and corroborated by the collective witness (the infallible church). . . . The place of authority, then, in Christianity is where these three realities meet and meet in a common and collective witness to Jesus Christ as Savior and Lord, all saying the same thing in different languages and in different ways.
>
> The place of authority at the junction of the three realities is more solid and substantial than if it were based on any one of the three alone. This is a "threefold cord [that] is not quickly broken." This brings the highest degree of certainty possible to a human being. It is not the precarious certainty of dogmatism; it is profoundly tested at each stage: the Word become flesh (the historical), the Word become experience (the subjective reality), and the Word become collective corroboration (the church witness). It is all with its feet on the ground; it has been put under life, and life has rendered and is rendering

a verdict to the degree it is being seriously tried. That verdict
is this: Jesus is Lord (ibid., 104–5).

A narrative theology of mission
in today's pluralistic contexts

Although E. Stanley Jones did not claim to be a theologian or a
missiologist, I submit in his own way he was both. His narrative methodology coupled with his own reflections have much to teach us about doing mission in a pluralistic context.

I see Jones's methodology as the interrelation of biblical text (what he
referred to as "objective reality"), individual Christian narratives (personal pilgrimage in a particular context) and the church (faith community—the stories and beliefs),[2] all based on a theology that is centered in
the Lord Jesus Christ. While he did not stress doctrine or the Bible in
his round-table conferences, Jones's firm faith in God's written word
undergirded his life and ministry. I believe, however, that his public emphasis on life experience and personal encounter remains an appropriate
approach to religious pluralism. His subjection of individual Christian
experience to the corporate narratives of the church provides a safeguard
against excess and heresy.

E. Stanley Jones's round-table methodology offers a viable approach
for mission in a pluralistic society, as well as a model for thinking
missiologically. At the same time, I want to be cautious not to overem-
phasize subjective experience to the detriment of objective truth. In my
openness to people of other faiths, I want to continue holding fast the
fundamentals of Christian faith. I resonate with Jones when he states
that his standard is Christ's mind as revealed in the Scriptures and as
unfolded by the indwelling Holy Spirit. I believe Jones models the delicate balance of holding fast the truth yet presenting that truth in a respectful, personal, gently compelling narrative in the midst of a whirl of
other truth-claims and faith stories.

I have had opportunity to share the Good News of our Lord Jesus
Christ with people of different religious faiths—nominal Christians,
Hindus, Muslims, Sikhs, secular atheists, Jews, Buddhists, Animists and
Jehovah's Witnesses—and different ethnic backgrounds and nationali-
ties. In a religiously pluralistic urban context we often do not have the
luxury to chose to whom we must present the reason for our hope. I do
accept that God may call persons to a specific group of people for linguistic and cultural reasons. Yet, as I discern the trends, heterogeneity
and plurality are becoming the norm of our society.

I see in Jones an admission that one tradition or nation cannot possibly hold the totality of truth, that we need to listen to the insights and stories from different cultures. At the same time I see in Jones an affirmation of the presence of absolute objective truth as incarnated in the person of Jesus Christ, and a focus on the living Christ as narratively manifest in the lives of people and in the church. I see his commitment to continue to "approximate" the truth of the gospel, and to make knowing, living and sharing the truth a lifetime commitment. In the midst of a pluralism of conflicting truth-claims, E. Stanley Jones encourages us to draw near and testify to the Reality incarnated in the person of Jesus Christ.

Notes

[1] For biographical data on E. Stanley Jones, I rely on Taylor 1982, Alphonse 1986, and Pickard 1994.

[2] See Van Engen 1996, 23, with the addition of "personal pilgrimage" as a fourth circle.

References

Alphonse, Martin Paul. 1986. "The Evangelistic Enterprise of E. Stanley Jones: A Missiological Review." Th.M thesis. Fuller Theological Seminary, Pasadena, California.

E. Stanley Jones. 1925. *The Christ of the Indian Road*. New York: Abingdon Press.

———. 1928. *Christ at the Round Table*. New York: Abingdon Press.

———. 1931. *The Christ of Every Road*. New York: Abingdon Press.

———. 1937. *The Choice Before Us* . New York: Abingdon Press.

———. 1946. *The Christ of the American Road*. Nashville, Tenn.: Abingdon-Cokesbury Press.

———. 1968. *A Song of Ascents: A Spiritual Autobiography*. New York: Abingdon Press.

Pickard, William M., Jr. 1994. "Jesus Christ and Religious Pluralism: Evangelical Theology for a Pluralistic Age." Unpublished manuscript.

Taylor, Richard. 1982. "The Legacy of E. Stanley Jones." *International Bulletin of Missionary Research* 6, no. 3: 102–7.

6

Charles H. Kraft

Ethnotheology in mission

LEVI T. DE CARVALHO

I felt lost. Not because I was working in the jungles of South America, but because all my training was proving insufficient in the face of the difficulties of conveying the gospel message to the Terena people of Brazil.[1] After almost one hundred years of missionary presence, a considerable number of church members still seek help from the shamans when someone is sick or demonized.

As a charismatic Christian worker, I initially believed I had all the training I needed to be a good missionary. My preparation had included research in linguistics, Bible translation theory, bilingual education, anthropology and communication theory. But in my actual ministry context I could not make sense of what was happening among the Terena Christians.

As part of my mid-career graduate research, I became acquainted with the teaching of Charles H. Kraft. His approaches seemed applicable to the issues I was facing in the field. I determined to learn more from him.

Levi T. De Carvalho, a Brazilian, has been a missionary among the Terena tribe of southwest Brazil since 1980. Currently he is working with the Terena tribal mission in cross-cultural training programs designed to equip native South American workers to reach indigenous groups in the Amazon region. DeCarvalho holds the Ph.D. from the School of World Mission, Fuller Theological Seminary, and currently works as a consultant in missiology and anthropology for several mission agencies in Latin America.

Setting the stage

Charles H. Kraft is a well-known anthropologist, linguist, Bible translator, communicologist, ethnotheologian and spiritual warfare specialist.
He is a well-rounded example of a multidiscipline Christian scholar. In
this chapter I focus on some of Kraft's missiological insights that apply
to my context of ministry and that help others in similar situations.[2]

Biographical overview

Charles H. Kraft was born on July 15, 1932.[3] He came to Christ when he
was 12, and he committed himself to missionary service soon thereafter.
His Ph.D. in anthropological linguistics from the Hartford Seminary
Foundation (1963) focuses on syntax in the Hausa language.

Kraft and his wife, Marguerite, served as missionaries in Nigeria, West
Africa, from 1957 to 1960. Kraft's main activities during this time revolved around language studies and encouraging the local church. He
learned the Hausa language and taught several courses for other missionaries. His main concern was the church among the Kamwe (Higi)
people. He was able to train and supervise Kamwe leaders, who participated in a major people movement that continues to this day. His cul-
ture-sensitive approach got him in difficulties with his mission, however,
so after returning home for furlough he received an "invitation" to re-
sign from the mission and remain in the United States.

Kraft taught linguistics and African languages, with a specialty in
Hausa, from 1963 to 1968 at Michigan State University, and from 1968
to 1973 at UCLA. In 1966–67 he returned to Nigeria to pursue field
linguistic studies on several Hausa-related languages, and in 1978 and
1980 he participated in a new translation of the Bible into Hausa. He
was also involved with the church in Nigeria on a short-term basis.

In 1968, during his first year at UCLA, Ralph Winter, at the time a
faculty member of the School of World Mission at Fuller Theological
Seminary, approached Kraft, asking if Kraft would like to team up with
Alan Tippett in teaching anthropology to missionaries and international
students. Kraft accepted the invitation, keeping both teaching jobs until
1973, when he resigned his position at UCLA. He has since taught at
Fuller in the areas of anthropology, intercultural communication, African studies, Christian ethnotheology, linguistics and spiritual warfare.

Kraft owes much to the influence of Eugene Nida and the *Practical
Anthropology*[4] group in helping him to deal critically with crucial issues in
the cross-cultural communication of the gospel.[5] Major influences on

Kraft's anthropology come from linguistics and psychological anthropology. Kraft's anthropological perspective serves as a lens through which he examines major issues related to intercultural and intracultural problems. Prominent themes in his teaching and writing are worldview theory, culture change, ethnotheology, power encounter, inner healing and application of all the above to general missiology.

Kraft on worldview and worldview change

Kraft defines worldview as the "structuring of the deepest level presuppositions on the basis of which people live" (1996b, 10). He believes people respond not to God's Reality ("big" R), but to "small r" reality—the reality people perceive and on the basis of which they interpret their experience.

I had to learn this truth the hard way. I thought I knew "big R" Reality; after all, I was a missionary! I wanted to teach the Terena the correct worldview—my worldview, of course! I had yet to acknowledge that my perception of reality was and still is only a fragment of God's Reality.

Often people accuse missionaries of intruding into other cultures and judging these cultures from the perspective of the missionaries' own specific ethos. Kraft speaks of "transcultural ethical standards" that "are the guidelines for correct behavior established by God," and "culture-specific ethical standards" that are "the small 'e' moral ideals . . . of a society that the members of that society are taught and expected to live up to" (1991b, 22).

Ethnocentrism, our tendency to judge everyone and everything according to our own standards, is an anthropological concept that should alert us to the danger of becoming arrogant in our evaluation of other people's behavior and thought patterns. I was doctrinally biased against combining a secular social discipline such as anthropology with the sacrosanct realm of theology. I could not see how any anthropological concept could be seen through Christian eyes. I did not know whether any bridge could connect the two.

Kraft's insights began helping me with this issue. He says it is possible to balance both the authority of God and the authority of human beings, "a perspective that holds to the ultimate authority of God, without denying either the importance of the delegation of certain authority to humans or the fact that on occasion God limits himself to that human authority" (1980, 243).

Revelation, for Kraft, has both a divine side, in the communication of truth proper, and a human side, in the process of discovering and appropriating this revelation. Christians (especially missionaries), while holding to a supernaturalistic view of reality, cannot dismiss the avalanche of anthropological data about the interplay between culture and human societies. "Christians can employ anthropological perspectives and methodology just as they have for years employed historical perspectives and methodology without fear of compromising their faith." An anthropologically informed Christian, he goes on, will "distinguish between relative cultural forms, in terms of which even transculturally valid Christian meanings must be expressed" (ibid.).

Such interdisciplinary cooperation is impossible as long as non-Christian anthropologists push for a naturalistic-humanistic perspective, while Christian anthropologists advocate, in Kraft's words, a "particular perspective on history and culture concomitant with their commitment to God. . . . The ultimate faith in God exercised by Christians is combinable with the anthropological perspective . . . on history and culture" (ibid., 144).

I wanted to test the bridge connecting anthropology and theology to see whether it could bear the weight of issues I was facing in the field.

In my first missionary years I had chosen a handful of Terena individuals and tried to transform them into a new breed of Christian leaders, which I believed the people needed. Most of them, however, either were ostracized by their people or chose to return to the old ways. What went wrong? I was dealing with issues of worldview change. I needed to understand how the Terena worldview works and how I could bridge the gap between their worldview and mine.

In terms of worldview change Kraft suggests the advocate for change should seek to understand the culture from the perspective of the people. Approval or ratification of cultural practices is not the issue but rather an attitude of respect for the other culture. He also cautions against trying to introduce too many changes at once. Only a minimum number of changes is necessary at the worldview level. Forcing immediate abandonment of culturally accepted practices may portray the Creator-God as opposing those values the social group holds dear. In my case, I had attacked Terena perceptions of community by pressuring some to act individualistically.

According to Kraft, in order to promote effective change cross-cultural workers should target opinion leaders rather than marginal individuals in the community. "God desires to see whole human groupings turning to him rather than simply a minimum number of relatively easily reachable fringe people" (1976, 20). And since both the cognitive and behavioral dimensions need to change, timing is important. Hastiness may provoke a serious disequilibrium if the first level of change does not consolidate itself before people move on to another level.

In my case, I felt I had failed. I was pushing for immediate changes without a prior understanding of the Terena worldview. I had not realized that since the Terena were a group-oriented society, extracting individuals from their social milieu and making them into self-sufficient *individuals* would never work in their context. I had yet to discover culturally accepted ways through which their leaders emerge and assume positions in society.

This and other issues had to do with the way in which Terena Christians were theologizing according to their own perception of God's message. The whole question was one of combining the "ethno" with theology. At this point I came across Kraft's seminal ideas about ethnotheology.

Kraft on ethnotheology

Kraft's article "Toward a Christian Ethnotheology" condensed the basic tenets of his approach to integration of theology and anthropology (1973, 109–26). He had personally experienced the challenges that Christian cross-cultural workers encounter all around the world as they propose to convey the Christian message in a culturally relevant way:

> We may conceive of a cross-discipline, labeled *Christian ethnotheology*, that takes both Christian theology and anthropology seriously while devoting itself to an interpretive approach to the study of God, man and divine-human interaction. From theology such a discipline would draw understandings of eternal (absolute) truths relating to each of the areas it treats. From anthropology it would draw cultural (relative) truths and perspectives concerning these areas. Such a discipline would have both a theoretical and a practical component, the latter of which might consist largely of the "harnessing" both of anthropology and of theology for the purpose of bringing about more effective cross-cultural communication of the Gospel of Jesus Christ (ibid., 110–11).

Early discussions of critical missiological themes by perceptive missiologists in the pages of *Practical Anthropology*[6] paved the way for the eventual gathering of a body of principles toward integration of theology and anthropology as Kraft proposed. Today the insights of Christian ethnotheology are being adapted in places where cultural issues press for a fresh rereading of Scripture. Theologians in the majority world, for one, are considering this possibility:

> The inculturation or cultural critical method . . . is ignited by the growing awareness that in the religious sphere (as also in other spheres of life) all peoples in their various socio-cultural milieux need self-knowledge, self-assessment, self-remedy and self-healing. . . .
>
> By cultural criticism of a religious text therefore, I mean an affirming indigenous hermeneutic that would help any people with a specific culture understand themselves as a people with a religious heritage and a future in which that heritage is to be expressed. . . .
>
> Biblical cultural criticism seeks to rid God's word of any form of "cultural imperialism" so that this word may be read and heard in languages other than Hebrew, Greek or Latin or any of the modern, imperialist, colonial languages (English, French, Spanish, German, Portuguese) (Mbachu 1995, 48–49).

Discussions about narrative theology are going on in both hemispheres. A combination of narrative criticism methods and ethnotheology, the inculturation approach, as it is known in some Catholic circles,

> involves a certain aspect of the narrative method which considers a narrative text as a story about some historical event that can be used to foster and promote values and beliefs worthy of emulation by the recipients or readers of the text. Hence the cultural critical method can be regarded as the centerpiece or the hermeneutical center around which the historical and literary methods evolve. The inculturation method is related to the historical critical method by its emphasis on the human cultures . . . and to the narrative method by its emphasis on the contexts of the story, its narrator or preacher or pastoral agent and its recipients or hearers or audience. This relationship to both the historical and contextual methods gives the inculturation method a growing popularity in the comparative study of the Church of Acts with the young local Churches of Africa, Asia and Afro-America (ibid., 50–51).[7]

I started asking myself, how do the Terena see the Scriptures? What assumptions about life, God, humanity and the spiritual world influence their reading of the biblical text? Is it possible they see things I cannot see because of my cultural biases? How does their preference for narrative over propositional thinking affect our communication of the gospel to them? What does their hermeneutical method consist of?

The methodological question was how could we "ethnotheologize" in our ministry contexts. Kraft indicates how a truly Christian ethnotheology should work:

> Christian ethnotheology would attempt to distinguish carefully what in Christian doctrine is supracultural revelation from God . . . and what is the cultural "enclothing" of this revelation in terms meaningful either to those who originally received the revelation or to those in another culture . . . to whom it has been transmitted in the Bible and interpreted by theologians. In so seeking to understand the message it would be necessary to divest the theological interpretation of such modifications as the pervasive influence of Greek philosophy on Western theology and the tendency to absolutize certain elements of western culture by attributing them (often wrongly) to Christian influence on our [American] culture (1973, 113).

Traditional anthropology shunned dealing with absolutes. Therefore, Christian ethnotheology cannot be left solely in the hands of secular anthropology. "Christian ethnotheology would seek to avoid relativizing God every bit as much as to avoid absolutizing culture. . . . Christian ethnotheology believes in absolutes—not as many as Western theology proposes perhaps, but far more than anthropology admits" (ibid., 116).

Can theology and anthropology be thus combined? As long as we hold culture as something negative (by identifying culture with the sinful world) and refuse to have an open attitude toward cultural relativity,[8] Christian ethnotheology will remain under suspicion.

Ethnotheology, meanwhile, needs the input of both theology and anthropology—the one to help define and circumscribe absolutes, the other to help define and circumscribe relatives. The ethnotheological conclusion, Kraft says, "may side with either, both, or neither of the source disciplines. . . . One of the major quests of Christian ethnotheology will be the understanding of what in Christianity is absolute, supracultural and valid for any church at any time, and that which is cultural, relative, and valid for a single culture only" (1973, 116).

The whole question of ancestor worship (as it is wrongly called) is one such issue among the Terena. The Western approach to spiritual realities has prevented many of us outsiders from even considering the issue among the Terena, let alone theologizing about it. Ethnotheological principles can help those of us who minister in such environments to propose fresh discussions on this theme.[9]

Nida's "relative cultural relativism" (1981, 50) states that all our Christian practices must be judged against God's absolutes. The danger is that people may either absolutize human institutions (on the part of theologians and missionaries) or relativize God (on the part of anthropologists). Exchanging one set of customs for another is not a prerequisite for communication of the Christian message.

The relationship between social structure and conversion, then, is crucial. Kraft suggests that people living in individualistic societies are likely to convert individually, whereas those living in group-oriented societies tend to convert in groups. "Conversion is a human process, even though Christians believe something cosmic takes place behind the scenes" (1992b, 263).

> In a group-oriented society, allegiance to family and clan is usually much higher than allegiance to oneself as an individual. One's personal security and hopes for the present and the future are felt to be inextricable from that social matrix. . . .
>
> In an individualistic society, however, one's allegiance to self may be much higher on the list. For some that allegiance will be above allegiance to the family/reference group. For others, it may be below. . . . So reference group considerations need to be taken very seriously in individualistic societies as well as in group-oriented societies in attempting to analyze and/or advocate Christian conversion (ibid., 274–75).[10]

For the Terena, conversion is not simply an individual matter, since all church groups are also family groups. It has been a paradigm shift for me to start thinking in terms of group decisions and group conversion. Theologizing among the Terena tribe has become a community event in which both culture and theology have a part to play.

Kraft on the "three encounters"

Kraft's ethnotheology came full circle for me when I came across his ideas about "allegiance, truth and power encounters." Initially discussed by Alan Tippett (1971, 16), the notion of power encounter was further extended by Kraft to issues of inner healing and deliverance both in Christian witnessing and maturing.[11]

> The concern of the truth encounter is understanding and the vehicle of that encounter is teaching. The allegiance encounter is focused on relationship and is mediated through witness. Freedom, then, is the aim of the power encounter and spiritual warfare is the vehicle (Kraft 1992a, 218).

The "three encounters" are closely related to Kraft's concept of "dual allegiance," a situation in which people, who may have "embraced a large amount of Christian truth , . . have not [yet] given up their pre-Christian allegiance and practice in the area of spiritual power. . . . So they continue with a 'bifurcated' Christianity characterized by dual allegiance and a syncretistic understanding of truth" (ibid., 219).

In the Terena context a clear syncretism is underway. Somehow we as missionaries have failed to keep the three encounters in balance. We have emphasized only truth and allegiance at the expense of power. Our assumption has been that once people understood the logic of Christianity they would pledge unswerving allegiance to Christ and immediately give up their former loyalty and practices in the realm of spiritual power.

When some Terena Christians need healing, however, or when someone in the family is demonized, what have we missionaries offered to them except a few medicines? So people seek the help of shamans who cater to their needs. What reason, then, would a shaman have to embrace Christianity? Don't church leaders and members seek out the shaman for spiritual help? What would happen if a converted shaman ever needed healing or deliverance from evil spirits? Would he or she have to seek the help of another shaman or backslide into shamanism once again?

> In a world in which most of its children have imbibed a focus on spiritual power with their mothers' milk, solid, lasting conversions to Christ are rarely achieved simply by presenting people with knowledge and truth (ibid., 228–29).

Lest the reader thinks that Kraft is being one-sided, he continues,

> As the Christian grows, all three kinds of encounters are significant, for each contributes to growth and assurance. Any relationship involves a continuing series of challenges to one's will, hopefully for the Christian, in ever-renewed pledges of

allegiance to Jesus Christ leading to an ever deepening relationship with him (ibid., 229).

Kraft compares these encounters to three arrows God has placed at the Christian's disposal to confront Satan's counterfeit arrows. The first time I confronted the powers of darkness among the Terena, I realized something was definitely missing in my quiver. The question was not simply one of spiritual battles, though. I needed new lenses to see what God was doing and what God is willing to do among the Terena people. Would I be a hindrance or a help in God's will for that people?

Conclusion

Kraft's principles have helped me to understand the Terena perspective on life. I was shocked to discover I had absolutized much more of my own culture than I had realized. I began trusting local leadership for the right timing in implementing effective change. Only now am I discovering the Terena process of leadership emergence.

By applying ethnotheological principles to that context, I am learning to avoid relativizing God as well as absolutizing culture. I am learning how to draw on the resources of both theology and anthropology in my cross-cultural ministry. I am still struggling with the issue of "groupness" and conversion. But I believe the balance comes through proper use of the three encounters.

I want to see the Terena pledging full allegiance to Christ, living out and understanding his truth and availing themselves of his power as they deepen their relationship with him. For me, the most exciting project, however, is participating with the Terena Christians in their own "ethnotheologizing." I no longer feel lost because in the jungles of South America. I am walking with the Terena in their journey with Jesus Christ.

Notes

[1] The Terena are an indigenous South American people group related to the Guaná. They number around 15,000 and live in scattered villages located mainly in the state of Mato Grosso de Sul, Brazil. Catholic, Protestant and Pentecostal missionaries have been working among them since the beginning of the twentieth century.

[2] I believe seminal ideas in missiology in the last 40 years or so have appeared mainly in journal articles, so I use only Kraft's articles as the basis for this essay. The reader who is not familiar with Kraft's writings may find this a useful

preliminary approach to his scholarly thinking in a few critical areas of missiology. A list of Kraft's major books is included in the references for this chapter.

[3] Biographical data come from personal interviews with Kraft.

[4] Initiated in 1953, *Practical Anthropology* became *Missiology* in 1973.

[5] Kraft was especially influenced by William Smalley, William Reyburn, Louis Luzbetak and Jacob Loewen.

[6] A collection of representative articles from that magazine was published by Smalley (1978).

[7] Mbachu's enthusiasm with the ethnotheological principles is shared by other African theologians and scholars (see her bibliography).

[8] Cultural relativity must not to be mistaken for cultural relativism, which does not admit any supracultural Reality or Truth but deems everything as relative.

[9] In the Terena context the whole universe revolves around the idea of the ancestors. Since missionaries chose to toss the issue aside as irrelevant or anathema, the people by and large continue to seek communication with the departed in such a way that the shaman becomes the central figure in this cultural drama. In Kraft's words, this is a case of "bifurcated Christianity."

[10] See also Kraft 1986, 12–15. Kraft's early article on conversion (1963, 179–87) established a hallmark in his thinking: "Much of modern missionary effort . . . has merely substituted Western culture for Hebrew culture as the *sine qua non* for God's acceptance of man" (1963, 183).

[11] Kraft outlines his conceptualization and understanding of the three encounters, their interrelationship and application for Christian witness. Basically there are three areas in which every Christian individual/community needs to grow and be permeated by God's grace: allegiance, truth and power. Without allegiance to Christ there is no salvation. For that allegiance to take shape and direction it needs to abide in the truth of God. In situations where Satan manifests his evil influence, sin overpowers the individual/community and sickness thwarts church growth, the power of God needs to be displayed to counter the enemy, witness to the world and strengthen the faith community (1992a, 215–30).

References

Kraft, Charles H. 1963. "Christian Conversion or Cultural Conversion?" *Practical Anthropology* 10, no. 4: 179–87.

———. 1973. "Toward a Christian Ethnotheology." In *God, Man and Church Growth*, ed. Alan R. Tippett, 109–26. Grand Rapids, Mich.: Eerdmans.

———. 1976. "Intercultural Communication and Worldview Change." Unpublished. School of World Mission, Fuller Theological Seminary, Pasadena, California.

———. 1979. *Christianity in Culture: A Study in Dynamic Theologizing in Cross-Cultural Perspective*. Maryknoll, N.Y.: Orbis Books.

———. 1980. "Conservative Christians and Anthropologists: A Clash of Worldviews." *Journal of the American Scientific Affiliation* 32 (September): 140–45.

———. 1986. "Conversion: Shaping Our Reality." *Theology, News and Notes* (June): 12–15.

———. 1988. *Communicating the Gospel God's Way.* Pasadena, Calif.: William Carey Library.

———. 1989. *Christianity with Power.* Ann Arbor, Mich.: Servant.

———. 1991a. *Communication Theory for Christian Witness.* Revised edition. Maryknoll, N.Y.: Orbis Books.

———. 1991b. "Receptor-Oriented Ethics in Cross-Cultural Intervention." *Transformation* 8, no. 1: 20–25.

———. 1992a. "Allegiance, Truth and Power Encounters in Christian Witness." In *Pentecost, Mission and Ecumenism: Essays on Intercultural Theology,* ed. Jan A. B. Jongeneel, 215–230. Frankfurt, Germany: Peter Lang.

———. 1992b. "Conversion in Group Settings." In *Handbook of Religious Conversion,* ed. H. Newton Malony and Samuel Southard, 259–75. Birmingham, Ala.: Religious Education Press.

———. 1992c. *Defeating Dark Angels.* Ann Arbor, Mich.: Servant.

———. 1993. *Deep Wounds, Deep Healing.* Ann Arbor, Mich.: Servant.

———. 1994. *Behind Enemy Lines.* Ann Arbor, Mich.: Servant.

———. 1996a. *Anthropology for Christian Witness.* Maryknoll, N.Y.: Orbis Books.

———. 1996b. "Culture, Worldview and Persons." Unpublished article adapted by Kraft from Kraft's *Anthropology for Christian Witness.* Maryknoll, N.Y.: Orbis Books.

Malony, H. Newton, and Samuel Southard, eds. 1992. *Handbook of Religious Conversion.* Birmingham, Ala.: Religious Education Press.

Mbachu, Hilary. 1995. *Survey and Method of Acts Research from 1826 to 1995.* Egelsbach, Germany: Hänsel-Hohenhausen.

Nida, Eugene A. 1981. *Customs and Cultures: Anthropology for Christian Missions.* Pasadena, Calif.: William Carey Library.

Smalley, William A., ed. 1978. *Readings in Missionary Anthropology.* Pasadena, Calif.: William Carey Library.

Tippett, Alan R. 1971. *People Movements in Southern Polynesia.* Chicago, Ill.: Moody.

———. 1987. *Introduction to Missiology.* Pasadena, Calif.: William Carey Library.

Tippett, Alan R., ed. 1973. *God, Man and Church Growth.* Grand Rapids, Mich.: Eerdmans.

Part II

MISSION *IN* THE WAY

This section portrays mission as relational. Mission occurs among the peoples and cultures of our world. The gospel story is mission in the street, an incarnational identification with the poor, sick, powerless and oppressed. Mission from the road—the place of action, pilgrimage, conflict and concern—is where life is lived, and where we meet Christ as we walk in the here and now of suffering humanity. Biblical theology of mission needs to be contextually appropriate to be mission *in* the way.

Quaker poet Nancy Thomas finds a friend in the Nicaraguan revolutionary Ernesto Cardenal. As a missionary to Bolivia, Thomas struggled to come to grips with the political turmoil and injustice surrounding the Aymara people. Through the life of this prophetic Catholic priest, Thomas begins to integrate mission in a revolutionary context. Using Cardenal's poetry, Thomas illustrates how, in a very Latin American style, he deals with Latin American issues. She suggests that Cardenal's life is one of incarnational mission, whereby he brings the kingdom of God to the poor of Nicaragua. Thomas's evaluation of Cardenal leads us to see a missionary who is walking *in* the way, passionately serving the mission of God to free his people.

Young Kee Lee's chapter flows from his concern for the church in Thailand. Rooted in Buddhist philosophy that encourages escape from suffering, Thai Christians have been ineffective in establishing Christianity in that country. On the other hand, the Korean church, born out of suffering, has experienced growth. Lee, a former Korean missionary to Thailand, asks, "Is there a connection between suffering and mission?" The author then examines suffering from a missiological perspective. Lee shows that Jesus' mission to the nations came through suffering, and his disciples may also be asked to suffer as part of the priesthood of the new covenant. This is an important aspect of mission *in* the way.

Mary Thiessen Nation, currently an urban mission consultant at the London Mennonite Centre, has seen and experienced intense suffering, working for over 20 years in the inner city of Los Angeles. Through the writings of Jürgen Moltmann she began to understand the tension between hope and despair among those suffering in the city. Thiessen Nation recognizes the importance of hope within despair, not merely the hope for something better after despair. This comes about as mission embraces suffering even as it fights it, letting the promise of the future influence and change the present.

Jude Tiersma Watson continues the theme of mission in the midst of human suffering as she discusses the life and work of Mother Teresa of Calcutta. If mission is to be relevant in the next century, we must know how to respond to the painful realities of our world. Mother Teresa provides an example of the church in mission as she responds to poverty and human need. Tiersma Watson, who lives and works incarnationally as an urban missionary in Los Angeles, points to the deep spirituality of the Missionaries of Charity, the prayer and joy that serve as a foundation for mission. She notes, through Mother Teresa's example, the place suffering plays in mission. And she highlights Mother Teresa's focused life, which enabled her to be a symbol of mission *in* the way.

Stanley Mutuka Mutunga's desire to search for a solution to Africa's urban challenges is the topic of the next chapter. The Kenyan missiologist recognizes economic, political, educational and social factors that contribute to the present disintegration of community values in cities. Mutunga analyzes the African idea of community and finds it to be essential for social and economic security, as well as a sense of identity and belonging. He then offers practical suggestions for churches to help in forming new inclusive communities in the cities.

After a summary of Hispanic and Latin American theologies, Daniel Rodriguez emphasizes the contribution these movements make to a theology of mission. This leads to the unique perspective of Mexican-descent Latinos living on the periphery of U.S. society. Focusing on the writings of Virgilio Elizondo, a prominent Hispanic theologian, Rodriguez describes what the Catholic academy has called a theology of *mestizaje*. This is a theology of liberation for Mexican Americans characterized by a fundamental search for identity, realizing that these people are doubly marginalized by reason of their participation in two distinct cultural groups. Mexican Americans, like Rodriguez, although living in exile and ambiguity, have a unique contribution as they discover God chooses the marginalized to be agents of mission *in* the way.

ROBERT L. GALLAGHER

7

Ernesto Cardenal

Poet and priest

NANCY J. THOMAS

I first "met" Ernesto Cardenal in the mid-1970s when a friend handed me his book *Salmos (Psalms)* and said, "Here, Nancy. I think you'll like this." I did. A poet myself, I felt as if I'd found a friend.

My husband, Hal, and I were in the middle of our second term as missionaries, working with the Aymara Friends Church in Bolivia. We struggled to come to grips with the country's political turmoil. The closer we grew to people, the more our hearts ached under the burden of injustice. At times we wondered if traditional missionary work (planting churches and training leaders) was even viable. Shouldn't we pour our lives into greenhouse projects, mobile clinics, relief work and other similar activities we were in no way equipped for but which seemed so crucial?

In the poetry of Ernesto Cardenal I met a person who, in a more profound and personal sense than I had yet experienced, grappled with the same issues.

About the same time I discovered Cardenal, the director of an interdenominational seminary in La Paz invited me to teach a creative writing course. Response to my class surprised and delighted me. Aymara men and women began to explore the possibilities of expressing their

Nancy J. Thomas served with the Friends Church in Bolivia for 18 years, where her work revolved around church planting, leadership training and encouraging Bolivian writers. A writer herself, she has published several volumes of poetry and writes regularly for magazines and devotional booklets. Nancy's Ph.D. research, completed in 1998, focuses on training writers in the Two-Thirds World to write according to their own unique styles and perceptions. She and her husband, Hal, have two children and a growing number of grandchildren.

own stories of struggle and hope—in short, their own deep spirituality—through writing. At the end of the class we formed the Bolivian Association of Christian Writers and began to publish a small interdenominational magazine.

I continue to read Ernesto Cardenal with a deepening appreciation. I search his story as well as his writing for insights on the missional integration of life and word in a revolutionary context.

Setting the stage

Ernesto Cardenal probably would not call himself a missiologist. He might not even call himself a missionary. But the controversial, contemplative priest-turned-revolutionary has certainly influenced the Latin American Catholic concept of mission.

The question of whether Ernesto Cardenal is a missiologist is perhaps irrelevant. A better question might be, What can missiology learn from Ernesto Cardenal. In this chapter I will attempt to look at the life and work of this extraordinary man through "missiological eyes."

The Revolution

Cardenal's personal story and writings cannot be understood apart from a grasp of the larger narrative of the times. In 1926, 2,700 U.S. Marines landed in Nicaragua to help bring about democratization. Nicaraguan General Cesar A. Sandino led a resistance movement that in 1932 managed to push out the "invaders." Sandino, however, was mysteriously assassinated shortly after the departure of the Marines, and the Somoza family came to power (see Bradstock 1987; Sand 1979).

The Somoza rise to power inaugurated a 43–year dictatorship that impoverished the country, increased infant mortality and did nothing to improve poor sanitary conditions and a 75 percent illiteracy rate (Sand 1979, 31–32). Political assassinations became the rule of the day. A growing revolutionary movement adopted the name of the martyred hero, Sandino: the Frente Sandinista de Liberación Nacional (FSLN) began training guerrilla warriors and planning the overthrow of the government, an event that took place on July 19, 1979.

In the years following 1979 reconstruction of the country was complicated by U.S. resistance to the Sandinista government and by the counter-revolutionary movement (the "contras"). In 1990 the Sandinistas lost the national elections and had to step down for the first time since the victory of 1979, but they remain a force in the country (Colás 1994, 164–65).

The role of the Catholic church

Since the time of the *conquistadores* the Latin American Catholic church has played a conservative role in support of the sociopolitical status quo, aligning itself with the elite. Historian Andrew Bradstock notes, "The price of this support included the [church] hierarchy's losing its right to engage in prophetic denunciation of injustice and oppression, thus leaving it open to charges of complicity in such excesses" (1987, 2).

This situation changed drastically in the twentieth century. After World War II new grassroots movements sprang up in the Catholic church, increasing in momentum after the Second Vatican Council and the sanction of liberation theology. These movements focused on evangelism, social justice and concern for the poor; they emphasized *concientización* (consciousness raising), lay activity, new ways of reading Scripture, and creation of Christian base communities (ibid., 3–5). The conservative element of the church hierarchy, however, continued in control.

In the 1970s many Nicaraguan priests who espoused liberation theology began supporting the Sandinista revolutionary movement. After the 1979 victory the FSLN invited three priests, Cardenal among them, to occupy posts in the new government cabinet, while many other priests and laypeople filled lower-level government positions (Cabestrero 1983).

The church hierarchy initially supported the priests' service in political office, following the tradition of allowing priests to engage in a "supplementary ministry" that, while not directly related to the priestly office, could be deemed necessary by the circumstances of history.

Within the first year of the new government, however, the conservative hierarchy of the Nicaraguan Catholic church withdrew its support. The bishops asked the three priests to step down from their government positions and resume their traditional roles. Cardenal and his companions refused to comply, seeing no contradiction between service to God and service to the people in the post-revolutionary government. The priests considered their continued government service to be in obedience to the will of God.[1] The bishops eventually gave in but ordered the priests to abstain from all official priestly ministry while in government service. The ensuing years saw increasing tension in the church over this issue.[2]

Biographical overview

Ernesto Cardenal was born in the Nicaraguan city of Granada in 1925.[3] As part of the wealthy elite, Cardenal experienced the privileges of education, travel and leisure. He studied literature at the National Autonomous

University in Mexico City and at Columbia University in New York. After a time of travel in Europe, he returned to Nicaragua, where he began to publish some of his poetry and to become interested in the revolutionary movement against the Somoza dictatorship. In 1954 he took part in an armed movement. An assault on the presidential palace failed, and several of Cardenal's friends were killed.

Cardenal's life turned around in 1956 when, at the age of 31, he experienced a profound religious conversion. He immediately decided to become a monk and entered a Trappist monastery in Gethsemani, Kentucky, where Thomas Merton became his mentor. Cardenal explains:

> I had a religious conversion, in which I discovered God as love. It was an experience of a loving faith, a falling in love. It made me want to live in the most isolated, lonely place I could find, to be alone with God. And I felt that the ideal place would be a Trappist monastery. So I entered the Trappists. There I renounced everything, even my interest in poetry and my interest in politics (Cabestrero 1983, 24–25).

But Cardenal's total renunciation was not to be. Merton encouraged the young monk to cherish the things that had always been important to him, perhaps sensing something of Cardenal's destiny. Cardenal continues,

> He [Merton] would get together with me for a spiritual conference—then instead of talking to me about "spiritual things," he'd start asking me about Somoza, or about the dictator of Venezuela, Pérez Jiménez, or the one in Colombia, and so on, or about his poet friends. And so our precious "spiritual direction" time all went by, "wasted." I'm sure he did this deliberately (ibid., 25).

Merton encouraged Cardenal to think about one day establishing a contemplative community in Nicaragua, and the two made concrete plans. Ill health forced Cardenal to leave Gethsemani after only two years, but the two maintained their friendship through correspondence until Merton's accidental death by electrocution in 1968. Shortly after Cardenal left the monastery, Merton sent him these prophetic words:

> What next? You must wait patiently, prayerfully, and in peace. No one can say yet whether you should enter another monastery. I do not know if you will be happy in the choir anywhere, since you do not sing. I advise you not to think too

much about whether or not you are happy. You will never
again reduplicate the feeling of happiness which you had here,
because it is not normal to do so. You would not have known
such happiness even if you had remained. Your life now will
be serious and even sad. This is as it should be. We have no
right to escape into happiness that most of the world cannot
share. This is a very grim and terrible century, and in it we
must suffer sorrow and responsibility with the rest of the
world. But do not think that God is less close to you now. I
am sure you are closer to Him, and are on the path to a new
and strange reality. Let Him lead you (Merton 1993, 113).

While preparing for the priesthood in Mexico and Colombia, Cardenal
reestablished himself as a poet.[4] He was ordained in Managua in 1965 at
the age of 40.

In 1966 Cardenal began an adventure that would profoundly affect
not only his own life, but that of the Catholic church in Nicaragua. In
that year he helped found a Christian community, Our Lady of
Solentiname, on an island in Lake Nicaragua. The community included
both singles and families. Labor combined with prayer and study as members participated in the life of the island as fishermen and farmers. Nicaraguan journalist José Arguello writes of the impact of the community:

The community of Solentiname . . . was not just a cultural or
political project; the deep significance of that experience is
theological. Through Cardenal's prophetic priesthood God
became present amid the campesinos of a distant corner of
Nicaragua and penetrated the history of our martyred and
oppressed people (Arguello 1985, 141).

Cardenal spent the next 10 years as priest of Solentiname. *El evangelio
en Solentiname* (1975/1982, "The Gospel in Solentiname") is a four-vol-
ume collection of discussions among the Solentiname campesinos of selected Bible passages. David Bosch calls this collection "a theology of
the people, a theology born out of reflections on the faith in the face of
the harsh realities of oppression, violence and the struggle for survival"
(1985, 126).

Another turning point in Cardenal's life came in 1970 when he went
to Cuba to participate in a poetry festival. He stayed three months and
experienced a "conversion" to communism as a "scientific method for studying society and changing it" (Cabestrero 1983, 31). He saw no contradiction in being both a committed Christian and a revolutionary communist:

"It was the gospel of Jesus Christ that made a Marxist of me. . . . I'm a Marxist who believes in God, follows Christ, and is a revolutionary for the sake of his kingdom" (ibid., 32). He defined "revolution" as "the efficacious practice of love of neighbor, in society and individually" (ibid.).

As the tension between the Somocistas and the Sandinistas increased, so did the revolutionary fervor of the community at Solentiname. One ramification of this was Cardenal's slow and painful change from pacifism (in the steps of his mentor, Thomas Merton) to the belief that violence was justified in an oppressive situation (Lefevere 1983; Cox 1985). Cardenal associated himself with the FSLN, becoming their spokesman abroad.

The campesinos of Solentiname also threw themselves into the revolutionary movement, and in 1977 some of them took up guns for actual combat. Cardenal was on a trip at the time. In a skirmish at the neighboring town of San Carlos, several of the Solentiname young men were killed. Others were captured and imprisoned. In an act of retaliation the National Guard destroyed Our Lady of Solentiname, razing all buildings except the church.

Word reached Cardenal abroad of the destruction of the community. He went into exile to continue his work for the FSLN in promoting the revolution.

With the victory of the revolution on July 19, 1979, the FSLN invited Ernesto Cardenal and two fellow priests, including his brother Fernando, to assume major roles in the post-revolutionary government. Cardenal accepted his post reluctantly. In an interview with Teófilo Cabestrero, Cardenal spoke of his work as minister of culture:

> Before I ever became minister of culture, before victory, I knew that ministry meant service, and minister meant servant. That goes for government ministry and ministers as much as for priestly ministry and ministers. . . .
>
> Now I happen to have this other ministry too, besides the priestly ministry. I have the job of promoting everything cultural in the country. I have the ministry of music, of poetry, of painting, of crafts, of theater, of folklore and tradition, of scholarly research of our whole national heritage—museums, libraries, magazines, cultural institutions, films, recreation, all those things. I have the ideological ministry. . . . And as Christ placed his Apostles in charge of distributing the loaves and fishes, I feel he's placed me in charge of spreading culture (Cabestrero 1983, 18–19).

In spite of the controversy his position occasioned in the hierarchy of the church, Cardenal held the position of minister of culture for 10 years, from 1979 to 1988. Ironically headquartered in the old mansion of Señora Somoza, Cardenal spearheaded the movement that aimed to bring the fine arts to the common people. Cardenal saw his government office as an expansion to the national level of the kind of awareness, self-expression and creative pride he had encouraged among the campesinos of Solentiname.

In 1988 Ernesto Cardenal retired from his government post to work in his hometown of Granada as director of Casa de los Tres Mundos, a cultural center (Cardenal 1993, author bio). He sums up his personal sense of mission and call by saying, "My religious calling is that of a contemplative and a prophet. . . . My vocation is one of union with God and service to the people, to build up his kingdom of life in love" (Cabestrero 1983, 34).

Cardenal the poet

Ernesto Cardenal is probably better known internationally as a poet than as a prophet, priest or cabinet minister. This would please him. In the interview with Cabestrero, he confessed, "I think my predominant calling (not the one God gave me later)—the one I was born with—is that of a poet, and it's as a poet that I'll be able to render the best service to the revolution" (ibid.).

Cardenal does not believe in "art for art's sake." His poetic documentation of the realities in Nicaragua has redemptive intentions. Marc Zimmerman observes that the prosaic, jagged and seemingly awkward style of Cardenal's poetry aims "to jar the reader, to refuse easy aesthetic harmonies, to provoke commitment, not applause, to demand completion not in literature, but in life" (1985, xxviii).

In an interview with Brazilian Catholic writer Frei Betto, Cardenal observed: "I have the same motivations as did the biblical prophets. The prophets were poets who wrote to denounce injustice and to proclaim the new kingdom. For me, poetry is just another vehicle. It is a form of preaching" (Betto 1979, 40).

In his poetry Cardenal prophetically denounces injustice.

> The Brazilian miracle
> of a Hilton Hotel surrounded by hovels.
> The price of things goes up
> and the price of people comes down.
> Handwork as cheap as is possible . . . .
> And in the Northeast their stomachs are devouring
> themselves.

> Yes, Julian, capital is multiplying like bacilli.
> Capitalism, the accumulation of sin,
> like the pollution of São Paulo
> the whiskey-colored miasma over São Paulo.
> Its cornerstone is inequality (1981a, xv).

He exposes twentieth-century idols, pointing out the corrupt idealism of "Miss Brazil on the screen/blotting out 100,000 prostitutes on the streets of São Paulo" (ibid., xiii).

Cardenal deals with Latin American issues in a very Latin American style. He adopted the term *exteriorismo* ("exteriorism") to describe his poetry, which has become a new poetic paradigm for a growing body of post-revolutionary Nicaraguan poets. He claims it is an objective, narrative, concrete poetry specifically suited to the realities of Latin America.

Zimmerman points out that the surface realism of the poetry of *exteriorismo* covers a core of idealism. "The harsh sounds of torture sessions and shootouts, the glare of National Guard searchlights and raw-bulbed Sandinista cell meetings all came together and were explicitly juxtaposed to a standard of truth and humanity" (1985, xi).

For Cardenal, this core of idealism centers in his deep belief in the love of God for all humanity, a love that seeks to reveal itself in the cosmos, in history, in the concrete events that make up contemporary life and, especially, in the sufferings of the poor. These themes weave through the body of Cardenal's published works.

In *Salmos* Cardenal applies the contemporary vocabulary of revolution to the Scriptures, as he seeks the coming of the kingdom of God on earth. He cries out,

> Lord O Lord my God
> why have you left me?
> I am a caricature of a man
> People think I am dirt
>   they mock me in all the papers
>
> I am circled
>   there are tanks all around me
> Machine-gunners have me in their sights
>   there is barbed wire about me
>   electrified wire
> I am on a list
> I am called all day
> They have tattooed me

and marked me with a number
They have photographed me behind the barbed wire
All my bones can be counted
        as on an X-ray film.
They have stripped me of my identity
They have led me naked to the gas-chamber
They have shared out my clothes and my shoes
I call for morphine
        and no one hears me
In my straitjacket I cry out
I scream all night in the mental home
        in the terminal ward
        in the fever hospital
        in the geriatric ward
        in an agony of sweat in the psychiatric clinic
In the oxygen tent I suffocate
I weep in the police cell
        in the torture chamber
        in the orphanage

I am contaminated with radioactivity
        no one comes near me
        for I am contagious

Yet
I shall tell my brothers and sisters
        about you
I shall praise you in our nation
and my hymns will be heard
        in a great generation
The poor will go to a banquet
and our people will give a great feast
    the new people
           yet to be born (1981b, 25).

Cardenal clearly identifies his mission with bringing about the kingdom of God on earth through the struggle for social justice.

The Military Police have told you
that all the Church should worry about is "souls."
But what about children starved by corporations?
How *shall they possess the earth* if the earth is owned by
    landlords?

Unproductive, esteemed only for real estate speculation
and fat loans from the Bank of Brazil.
There He is always sold for Thirty Dollars
on the River of the Dead.
The price of a peon.
In spite of 2,000 years of inflation (1981a, xi).

Cardenal sees Christ identifying with the suffering of the poor: "With no news because of censorship, we know only: there where the helicopters gather is the Body of Christ" (referring to the dropping of victims from helicopters as a form of extermination) (ibid., xv). He identifies himself with Christ in becoming a "subversive" on behalf of justice and the poor, sometimes against official church practice. In a poem dedicated to a prominent Brazilian bishop, Cardenal writes:

Bishop, we are subversives
a secret code on a card in a file who knows where,
followers of the ill-clad and visionary proletarian,
a professional agitator, executed for conspiring
        against the System.
It was, you know, a torture intended for subversives,
the cross was
for political criminals,
not a cluster of rubies on a bishop's breast (ibid., xiv).

In this same poem, Cardenal looks toward the coming of the kingdom:

A new order.
Or rather a new heaven and a new earth.
New Jerusalem. Neither New York nor Brasilia.
A passion for change:
the nostalgia of that city.
A beloved community.
We are foreigners in Consumer City.
The new person, and not the new Oldsmobile (ibid.,
        xiii).

Cardenal from a missiological perspective

David Bosch includes Ernesto Cardenal in his list of "Contextual Missionary Theology from Orbis," looking primarily at the contribution of

El evangelio en Solentiname (Bosch 1985, 125–26). It provides an example of mission theology from the bottom up, springing from the life of a people as they relate their experience of oppression and struggle to the content of the Scriptures.

I am aware that any consideration of Ernesto Cardenal as a missiologist will be controversial. His espousal of liberation theology, including use of violence to achieve the ends of revolution, contributes to the issues that divide Christians. His position on the authority of Scripture is not clear, and his concept of "evangelization" does not seem to have much to do with spiritual transformation. Even so, we still have much to learn missiologically from this poet-priest.

Rather than speaking of missiology in general terms, it may be that Cardenal provides an example of missiology in the specific context of revolution, where old answers and methods are no longer adequate. The Catholic tradition of the "supplementary ministry" in times of crisis has something to teach us.

Cardenal's experience in Solentiname exemplifies incarnational mission and contextualization. Cardenal crossed social-class barriers to minister alongside the farmers and fishermen of the islands. He encouraged the local people as a community to interact with the Scriptures, relating them to their own experiences in a three-fold interaction of biblical text, faith community and missional context (Van Engen 1996).

José Arguello says of the Solentiname community, "[Cardenal's] campesino community experience turned the church of Nicaragua back to its mission of bearing and announcing the Kingdom that Jesus promised to the poor. God returned and was authentically revealed in Solentiname" (1985, 141).

Cardenal also models use of narrative in mission. He clearly understands the reality of history and the power of story, both as a way of interpreting reality and of communicating hope. And his "mission" of "horizontal communication," of empowering the people to discover and express their own voice, is a model to be taken seriously.

Finally, Ernesto Cardenal exemplifies integration. He unites sacred and secular in mission, though the union is often uncomfortable for the contemplative monk turned cabinet minister. He also seems to integrate doing with being and praying. We see Cardenal, in the middle of the activity and struggle, reflecting, pondering, asking questions, seeking a clearer path.

Especially significant for me as a writer and trainer of writers, Cardenal as a writer in mission achieves a unity of form, content and context. Better than any systematic theology could have done, his very Latin American poetry ("teo-poesía," in the words of José Arguello [ibid.]) cries out with the pain of his people and, at the same time, shows the footprints of God in the midst of the rubble.

Cardenal as a missiological model is perhaps weakest at the point of bringing the Scriptures, in their own terms, to bear on the context and on the mission of the church in that context. This reflects the Catholic doctrine of natural theology that hears the voice of God equally in nature, culture and the Scriptures. An evangelical perspective would place the Scriptures above the first two, while not denying them.

Nevertheless, I find myself deeply moved by the example of Ernesto Cardenal as a person whose life and words passionately serve the mission of God to free his people. I can picture him among my Aymara sisters and brothers in La Paz, holding a poetry workshop. He would prod them to recognize and express the concrete ways God speaks in their pain and joy. Through their struggles would emerge new stories, songs and sermons that would reveal the face of God as we have never before seen it. The whole church would be enriched.

Notes

[1] Note in the priests' public "Confession of Faith," issued June 8, 1981, in response to an ultimatum by the bishops.

[2] For more on the controversy within the Nicaraguan Catholic church, see Cabestrero 1983; Cox 1983; Bradstock 1987; Foroohar 1989.

[3] Biographical material about Cardenal is taken primarily from Cabestrero 1983; Cox 1983; Zimmerman 1985.

[4] See the references at the end of this chapter for a list of Cardenal's publications.

References

Arguello, José. 1985. "Cardenal's Theo-Poetry." *Christianity and Crisis* 45, no. 6: 141–43.

Bausch, William J. 1984. *Storytelling: Imagination and Faith*. Mystic, Conn.: Twenty-Third Publications.

Betto, Frei. 1979. "Ernesto Cardenal, Poet/Priest of the Nicaraguan Revolution." *The Other Side* 15, no. 9: 39–41.

Bradstock, Andrew. 1987. *Saints and Sandinistas: The Catholic Church in Nicaragua and Its Response to the Revolution*. London: Epworth.

Cabestrero, Teófilo. 1983. *Ministers of God, Ministers of the People*, trans. R. Barr. Maryknoll, N.Y.: Orbis Books.

Cardenal, Ernesto. 1969a. *Oración por Marilyn Monroe y otros poemas (Prayer for Marilyn Monroe and Other Poems)*. Medellín, Colombia: La Tertulia.

———. 1969b. *Homenaje a los indios americanos (Homage to the American Indians)*. Managua: Universidad Nacional Autónoma de Nicaragua.

———. 1974a. *La Vida en el amor (Life in Love)*. Buenos Aires: Carlos Lohlé.

———. 1974b. "Prólogo." In *Poesía Nueva de Nicaragua (New Poetry of Nicaragua)*, ed. Ernesto Cardenal, 9–11. Buenos Aires: Lohlé.

———. 1977. *Apocalypse and Other Poems*, ed. Robert Pring-Mill and Donald D. Walsh. New York: New Directions.

———. 1981a. "Letter to Bishop Casaldáliga," trans. Donald D. Walsh, Preface to Teófilo Cabestrero, *Mystic of Liberation: A Portrait of Pedro Casaldáliga*. Maryknoll, N.Y.: Orbis Books.

———. 1981b. *Psalms (Salmos)*. New York: Crossroad/Continuum. (Originally published in 1969.)

———. 1984. *The Gospel in Solentiname*. 4 volumes, trans. Donald D. Walsh. Maryknoll, N.Y.: Orbis Books. (Originally published in 1975.)

———. 1985. *Flights of Victory/Vuelos de Victoria*, ed. and trans. Marc Zimmerman. Maryknoll, N.Y.: Orbis Books.

———. 1993. *Cosmic Canticle*, trans. John Lyons. East Haven, Conn.: Curbstone. (Originally published in 1989.)

Colás, Santiago. 1994. *Post Modernity in Latin America: The Argentine Paradigm*. Durham, N.C.: Duke University Press.

Cox, Harvey. 1983. "Who Is Ernesto Cardenal?" *Christianity and Crisis* 43, no. 5: 108–9, 126–27.

Foroohar, Manzar. 1989. *The Catholic Church and Social Change in Nicaragua*. Albany, N.Y.: State University of New York Press.

Lefevere, Patricia. 1983. "Daniel Debates Peace from Prison." *International Review of Mission* 72, no. 288: 59–60.

Merton, Thomas. 1993. *The Courage for Truth: The Letters of Thomas Merton to Writers*, ed. Christine M. Bochen. New York: Farrar, Strauss, Giroux.

Sand, Faith Annette. 1979. "Nicaragua: Christians and the Struggle for Justice." *The Other Side* 15, no. 9: 31–33.

Van Engen, Charles. 1996. Syllabus, handouts, lecture notes for the class "Theologizing in Mission" (MT537). School of World Mission, Fuller Theological Seminary, Pasadena, California.

Zimmerman, Marc. 1985. "Ernesto Cardenal After the Revolution." "Introduction." In Ernesto Cardenal, *Flights of Victory/Vuelos de Victoria*. Maryknoll, N.Y.: Orbis Books.

8

A missiological perspective on suffering

YOUNG KEE LEE

My wife and I went from Korea to Thailand as missionaries in 1986. We were sent to work in church planting and leadership training. Early in our missionary career we realized Thailand was a difficult mission field and results would be difficult to win. We learned that, although Protestant missionaries have been working there for more than 170 years, evangelical Christians make up only 0.3 percent of the population. I pondered the contrasts between Thai culture and Korean culture and noted the very different responses to the gospel in the two countries. I began searching for the reasons for this difference.

I discovered Thai culture is deeply rooted in Buddhist philosophy. Hinayana Buddhism aims at individual *nirvana*,[1] an escape from every kind of suffering and trouble in this life. Thai people speak of their culture as having the three characteristics of *Sanuk, Sabaay* and *Saduak*— Thai terms that roughly mean "having fun," "comfortable feeling of peace," and "convenience of life," respectively. Thai Christians exhibit this mentality of *Sanuk, Sabaay* and *Saduak*.

In Korea, the Christian faith has been firmly established in the midst of persecution and suffering, yet the Korean church has grown strong and has now become a major missionary force in the majority world.

The difference between these two historical backgrounds has made me rethink the relationship between Christian mission and suffering from

Young Kee Lee, originally from Korea, has served as a missionary to Thailand. His Ph.D. research focuses on the missiology of suffering and martyrdom. Lee plans to continue his missionary service in Asia, perhaps in China, as well as in Thailand, where he will minister in the areas of raising up national church leadership and training cross-cultural pioneering missionaries.

a biblical perspective. Is there a connection between suffering and effective ministry in mission? In this chapter I examine two aspects of suffering from a missiological point of view: how the ministry of Jesus expanded, through suffering, to touch the nations, and the place of suffering in the New Covenant concept of the priesthood.

Jesus' ministry through suffering

Jesus' death on the cross can be seen as "God's wisdom, secret and hidden, which God decreed before the ages for our glory" (1 Cor. 2:7). The apostle Paul boldly preached Christ crucified, a stumbling block to Jews and foolishness to Gentiles, because Paul knew Christ was the answer for both groups—the power of God for the Jews and the wisdom of God for the Gentiles (1 Cor. 1:23–24). A similar statement could be given concerning Jesus' ministry through suffering. John Stott clearly states the secret of the effectiveness of mission:

> The place of suffering in service and of passion in mission is hardly ever taught today. But the greatest single secret of evangelistic or missionary effectiveness is the willingness to suffer and die. . . . But the servant must suffer if he is to bring light to the nations, and the seed must die if it is to multiply (1986, 322).

Limited ministry before suffering

There has been much discussion about whether or not Jesus intentionally directed any of his ministry to the Gentiles before the cross. As Jesus sent out the twelve apostles to preach the gospel of the kingdom, he instructed them, "Go nowhere among the Gentiles, and enter no town of the Samaritans, but go rather to the lost sheep of the house of Israel" (Matt. 10:5–6). This priority in Jesus' ministry is also seen in the episode with the Canaanite woman who came to Jesus requesting that he heal her demon-possessed daughter. Jesus responded at first, "I was sent only to the lost sheep of the house of Israel. . . . It is not fair to take the children's food and throw it to the dogs" (Matt. 15:24, 26). These references show that Jesus' ministry was limited in scope at that time.

Many missiologists have discussed the issue of the limited ministry of Jesus' earthly life. Scholars such as David Bosch and Johannes Verkuyl have grouped their arguments around the concept of centripetal/centrifugal mission. At first, Israel's relationship to the nations is centripetal, drawing them to itself. But after the messianic prophecies of the Old Testament are fulfilled and all the various strands meet in the Man from Nazareth, the relationship of Israel to the nations becomes centrifugal, actively reaching out. Verkuyl describes it this way:

> I see Jesus itching with a holy impatience for that day when all the stops shall be pulled as the message goes out to the Gentiles. For a time he restricts his message to the lost sheep of the house of Israel, knowing that certain conditions must be met before the message goes out to the *goyim* (1978, 104).

Bosch goes even further to lay a biblical foundation for the Gentile mission when he says, "There would have been a Gentile mission in the post-Resurrection period even if the historical Jesus had had no contact with non-Jews and had said nothing about them" (1980, 48). Bosch does not base his foundation for mission on the Great Commission. Instead, he places the foundation for mission in God's compassion and mercy as expressed in the biblical record of Jesus' earthly ministry (ibid., 57).

I think Verkuyl and Bosch rightly saw the missionary dimension of Jesus' earthly ministry as based on God's mercy and compassion. However, they did not show clearly enough why and how the turning around of Jesus' ministry was made to all nations. What was the instrument that eventually let Jesus reach out to the ends of the earth? It is at this point we see the instrumentality of suffering in Jesus' ministry.

Expanded ministry through suffering

Keeping in mind the limited scope of Jesus' ministry before his suffering on the cross and his resurrection, let us now look at the expansion of Jesus' ministry after the cross. After his crucifixion and resurrection, Jesus commanded his disciples to "go into all the world and proclaim the good news to the whole creation" (Mark 16:15). The Great Commission is given to his disciples only after his suffering and death on the cross.[2] Could we see Jesus' suffering and death on the cross as the vehicles of expanding his ministry from one nation, Israel, to "all the world"?

A suggestion for the instrumentality of suffering may be seen in Jesus' words to his disciples before the cross: "The hour has come for the Son of Man to be glorified. Very truly, I tell you, unless a grain of wheat falls into the earth and dies, it remains just a single grain; but if it dies, it bears much fruit" (John 12:23–24). Jesus remained a single grain while he was doing limited ministry in one nation, Israel, but after suffering Jesus produced much fruit whereby he expanded his ministry to all nations. He taught his disciples that "the Son of Man must undergo great suffering . . . and be killed, and after three days rise again" (Mark 8:31–32; see also Matt. 16:21–28; Luke 9:22–29). And after his resurrection, while on the road to Emmaus, Jesus asked the two disciples, "Was it not necessary that the Messiah should suffer these things and then enter into his glory" (Luke 24:26)?

We need to understand the context in which Jesus spoke the words in John 12 about the grain falling to the ground and dying. The Greek visitors who came up to Jerusalem to worship at the Passover feast probably saw the triumphal entry of Jesus and felt its impact on the whole city. They may have heard the Pharisees say to one another in frustration, "You see, you can do nothing. Look, the whole world has gone after him" (John 12:19). The Greeks were probably impressed, for they requested that Philip and Andrew arrange an interview with Jesus. It was in this context that Jesus spoke those remarkable words concerning his suffering and death, indirectly refusing their request for an interview.

Jesus told the people the kind of death he was about to die when he said, "And I, when I am lifted up from the earth, will draw all people to myself" (John 12:32). In this statement, "all people" is mentioned to show that the scope of his ministry would be expanded. Perhaps this was his answer to the Greek visitors who sought an interview. Jesus never saw his suffering on the cross as a failure or a regress in mission, but rather as an instrument for touching the nations in mission and as a vehicle of glorification (cf. John 12:23).

Verkuyl saw the cross and resurrection of Jesus Christ as the foundation for worldwide mission:

> On his cross Jesus vicariously endured God's judgment which was properly due to Israel and the Gentiles. His resurrection likewise brought about a liberating rule, and the lines thus become extended to reach the whole worldwide community of nations and peoples. Jesus' cross and resurrection are the bases for a worldwide mission. For these reasons, interspersed with reports of his cross and resurrection, are the mandates to carry the message to all peoples (1978, 104).

However, Verkuyl misses the dynamics of suffering in his observation. The theme of touching the nations through suffering has been revealed in many places in the Bible. The story of Joseph in Genesis is a good example. The Suffering Servant of the Lord in Isaiah is clearly described as accomplishing his God-appointed mission through vicarious suffering. In the same way, Jesus not only accomplished God's redemptive mission through his suffering but also multiplied his ministry through the instrumentality of suffering.

Suffering in the New Covenant priesthood

In order to understand the missiological implications of Jesus' suffering for the ministry of his disciples, we need to explore the concept of priesthood in the New Covenant. The ministry aspect of Jesus' suffering is based on the concept of Jesus' high priesthood, as revealed in the New Testament epistles.

Understanding the Christian priesthood

The most explicit statements of the priesthood of believers are found in 1 Peter and Revelation. In 1 Peter 2:4–5 Christians are described as "a holy priesthood": "Come to him, a living stone, though rejected by mortals yet chosen and precious in God's sight, and like living stones, let yourselves be built into a spiritual house, to be a holy priesthood, to offer spiritual sacrifices acceptable to God through Jesus Christ" (1 Pet. 2:4–5).

The apostle Peter describes the Christian identity in the statement, "But you are a chosen people, a royal priesthood, a holy nation, God's own people, in order that you may proclaim the mighty acts of him who called you out of darkness into his wonderful light" (1 Pet. 2:9). In Revelation we also find the phrase "a kingdom and priests" (Rev. 1:5–6, NIV).

These passages are quoted from Exodus 19:5–6, when God entered into covenant with the people of Israel: "'Now then, if you will indeed obey My voice and keep My covenant, then you shall be My own possession among all the peoples, for all the earth is Mine; and you shall be to Me a kingdom of priests and a holy nation.' These are the words that you shall speak to the sons of Israel" (NASB).

The notion of "royal priesthood" in 1 Peter 2:9 comes from the Septuagint translation of Exodus 19:6. Although the original Hebrew implied "a kingdom ruled by priests" or "a kingdom of those who serve as priests," the Septuagint translated it a "royal priesthood" (*basileion hierateuma*). Richard D. Nelson points out that in this way the center of gravity shifted from the priestly polity related to the nature of the nation to the concept that the entire community makes up a collective company of priests with royal authority. What was a "priestly realm" in Hebrew now became a "regal body of priests" in Greek (1993, 159).

To establish an argument on the Christian priesthood, Nelson relates the spiritual lineage of Jesus' priesthood to 1 Samuel 2:35: "I will raise up for myself a faithful priest, who shall do according to what is in my heart and in my mind. I will build him a sure house, and he shall go in and out before my anointed one forever." Nelson insists that the author of 1 Peter had this verse in mind when composing 2:5: "like living stones, let yourselves be built into a spiritual house, to be a holy priesthood, to offer spiritual sacrifices acceptable to God through Jesus Christ" (ibid., 163–65).

One problem in convincing the readers of 1 Peter that they were truly the chosen people must have been genealogical. The apostle Peter seeks to handle this first in 1:23, reminding them of their spiritual birth: "You have been born anew, not of perishable but of imperishable seed, through the living and enduring word of God" (1 Pet. 1:23). This problem of genealogy becomes acute in the notion of priesthood, since Aaronic ancestry was fundamental to the Hebrew priesthood. Any claim of a new priesthood would immediately raise the question of genealogy. Therefore, Nelson contends that 1 Peter emphasizes the "spiritual" nature of the Christian priesthood:

> As was the case when Zadok's house succeeded that of Eli, 1 Peter asserts, you Christians are being established as a priestly house or lineage. However, your lineage is "spiritual," not according to the flesh like that of Aaron and Zadok. As a spiritual house it is a lineage that rests on divine power, not human descent (ibid.).

Thus the concept of the Christian priesthood is established in the New Covenant, along with the concept of Jesus' high priesthood.

Christian priestly ministry in suffering

Nelson makes a good argument for the identity of Christians as "a holy priesthood." However, I contend that the priestly ministry of the Christian community deserves more attention in terms of the missiological implications of Christian suffering. 1 Peter 2:9 shows the major priestly duty when it states "that you may proclaim the mighty acts of him who called you out of darkness into his wonderful light." Proclaiming the gospel is the primary duty of the Christian community. Nelson recognizes the emphasis on evangelism in 1 Peter 2:12 and 3:1–2 regarding testimony of good lives, and in 3:15 regarding verbal testimony, but unfortunately he misses 5:1, which addresses being a witness of Christ's sufferings (ibid., 162–65).

1 Peter 2:4 talks about coming to Jesus, the living stone—rejected by men but chosen by God and precious to him. This verse and those that

follow extend the idea of Jesus' sufferings to his followers. Jesus is the model, as 1 Peter 2:21 clearly indicates: "For to this you have been called, because Christ also suffered for you, leaving you an example, so that you should follow in his steps." Hebrews 13:12–13 also speaks of the suffering of Jesus' disciples as they come to the Lord of suffering: "Therefore Jesus also suffered outside the city gate in order to sanctify the people by his own blood. Let us then go to him outside the camp and bear the abuse he endured."

The idea of suffering on the part of Jesus' disciples brings us to the concept of the cross. The cross is seen as the central focus of Jesus' discipleship. Jesus taught his disciples, "If any want to become my followers, let them deny themselves and take up their cross and follow me" (Matt. 16:24). Jesus' disciples are to follow the example of their Master, sometimes even to the point of death.

But how is this theme of suffering connected to the concept of the Christian priesthood? In the concept of the Old Covenant priesthood we find self-renunciation in service to God and human beings, but not the cross in the sense of self-sacrifice:

> He said of his father and mother,
>   "I have no regard for them."
> He did not recognize his brothers
>   or acknowledge his own children,
> but he watched over your word,
>   and guarded your covenant.
> He teaches your precepts to Jacob
>   and your law to Israel.
> He offers incense before you
>   and whole burnt offerings on your altar
>   (Deut. 33:9–10, NIV).

Compare this description of priests with that of Jesus' disciples:

> Whoever comes to me and does not hate father and mother, wife and children, brothers and sisters, yes, and even life itself, cannot be my disciple. Whoever does not carry the cross and follow me cannot be my disciple (Luke 14:26–27).

Both priests and disciples deny themselves for the sake of God's people in dedicated service to God. The major difference between the Old and New Testaments at this point lies in the cross-bearing of the disciples of Jesus. The apostle Paul urged Christians to offer their bodies as living sacrifices, holy and pleasing to God, and to live a transformed life (Rom. 12:1–2). The apostle Peter also reminds the Christian community of its status as "a holy priesthood, to offer spiritual sacrifices acceptable to God through Jesus Christ" (1 Pet. 2:5).

How can we offer "spiritual sacrifices acceptable to God"? First, spiritual sacrifices are to be offered to God "through Jesus Christ," so that they may be acceptable to God, because we can only be sure of our acceptance before God through the redemptive work of Christ on the cross. Concerning the mediation of Jesus Christ in our offering spiritual sacrifices, Hans Küng writes:

> "Through him" (Heb. 13:15) the faithful are to offer sacrifices. But the whole idea of sacrifice has undergone a radical change: no longer are sacrifices made by men from their own strength, but through the mediation of Christ; they are no longer sacrifices of atonement (nothing can be added to the atoning sacrifice of Christ), but sacrifices of thanks and praise for what Christ has perfected; not sacrifices of external gifts, but the offering of oneself (1976, 472–73).

Spiritual sacrifices in the New Covenant are those brought about by the Holy Spirit. The role of the Holy Spirit is crucial in offering "spiritual sacrifices acceptable to God." We can understand these spiritual sacrifices in terms of the priestly ministry of the Christian community in preaching the gospel in the world. Paul sees his preaching as a priestly ministry: "to be a minister of Christ Jesus to the Gentiles in the priestly service of the gospel of God" (Rom. 15:16a). Paul also could say that his life was poured out like a drink offering in the ministry of preaching the gospel of God (2 Tim. 4:6). We are called to suffer for the preaching of the gospel, just as Paul was called (see Acts 9:16).

The purpose of suffering in discipleship to Jesus is not only for the atonement of sins before God, which was accomplished through the sacrifice of Jesus on the cross once for all. It is also for the witness of Jesus and of the gospel in the world. Christian discipleship is established for the fulfilling of God's mission, and, in the course of fulfilling that mission, suffering is inevitably involved as God's way of doing mission in the world. Suffering is not a goal in itself, but rather should be understood as a means of mission in this world. C. Rene Padilla has noted that

> Christian mission and Christian discipleship are two sides of the same coin. Both derive their meaning from Jesus, the Crucified Messiah, who even as Lord remains crucified. The

Christian mission is the mission of those who have identified
themselves with the Crucified and are willing to follow him
to the cross. Mission is suffering (1982, 338).

Regarding the priestly act of worship for the world, Emilio Castro
states, "A community worships God not for its own edification only, but
as the priestly people of God praying for the good of all mankind" (1978,
87). Orlando Costas also explains the nature of active involvement in
mission in this world through a spirituality of suffering (1982, 171–72).

Intercessory prayer provides a missiological link between priesthood
and suffering. We see Jesus, our High Priest, interceding for the salvation of people at the right hand of God. Since the Christian priesthood
derives its meaning and purpose from the example of the high priesthood of Jesus, another missiological implication of participation in Jesus'
suffering is active involvement in mission through intercessory prayer.
We are called to the hard task of interceding with Jesus in the Spirit for
the salvation of the world, standing before God in the gap to divert God's
wrath into blessing. God is searching for persons who can give themselves to this ministry. As the prophet Ezekiel wrote,

> And I sought for anyone among them who would repair the
> wall and stand in the breach before me on behalf of the land,
> so that I would not destroy it; but I found no one. Therefore I
> have poured out my indignation upon them; I have consumed
> them with the fire of my wrath; I have returned their conduct
> upon their heads, says the Lord GOD (Ezek. 22:30–31).

Ministry through instrumental suffering

Mission through suffering is like sowing seeds in tears (cf. Ps. 126:5–6).[3]
One reason for the remarkable growth of the church in Korea in the
1960s through the 1980s was the fact that the church's founders in faith
sowed in suffering. What happens if a farmer does not sow seed in the
spring? There is no harvest in the fall! Perhaps this is what is happening
today in Korea. We hear sad news that the growth of the Korean church
has reached a plateau and may even be declining. Could it be that this
situation can only be corrected by a new emphasis on Christian discipleship and priesthood from the perspective of the Cross?

The Thai church also desperately needs an understanding of mission
through suffering. Thai Christians have never confronted their context
of nationalistic Buddhism with the gospel of a crucified Jesus Christ, a

gospel that is confrontational by its very nature (Sterk 1992, 74–76). The Christian mission in places like Thailand needs to address deep worldview issues, such as those connected with Buddhist philosophy. The biblical perspective on suffering needs to confront and convert the Thai church and the Thai culture.[4] Only then can we expect a more effective and productive ministry in that nation.

In this chapter we have seen how the ministry of Jesus expanded to "all nations" and multiplied in the ministries of his disciples through the instrumentality of suffering. I have proposed that the concept of Christian priesthood be developed into a missiological paradigm of ministry through instrumental suffering. Just as Jesus' high priesthood was involved in suffering in God's redemptive mission, so the Christian priesthood includes suffering for the sake of the ministry of the gospel.

We need to recover the positive meaning of suffering in God's mission as revealed in the Bible. We need a deeper understanding of the instrumentality of suffering in Christian mission to promote more effectively the advance of the gospel.

Notes

[1] *Nirvana* is a word from the Sanskrit describing "the blowing out from the flame of life through reunion with Brahma," which Buddhists hold as the highest state of perfect blessedness achieved by the extinction of individual existence or by the extinction of all desires and passions of this life.

[2] See the references in Matt. 28:16–20; Mark 16:14–20; Luke 24:45–49; John 20:21–23; Acts 1:8–9.

[3] Psalm 126 declares the joy brought by God's restoration of Israel's fortune after the Babylonian captivity. The writer of the psalm compares the joy of God's restoration to the joy of reaping a harvest, but only after having sown the seed in tears. We can apply this pattern to pioneering in mission work through suffering, followed by the subsequent joy of fruitful ministry.

[4] While in Thailand I did find some Christian leaders who were making a self-sacrificial commitment. We need to encourage and build on such people.

References

Bosch, David J. 1980. *Witness to the World.* Atlanta, Ga.: John Knox Press.

Castro, Emilio. 1978. "Liberation, Development and Evangelism: Must We Choose in Mission?" *Occasional Bulletin* 2, no. 3.

Costas, Orlando E. 1982. *Christ Outside the Gate: Mission Beyond Christendom.* Maryknoll, N.Y.: Orbis Books.

Küng, Hans. 1976. *The Church*. Garden City, N.Y.: Image Books.

Nelson, Richard D. 1993. *Raising up a Faithful Priest*. Louisville, Ky.: Westminster/ John Knox Press.

Padilla, C. Rene. 1982. "Biblical Studies." *Missiology* 10, no. 3.

Sterk, Vernon J. 1992. "The Dynamics of Persecution." Ph.D. dissertation. Fuller Theological Seminary, Pasadena, California.

Stott, John R. W. 1986. *The Cross of Christ*. Leicester, England: InterVarsity Press.

Verkuyl, Johannes. 1978. *Contemporary Missiology: An Introduction*. Grand Rapids, Mich.: Eerdmans.

9

Jürgen Moltmann and a missiology of hope

Embracing the tensions

MARY THIESSEN NATION

My despair was understandable. During the previous month, my friend's brother was murdered at his job, my home in the inner city of Los Angeles was broken into three times, and I moved away from the neighborhood where I had lived and ministered for almost 18 years. I felt fear, grief, loneliness and exhaustion.

Who was I, if I was no longer a missionary? To what extent were the accusations hurled at our missionary community, accusations of paternalism and cross-cultural insensitivity, also true of me? Why had some of my co-workers burned out? Why had others left in disillusionment and anger?

Fortunately, within the despair I also heard the call to hope. I remembered the vibrant celebrations in our missionary community and the sustaining spirituality of my neighbors in the city. I could not deny that daughters of prostitutes had become minister's wives, victims of family abuse were providing homes for the lonely, those who once knew the bondage of fear and revenge had become agents of reconciliation.

Hope and despair intertwined in my spirit. The memory of God's presence in my darkest hour, when threats of dismemberment had nearly

---

Mary Thiessen Nation grew up in a rural Canadian Mennonite community. She served in Los Angeles from 1973 to 1992 with World Impact, Inc., an interdenominational urban mission organization. She presently works in the London Mennonite Centre, where her husband, Mark, is director. Her research focuses on developing a missiology of hope for urban centers.

paralyzed me, gave me a foundation of hope upon which I drew in count-
less visits with women who had been raped, abused or abandoned. But I
also wrestled with the absence of God. I thought often of my friend's
mother. After experiencing frequent rejection by men, being robbed by
her own son, failing to find meaningful work and, most recently, learning of the murder of her youngest son, she had given up. She no longer
talked about the future. She no longer talked much at all.

Yes, I knew both hope and despair. The more I pondered, the more
the two seemed intimately related. One did not merely follow the other,
nor did the presence of one mean the absence of the other. When in the
following months I confessed my avoidance and apathy, admitting I did
not want to pour out my life again, I wept. But wait. Was my weeping
not in fact a sign of hope? Clearly I still cared.

My encounter with hope through Moltmann's life

In the time following my move, I discovered Jürgen Moltmann, a German theologian who wrote about hope. The opening words of his book
The Passion for Life captivated me: "Where Jesus is, there is life. There is
abundant life, vigorous life, loved life, and eternal life. There is life-be-
fore-death" (1978, 19). In my own experience, such passion and celebration had lessened of late.

I read on eagerly: "When passionate devotion to life is missing, the
power to resist is paralyzed. . . . Apathy is a terrible temptation. Promis-
ing to spare us death, it in fact takes away our life" (ibid., 22, 26). Moltmann
articulated my inner struggle. I noted that he identified some of those
things which had destroyed my zest for life, both within my mission organization and within the city. I searched for more of his writings.

To my delight I found Moltmann's personal testimony in *Experiences
of God*. At 18, Moltmann planned to study mathematics and physics. Instead, he was drafted to serve in the German army under Hitler. Twice
his anti-aircraft unit was hit by mortar fire. Both times he was the only
one left alive. He was captured by the Allies and subsequently spent four
years as a prisoner of war.

He said of his years in prison, "We lost our names and became numbers. We lost our home and our country; we lost our hope and our self-
consciousness; and we lost our community" (1978, 97). These words reso-
nated with the despair I had seen in the city among the oppressed. I
recognized the despair my parents had tasted in their flight from Russia
to Canada, a despair shared by multitudes who experience homelessness
and alienation. Moltmann recounts, "I saw how other men collapsed

inwardly, how they gave up all hope, sickening for the lack of it, some of them dying. The same thing almost happened to me" (1980, 7).

What spared Moltmann's life was "a rebirth to new life thanks to a hope for which there was no evidence at all" (ibid.). He did not experience any sudden conversion, but writes that "the experience of misery and forsakenness and daily humiliation gradually built up into an experience of God" (ibid.). A chaplain in the prison gave him a New Testament with an appended Psalter. In the Psalms he found words for his suffering and a God who is "present most of all behind the barbed wire" (ibid., 8). I sensed Moltmann could aid my search for an understanding of the dynamic between hope and despair.

I was both comforted and disturbed to read further, "Whenever in my despair I wanted to lay firm hold on this experience, it eluded me again, and there I was with empty hands once more. All that was left was an inward drive, a longing which provided the impetus to hope" (ibid.). I had known this kind of longing. "At the same time, even this hope cut two ways; on the one hand it provided the strength to get up again after every inward or outward defeat; on the other hand it made the soul rub itself raw on the barbed wire, making it impossible to settle down in captivity or come to terms with it" (ibid.). Had I not witnessed this fierce hope in the mothers of gang members?

These experiences with God convinced Moltmann that renewal can be our response to destruction and despair. He writes, "Some of us found behind the barbed wire the power of a hope which wants something new, instead of seeking a return to the old" (ibid., 6). Upon his release, however, he was deeply disappointed to find the church in West Germany was seeking reconstruction rather than a new beginning.

After careful theological study, a subsequent pastorate, and eventually a doctoral thesis, in 1964 he wrote *Theology of Hope*.[1] This seminal work seemed to give voice to a universal yearning. It was reprinted six times in its first two years of publication. Its message endured the disappointed hopes of the world in the later 1960s. The book's success led to fruitful ecumenical and international dialogue.

Could Moltmann's insights provide a theological foundation for a missiology of hope for me? For my friends? What would he offer concerning the relationship between hope and despair among those suffering in the inner city?

Theology of hope: Hope in mystery

As I studied Moltmann's writings, I learned eschatological hope provided the foundation of his theology. But this future orientation was neither mystically futuristic nor utopian. Instead, it wrestled with contradictions between the promised and the actual.

It was a theology that included a sense of tentative certainty, because it remained closely tied to his experiences of God amid personal powerlessness and isolation. He determined to write not only as an academician, or even as a pastor, but also as a prisoner.

I noted that what Moltmann called a dialectical[2] theology permeated his early writings. In my search for the connections between Moltmann's theology and stories in the city, I discovered three areas in which Moltmann exposes a tension that sheds light on the dynamics between hope and despair. These are the relationship between the promised future and the actual past, present and future; between the Crucifixion and the Resurrection; and between death and the new creation.

The past, present and future as shaped by the promised future

Moltmann suggests that eschatological hope informs and shapes the past, present and future. He shows how this dynamic interrelationship is sustained throughout the biblical text (1994, 130). Promises concerning the future kept Israel moving forward. Prophetic references to the pending day of Yahweh and the apocalyptic visions of a new heaven and earth helped Israel understand and interpret its stories. The teachings of Jesus about the present and coming kingdom of God included implications for the immediate situation of his audience. And Paul's emphasis on the promise of final vindication, as well as John's visions, all infused the past with meaning and called for faithfulness and hope in the present.

Concerning the impact of eschatological hope on the past, Moltmann writes:

> Yahweh's faithfulness in the past is recalled and recounted to the "children of the future" (Ps. 78:6), in order that the "people which shall be created" may praise Yahweh and recognize his lordship for their own present and future (Ps. 71:18; 102:18). Thus it is in order to awake confidence in Yahweh's faithfulness in the future that the historic experiences of former times are recounted (1993, 297).

Our vision of the future enables us to critique the past, to reinterpret it and build upon it.

Eschatological hope also informs the present. When Moltmann claims that "Christianity is completely and entirely and utterly hope—a looking forward and a forward direction; hope is not just an appendix," he deduces that this means it calls for "a new setting forth and a transformation of the present" (1980, 11). The coming kingdom, the promised new heaven and earth, and the resurrection of the dead, do not merely describe a future event. They set us in the direction of the future and invite us to participate in the transformation of the present in light of future reality. This does not preclude the radical newness of the coming kingdom and the new creation but points to the power of that kingdom to touch the present one. Our enduring hopes kindle our daily hopes. Our daily hopes quicken our enduring hopes.

How does this dynamic nature of eschatological hope inform my search for the relationship between despair and hope? It causes me to recognize the possibility of hope within despair, not merely the hope for something better after despair. Both despair and hope invite me to choose to live creatively in ways consistent with my vision of the future and in ways that prepare the world for the fulfillment of that vision. In this way despair calls out hope while hope embraces despair.

The resurrection of Christ and the crucified God as a paradox

A second area of vibrant coexistence within Moltmann's theology of hope relates to the Crucifixion and Resurrection. Richard Bauckham, a leading interpreter of Moltmann, expresses this association as follows:

> For Moltmann, the cross and the resurrection of Jesus represent total opposites: death and life, the absence of God and the nearness of God, godforsakenness and the glory of God. Jesus abandoned by his Father to death and Jesus raised by his Father to eschatological life in the divine glory represent an absolute contradiction, yet it is the *same* Jesus who was crucified and is now raised (1995, 33).

The contradiction between the Cross and the Resurrection corresponds to the discontinuity between human experience and the promised future. In the Cross, Jesus identifies with present reality—its subjection to sin, suffering and death. In the Resurrection, Jesus opens the whole world to its future and guarantees all other promises will be fulfilled. The coming kingdom of righteousness and glory, the new creation of all life, and the resurrection of the dead are declared a certain coming reality by Christ's resurrection. Because the resurrection of Christ goes as far as hope can go–to God's triumph over death—it encompasses all lesser hopes for the realization of God's righteousness within history (Moltmann 1993, 33–34).

But lest we mistakenly think Moltmann is proposing mere optimism in light of the Resurrection, and activism in response to future possibilities, we must note his concurrent wrestlings regarding the crucifixion of Jesus. The fruit of this struggle, as articulated in *The Crucified God* (1974), offers God's presence and suffering within despair, not just his final resolution of despair. As a result, despair contains both the presence of hope and the creation of hope. We need not understate or invalidate the depths of despair by prematurely pointing to the promised future, or even by taking action. Hope within contradiction, hope during abandonment, hope before resolution—all these drew me to study further.

The new creation and the struggle with death

A third productive area of Moltmann's wrestlings deals with his understanding of the present reality and its relation to the new heaven and the new earth. He suggests that the eschatological kingdom represents a radically new future in which there is life for the dead, righteousness for the unrighteous and a new creation in place of this creation that is subject to evil and death. The future is neither a fulfillment of the possibilities of the present nor the achievement of utopian ideals. It is a new creation.

At the same time, the new creation is not unrelated to the present one. It is this one born anew. The apostle Peter writes, "Blessed be the God and Father of our Lord Jesus Christ! By his great mercy he has given us a new birth into a living hope through the resurrection of Jesus Christ from the dead" (1 Pet. 1:3). Moltmann suggests this rebirth is not limited to humans: "With Christ's rebirth, the rebirth of the whole cosmos begins, not just the rebirth of human beings (Matt. 19:28). His dying and his 'coming alive again' represent a transition, a transformation, a transfiguration, not a total breach and a radical new beginning" (1994, 84). Christ is "the firstborn from the dead" (Col. 1:18)—the other rebirths follow.

Therefore, the promise of a new creation includes within it the ability to confront death in all its forms. Moltmann says it this way:

> In the perspective of human history the raising of Christ *from the dead* means that the general raising of all the dead has begun. But that is only the personal side of the hope. In the perspective of nature, the raising of Christ means that the destructive power of death, which is anti-God, is driven out of creation. Death is "destroyed" (1 Cor. 15.26), and in the new creation there will be no more death. That is the cosmic side of the hope (1994, 85).

But once again we encounter no simple resolution. Within the present situation, the Spirit co-suffers with creation in its bondage to decay. We too suffer with the Spirit and in solidarity with nature. The possibility of rebirth, however, keeps each experience of despair alert to an infusion of new life. But it does not expect that things will reach their ultimate fulfillment within present reality. It expects everything will someday be reborn by the Spirit.

By respecting this unresolved condition, we do not give in to despair when we fail to see the new creation in present events. But because all things will someday be reborn, we recognize their value and commit ourselves to working now toward their transformation. All of creation and history are moving toward the future of the risen Christ. As Moltmann states it, "The Christian faith lives from the raising of the crucified Christ and reaches out towards the promises of Christ's universal future" (1980, 11–12). The resurrection is hope's foundation and the *parousia* defines hope's horizon.

What does this restless theology offer to a missiology for urban centers? How can mission embrace the tensions between the promised future and present reality? How can both the Crucifixion and Resurrection infuse us with hope within despair in the city? How do new creation and death coexist?

A hopeful missiology

Moltmann reminds us it is the Spirit's mission to strive within the world to resolve the discontinuity between what is and what is to come. This same impulse must define and characterize the mission of the church. Only then will mission be able to embrace and address despair hopefully.

The Spirit's mission

Mission that understands that the promised future has the power to shape history will be actively involved within this history. Salvation will be understood as *shalom*, which "does not mean merely salvation of the soul, individual rescue from the evil world, comfort for the troubled conscience, but also the realization of the eschatological *hope of justice*, the *humanizing* of man, the *socializing* of humanity, *peace* for all creation" (Moltmann 1993, 329).

Those who embrace both the Cross and the Resurrection in mission will engage in solidarity and resistance. They will delight in awareness that "the resurrection of Christ is not merely consolation in suffering; it is also the sign of God's protest against suffering. . . . Instead of being reconciled to existing reality they [the people of hope] begin to suffer from it and to resist it" (Moltmann 1980, 12). The people of hope will choose to live in "critical opposition" to evil even as they live in "creative expectation" of the future resurrection of all things.

Mission that envisions the coming transformation of all reality thrusts believers into the reality of the future they hope for. "The hope makes the Christian Church a constant disturbance in human society. . . . It makes the Church the source of continual new impulses towards the realization of righteousness, freedom and humanity here in the light of the promised future that is to come" (Moltmann 1993, 22).

Hope gives mission its vision and impetus; despair defines the context of its activity.

The spirit of mission

Sprinkled throughout Moltmann's writings are invitations to a spirit of mission that lives faithfully within the contradictions of life. It is a spirit that resists the temptation to offer answers when only presence provides peace. At the same time, it is a spirit of expectation that seeks to prepare the world for its promised future, resisting the temptation to polarize aspects of mission like evangelism and social action. It participates in both contemplation and political struggle, and it is keenly aware of both the transcendent nature of faith and the call of faith to solidarity (Bauckham 1995, 223–24). It recognizes the "not yet" of human history and chooses to bind up the world's wounds in anticipation of their final eschatological healing (Moltmann 1977). It engages in the liberation of others in anticipation of their final transformation.

> We show our hope for the life that defeats death in our pro-test against the manifold forms of death in the midst of life. It is only in the passion for life and our giving of ourselves for its liberation that we entrust ourselves utterly to the God who raises the dead (Moltmann 1980, 32).

Mission that hopes for bodily and earthly resurrection is prepared to spend. It is willing to sacrifice itself in the work of the reconciliation of the world with God and God's future. Such sacrifice is possible when the dual images of Christ in the crucifixion and resurrection are kept to-gether. Moltmann warns, "Without the brother in our fears there is no fellowship with Christ; without the redeemer in *his* fear there is no lib-eration from ours" (1994, 56).

As mission is able to be present in despair, it will be a sign of hope in the despair. Since "the lively hope appears more frequently at the breaking points of life than at the consistent unity of the whole" (1978, 41), hope will be most evident in the midst of intense despair. According to Moltmann, the missionary who accepts his or her own suffering, and does not run away from it, shows the power of hope (1980, 74).

Embracing the tension

We must embrace both hope and despair even as we work within the tension and toward its final resolution. Otherwise Christian mission will not be faithful to both the Cross and Resurrection. Moltmann warns that

> the orientation to the beyond which wants to have God without his kingdom, and the salvation of the soul without the new earth, ends up basically only in establishing an orientation to this world which builds its kingdom without God and wants to have the new earth without a new heaven. The worldless God of the one and the godless world of the other, the faith without hope of the one and the hope without faith of the other, mutually confirm each other. But in this split the Christian faith is corrupted and ruined (1978, 42).

I appreciate Moltmann's attempt to remember his own experience as a prisoner of war while writing on the theology of hope. Moltmann's willingness to allow despair and hope to be simultaneously present invites us on a journey vibrant with energy and expectation.

A return to the opening testimonies

During the time I was reading Moltmann, I learned of the murder of my friend's sister. I experienced again the intertwining of despair and hope.

Few people knew my friend's sister. She was the daughter of immigrants. Her baby's father had abandoned them. She moved to a neighboring state with her mother and baby. She was lonely. She did not feel beautiful. But she loved her mother and her child. She accepted a job at a local restaurant, and because she was dependable, she was entrusted to carry several thousand dollars home with her at the close of each working day.

When an attractive man befriended her, she was delighted. She naively felt honored by his love for her, a love he claimed prompted him to take out a life insurance policy on her. Misplaced hope cost her her life. He killed her for one day's profits—and possibly for the life insurance money.

Where is the hope in this gruesome tragedy? After my friend related the few known details of her sister's murder, she said, "Mary, I'm so proud of my sister. She fought to the end. She's always been a fighter." I sat in shocked silence. My friend interpreted the blood and skin and hair under her sister's fingernails as signs of life! It was clear to her that her sister wanted to live. My friend continued: "This gives me hope to keep on. To keep fighting and working and trying."

I was startled to hear the word *hope* in the context of a murder. When I expressed my confusion to another woman in the inner city, her immediate response was, "Oh, yes, that story gives me hope. That girl kept hoping to the end. When I hear of people fighting like that, I know I can make it through my little things."

The murdered girl had not despaired of life. Her will to live had endured. She died only because her life was taken from her. In her struggle for life, others found hope and courage.

As I wrestled with this event, I experienced again the almost dizzying tension between despair and hope. Despair invited me to denial, to categorize this murder with the bizarre, the infrequent, the unlikely to be repeated.

But further reflection reminded me that my friend's hope lay not merely in her sister's struggle to live. My friend had also chosen life—she had chosen life by crying out to God, by meeting often with her pastor, by calling me and recounting in detail the story of her sister's life and death, by fighting for the best home for her sister's baby, and by discussing options she herself had for the future. She also expressed assurance of her sister's future rebirth, of seeing her sister again. She understood that death did not have the final word. The promised future affected my friend's past, her present, and her future.

I have learned from my friends in the city that fighting to live is an expression of the value of life now and of the life that is to come. It has become clear to me that I could name and judge the murders as gross evil, and I could be enraged at them, even as I simultaneously believe in grace and forgiveness. Moltmann has invited me to live with the unrest of evil and the shalom of grace at the same time.

Hope calls me to fight for life in a world where poverty, loneliness and misplaced hopes can end so tragically. It also calls me to protest and resist where desperation, calculated evil or the demonic can incite someone to terminate another person's life for a few thousand dollars. Hope calls me to wrestle honestly with rebirth and healing for both victims and murderers, but to do so while facing the despair and hope of both.

With Moltmann in the prison camp, I find myself joining my friends in the city as we "rub our souls raw on the barbed wire" of oppression, fear and despair. Together we accept the discomfort of hope and receive the courage not only to keep living, but to talk of the future; to share peace, comfort and love; to articulate our desires for fruitfulness and fulfillment. Despair itself becomes embraceable. The bruised hands of the crucified and risen Lord lead us as we cling to the righteousness that is already here and reach for the shalom that is surely coming.

Notes

¹ I use the 1993 edition of *Theology of Hope* throughout this chapter.

² Moltmann borrows the term *dialectic* from Hegel, a philosopher whose teachings influenced Moltmann's early writings. Studies in recent years of Moltmann's reference to dialectic have produced multiple interpretations and some confusion. I am indebted to Moltmann's use of the term for my discovery of the complex tension, paradox, and mystery that I knew intuitively to be present in the relationship between hope and despair. I have chosen not to use the word *dialectic* because of its confusing connotations, particularly its suggestion that the elements in tension are untenable, that they cannot be held together. I hope to remain true, however, to the mystery and contradiction of which Moltmann made me aware.

References

Bauckham, Richard. 1995. *The Theology of Jürgen Moltmann*. Edinburgh: T & T Clark.

Moltmann, Jürgen. 1974. *The Crucified God: The Cross of Christ as the Foundation and Criticism of Christian Theology*. New York: Harper & Row.

———. 1977. *The Church in the Power of the Spirit*. New York: Harper & Row.

———. 1978 *The Passion for Life: A Messianic Lifestyle*. Philadelphia: Fortress Press, 1978.

———. 1980. *Experiences of God*. Philadelphia: Fortress Press.

———. 1992. *The Spirit of Life: A Universal Affirmation*. Minneapolis: Fortress Press.

———. 1993. *Theology of Hope: On the Ground and the Implications of a Christian Eschatology*. Minneapolis: Fortress Press.

———. 1994. *Jesus Christ for Today's World*. Minneapolis: Fortress Press.

10

Mother Teresa

To suffer with joy

JUDE TIERSMA WATSON

My fascination with Mother Teresa began long before I moved into a poor immigrant neighborhood near downtown Los Angeles. Many things about this woman intrigued me: her dedication to the poor; her ability to live a life of quiet reflection in the midst of intense activity; and, especially, her capacity to know joy in the depths of human suffering. Seeing her words lived out by the sisters of the Missionaries of Charity I encountered heightened my interest.

In Kathmandu, Nepal, the sisters ran a home for the destitute and dying, as well as a home for children. I met Reyna there as I was serving a two-year mission assignment. Like all the sisters, Reyna worked in either house, wherever she was needed—long hours of strenuous work. What I remember about Reyna was her radiant, ever-present smile. One time we brought her yet another malnourished baby who needed care until he was strong enough to return to his village. The home for children was just being set up, and already there were far more children than beds. Yet Reyna turned for a moment from the other 30 hungry children to lovingly hold the new addition. "There's always room for one more," she said with her characteristic smile. I was amazed. I felt tired just watching her.

Jude Tiersma Watson immigrated from the Netherlands to the United States as a child. She has served as a missionary to the Netherlands and Nepal. Currently she and her husband, John, live and work in an immigrant neighborhood near downtown Los Angeles as a part of Inner Change L.A. Her doctoral research, completed in 1999, integrated urban studies, mission theology, youth in the graffiti culture and narrative methodology.

Some years later, in Mexico City, I arrived in a van with other North Americans ready to volunteer in a Missionaries of Charity center. A young girl ran up to greet us, exuberant and beaming. She seemed completely unaware that her face had been severely burned, that most people's reaction would be to turn away from her. The joy of the sisters was reflected in the face of this young one. What unconditional love she must have experienced from the sisters to radiate such confidence.

At the end of the twentieth century neither poverty nor suffering is diminishing. If mission is to be relevant in the twenty-first century, we must know how to respond to the painful realities that surround us. Mother Teresa is one person to whom we can turn as an example of the church in mission responding to poverty and human need. In an increasingly complex world, she showed us the way to simplicity. In a world where the poor are greeted, if at all, with paternalism, she shows us that to care for the poor is doing "something beautiful for God."[1] In a world filled with noise, she lived a life of quiet contemplation in the midst of active engagement. In a world starving for love, she lived out the Great Commandment to love God and neighbor.

Thus it was with great anticipation I began this chapter, immersing myself in the words of Mother Teresa. I soon discovered, however, that the outward simplicity of her words disguised the difficulty of my task. Several times I chose a new topic. Other times I tried to approach my "subject" with academic objectivity, thus creating distance and lessening the discomfort of getting too close but running the danger of losing the essence of this woman. To be true to Mother Teresa, I needed to encounter her with my heart. And as I approached, I discovered "that my journey toward the poverty of the poorest turned out to be an agonizing journey into my own spiritual poverty" (Mother Teresa 1986, xi).

The call within the call

Mother Teresa was born in 1910 as Agnes, the third child in an Albanian peasant family in Skopje, Macedonia, in the former Yugoslavia. Her father died of an apparent poisoning when she was only nine years old. Despite this tragedy, Mother Teresa remembered her family as united and happy. Her mother loved God and was very involved in the local Catholic parish. According to her brother, their mother also modeled generosity, never letting any of the poor who came to their door leave without something to eat.

At the age of 12, Agnes received her first gentle calling to the missionary life. But she was content with her life and did not want to become a nun. A few years later, however, she received a clear calling and at 18 joined the Sisters of Loreto, an Irish order. She was drawn to their missionary work in India. After a short time in Ireland, she journeyed to Calcutta. She would never see her mother or sister again. In Calcutta she taught at St. Mary's High School and later became headmistress of the school.

In 1946, while on a train to Darjeeling for a retreat, young Sister Teresa had a "day of inspiration." She clearly felt a call within her call— a call to give up all, to leave her beloved convent and to follow Jesus into the slums to serve him among the poorest of the poor. "At Loreto," she said, "I was the happiest nun in the world. Leaving the work I did there was a great sacrifice" (1987, 39).

These were difficult and violent days as India struggled for independence. The streets of Calcutta were bloody from the conflict between Muslims and Hindus. Sister Teresa received her "call within a call" one month after the worst riot in Calcutta's history. Once she received permission from her superiors to begin her new work, she put on the cotton sari, the clothing of the poor. In the beginning she was often tempted to give up. She tells of bringing her food with her to a convent, knocking on the door as though she were a beggar, and asking for water to go with her meal. She received water but was told to go behind the building, where she ate her food like one of the poor (Egan 1994, 66).

One day she wrote in her journal, "God wants me to be a lonely nun, laden with the poverty of the cross. Today I learned a good lesson. The poverty of the poor is so hard. When I was going and going until my legs and arms were paining, I was thinking how the poor have to suffer to get shelter" (ibid.). Other missionaries thought she was crazy. She was tempted to return to the security and comfort of the Loreto Convent, but she knew she had to say yes to the call within her call.

The Missionaries of Charity were initiated as an order in 1950. Ten young women, all from affluent families, began their novitiate. Those who knew her at this time say Mother Teresa had delicate health and was not at all extraordinary, certainly not one likely to be chosen to lead an order that would make such an impact on the world.

By 1952 the first Home for Dying Destitutes was opened in Kalighat, a Hindu temple in Calcutta. Shortly thereafter, the sisters opened a home for abandoned children. By 1965, 300 sisters had joined the order. This same year the first home was opened outside of India, in response to requests from local bishops in Venezuela. During the next years, houses were opened in Sri Lanka, Tanzania, Rome and many other places around the world.

Mother Teresa traveled to Italy in 1960 to be reunited with her brother and meet his Italian wife and their daughter. Teresa's mother, plagued by failing health, also longed to see her daughter again, but the Albanian government refused to grant visas. Both her mother and sister died before they could be reunited with her.[2]

In 1979 Mother Teresa was awarded the Nobel Peace Prize, in addition to the many other awards she received. In a world of increasing selfishness, she shone as a symbol of a life given to the service of others. When asked how she accomplished all this, she replied, "I was so sure then [in the early days], and I'm still convinced, that it is he and not I" (Muggeridge 1977, 65). With her standing as a world figure, she never lost her humility and the calling to "the small things"—her calling to serve God by following Jesus to the poorest of the poor.

A story is told of Mother Teresa that captures much of who she was. One day she was to address a conference on world hunger. She and the sister who accompanied her got lost in the city streets on the way to the hotel. When they at last found the back of the hotel, late for the meeting, they discovered a man dying of hunger. Rather than hurry straight into the conference, they cared for the man. As they later walked into the conference hall, large screens projected statistics on world hunger. Mother Teresa remarked that when we look at such numbers, we can get lost in them while someone may be dying at our doorstep.

The Missionaries of Charity

"For I was hungry and you gave me food, I was thirsty and you gave me something to drink, I was a stranger and you welcomed me, I was naked and you gave me clothing, I was sick and you took care of me, I was in prison and you visited me. . . . Truly I tell you, just as you did it to one of the least of these who are members of my family, you did it to me" (Matt. 25: 35–36, 40).

That the order founded by Mother Teresa sees itself as missionary is made clear in its name—the Missionaries of Charity. The order has never strayed from its original calling, that of free heartfelt service to the poorest of the poor. Jesus' words in Matthew 25 serve as their guiding text. Part of their constitution reads:

We are called the "Missionaries of Charity." A missionary is one sent with a mission—a message to deliver. Just as Jesus was sent by his Father, we too are sent by Him, filled with his Spirit to be witnesses of His gospel of Love and Compassion in our communities first, and then in our apostolate among the poorest of the poor all over the world (Tangha 1989, 109–10).

Just as the purpose of their mission is clear, equally clear is their means of mission. The *way* something is done is as important as *what* is done. Goal and means are inseparable. "We must do small things for one another with great love," Mother Teresa was fond of saying. This love flowed from her deep sense of "being" in Jesus. Thus in Mother Teresa, and in the order she founded, we see integration of the "doing" and "being" of mission.

This integration of being and doing is further reflected in the description of the missionaries found in their constitution.

> As missionaries we must be
> — carriers of God's love, ready to go in haste in search of souls,
> — burning lights that give light to all men,
> — the salt of the earth,
> — souls consumed with one desire: Jesus,
> — fearless in doing the things He did and courageous in going through danger and death with Him, and for Him,
> — ready to accept joyously to die daily if we want to bring souls to God, to pay the price He paid for souls,
> — ever ready to go to any part of the world at any time,
> — always ready to respect and appreciate unfamiliar customs of other peoples, their living conditions and language, willing to adapt ourselves,
> — happy to undertake any labor and toil and glad to make any sacrifice involved in our missionary life (ibid., 110).

True to their vow of poverty, each sister owns no more than will fit into a small box. That includes only three saris—two everyday saris (one to wear while the other is being washed), plus one for special occasions. Each sister also has a Bible, a prayer book, a song book, a cup and dish, a pillow, two sheets, a rosary and a crucifix pin. When they go visiting, they never accept food or drink because the poor don't have these luxuries. Their poverty allows them to understand the plight of those they serve. It also guards against paternalism, since they give out of their lack, not their plenty. According to Mary Poplin, who spent several months with the sisters in Calcutta, "Their elected poverty is a reparation, in part, for the materialistic sins of the world" (1996, 5).

However, Mother Teresa insisted that not all people are called to poverty. Some are called to live in castles. All are called to be holy. She said, "What you do, I cannot do. What I do, you cannot do. But together, we can do something beautiful for God" (Egan 1994, 97).

Mother Teresa was very clear that the work the sisters do is not social work. Outwardly it may appear that way, but the motivation is clearly distinct. The sisters do all they do for Jesus. Likewise she was clear, contrary to popular perception, that her calling was not from the poor or to the poor. The call of the Missionaries of Charity is to follow Jesus, who calls them to the poor. "If he calls me to the rich," said Mother Teresa, "I will go to the rich" (Petrie).

What missiology learns from Mother Teresa

Looking at Mother Teresa in a missiological light raises significant questions. What does missiology look like in the context of traditional oral cultures, amid people who prefer the spoken word and storytelling to written discourses? How is mission expressed in such contexts?

Mother Teresa came from peasant stock. Malcolm Muggeridge says this was apparent in her appearance and her down-to-earth way of looking at things (1977, 16). Her idea of learning was to "come and see." A priest from Belgium recounts a story of Mother Teresa's visit to Belgium. They were discussing the lack of people going into religious vocations. He was explaining in carefully chosen language the various reasons. After listening for a moment she interrupted him and said, "Father, all of you back there in Europe talk too much and put on too many airs. You would do better to talk more about Jesus" (Tangha 1989, 41).

Although Mother Teresa was intelligent and articulate, she had little time or desire to write her thoughts. We read in the introduction to one of her books: "It is only fair to confess that not everything that appears in these pages has been written by Mother Teresa for a book. We should actually say that she has not written anything for a book" (González-Balado 1987, vii). Her life in all its intensity was devoted to the poorest of the poor (who probably wouldn't read her books). It is the efforts of others, "born of the desire to make known the words that have been lived by Mother Teresa before they were ever written or uttered" (ibid., viii) that have produced various books featuring what others have collected of her words. They are words that have been refined in the heat of Calcutta streets.

Yet her missional action was not without reflection. Action and reflection were a simultaneous process for Mother Teresa. Her reflection, however, was not academic or scholarly. Certainly it could not be seen as the "study" of mission in the stream of Dutch missiologist Johannes Verkuyl and other European missiologists. It began and ended in action. While Verkuyl does make the statement that "if study does not lead to participation , . . missiology has lost her humble calling" (Verkuyl 1978, 6), yet study even leading to participation was not part of Mother Teresa's vocation.

It is perhaps closer to the kind of missiological reflection that Orlando Costas calls us to: "Missiology is fundamentally a praxeological phenomenon. It is a critical reflection that takes place in the praxis of mission. . . . [It occurs] in the concrete missionary situation. . . . Missiology arises as a part of a witnessing engagement to the gospel in the multiple situations of life" (1976, 8).

While this is close to what the Missionaries of Charity do, their reflection isn't exactly "critical reflection." The reflection of Mother Teresa, and now her sisters, is a reflection that takes place deep in the heart of a person sitting, like Mary, at the feet of Jesus. For this reason, the sisters start each morning with prayer. This spirit of the morning prayers remains with them throughout their long days. While accomplishing their many tasks, they are constantly aware of Jesus and offer every action in dedication to him. Thus they are accomplishing many tasks, as Martha needed to do, with Mary's heart of devotion.

Whether or not we consider Mother Teresa a missiologist, missiology can learn some significant lessons from this dedicated missionary. In her life and work we encounter the first lesson—a deep spirituality serves as a foundation for mission. This foundation is never clearer than in the motivation of the sisters. All they do is clearly done for Jesus, always with a smile.

Their deep spirituality is also seen in their attitude of joyful obedience. They take a vow of obedience, but it is an obedience with great joy. "That's the spirit of our Society, that total surrender, loving trust and cheerfulness. We must be able to radiate the joy of Christ, express it in our actions. If our actions are just useful actions that give no joy to the people, our poor people would never be able to rise to the call we want them to hear, the call to come closer to God" (Egan 1994, 37–38).

Concerning the centrality of joy to the mission of "catching souls," Mother Teresa said:

> Joy is prayer–Joy is strength–Joy is love–Joy is a net of love
> by which you can catch souls. God loves a cheerful giver. She
> gives most who gives with joy. The best way to show our
> gratitude to God and the people is to accept everything with

joy. A joyful heart is the normal result of a heart burning with love. Never let anything so fill you with sorrow as to make you forget the joy of Christ Risen (Muggeridge 1977, 49–50).

Prayer is also essential to this spirituality. On prayer, Mother Teresa said:

It is not possible to engage in the direct apostolate without being a soul of prayer. We must be aware of our oneness with Christ, as he was aware of his oneness with the Father. Our activity is truly apostolic only in so far as we permit him to work in us and through us, with his power, with his desire, with his love. We must become holy, not because we want to feel holy, but because Christ must be able to live his life fully in us. . . . Love to pray—feel often during the day the need to pray, and take trouble to pray. Prayer enlarges the heart until it is capable of containing God's gift of himself. Ask and seek and your heart will grow big enough to receive him and keep him as your own (ibid., 47–48).

This devotion to prayer complements the sisters' life of action. It is through prayer, offered with joy, that their souls draw the grace and strength they need for their lives of sacrifice. While in other mission circles there is currently a strong prayer movement, what is especially notable about this society is the lack of a dichotomy between prayer and work. The sisters are contemplatives in the heart of the world.

Another lesson from Mother Teresa concerns the place of suffering in this world, and in the lives of missionaries. Evangelical missiology does not often address this topic, but it must be considered in a world of Rwanda, Bosnia and the violence in our cities. The reason to address suffering is not only contextual but also textual. Despite evangelical silence, the Scriptures are not silent. Any biblical theology of mission must take suffering seriously.[3]

According to Mother Teresa, suffering is a necessary part of the mission work of her order. Without suffering it would just be social work—good and helpful, but not the work of Jesus Christ, not a part of redemption. "A symbol of hope in the midst of almost overpowering darkness and poverty, Mother Teresa teaches that suffering can be turned to good to produce true joy in the heart of a believer" (Egan 1994, 19).

While many people question the suffering of the innocent, and many of us in Western society actively avoid all kinds of pain, Mother Teresa believed the suffering of God's servants is connected to the suffering of

Jesus. She called it co-redemption (ibid., 56). This perspective gives meaning to suffering and helps us become more like Jesus. This is why joy is possible in the midst of suffering. It is in the acceptance of suffering as a gift that joy is possible. "To the missionaries suffering encourages them to learn new responses, to seek forgiveness, to turn to God, to think like Christ, and to rejoice that the suffering has produced a good work in them" (Poplin 1996, 11). Thus, the sisters are able to face seemingly endless human misery and care for people with radiant, smiling faces.

Here we see another lesson from Mother Teresa for missiology. She led an active but focused life. For 50 years she was sure of her call, and she lived according to that call. Despite the need, she did not fight oppressive structures.[4] Although she loved the Word of God, she did not develop a biblical theology covering both Old and New Testaments. She didn't do the kind of research and critical reflection a missiologist might. Despite criticisms of what she did not do, she stayed true to the call she was given. She led a movement that is just as focused as she was, that has the same unity of heart and purpose. The peace and joy that radiated from her radiates from her sisters as well. Long before the word was popular, she was a *mentor* to many, both inside and outside her order.

Conclusion

Last week, steeped in the story of Mother Teresa, I encountered the Penny Lady on my way to the Lucky Buy discount store. Many people in my Los Angeles neighborhood are a joy for me to greet on an evening errand—children playing in the streets, women going to the market, the homeless pushing their shopping carts in the never-ending search for cans. But the Penny Lady I avoid. After a few instances of verbal abuse when I didn't give her anything, I began crossing to the other side of the street whenever I saw her. Just like the priest and the Levite. But recently, with chagrin, I have heard the words of Jesus: "Whatever you do for one of the least of these, you do for me."

This time I chose not to cross the street. I sat next to her at the bus stop. Perhaps we would have a significant encounter. Perhaps not. Her mind seems far "gone," and I wonder what she is actually capable of. I decided just to sit with her and sense the presence of Jesus.

Notes

[1] This is one of Mother Teresa's favorite phrases and also serves as the title of Malcolm Muggeridge's book about her (1977).

[2] An enduring dream came to pass in 1991, however, when the Missionaries of Charity were allowed to begin work in Albania.

[3] See Isaiah 53, Hebrews, and Job. Note also the essay by Young Kee Lee in this volume.

[4] While some have argued that Mother Teresa should have accepted suffering less and helped to fight the injustice that is the cause of much suffering, she said that was not her call—important, but not her call.

References

Allegri, Renzo. 1996. *Teresa of the Poor: The Story of Her Life.* Ann Arbor, Mich.: Servant Publications.

Costas, Orlando. 1976. *Theology of the Crossroads in Contemporary Latin America: Missiology in Mainline Protestantism, 1969–1974.* Amsterdam: Rodopi.

Egan, Eileen, and Kathleen Egan, O.S.B., eds. 1994. *Suffering into Joy: What Mother Teresa Teaches About True Joy.* Ann Arbor, Mich.: Servant Publications.

González-Balado, José Luis. 1987. "Introduction." In Mother Teresa, *Heart of Joy: The Transforming Power of Self-Giving*, vii-viii. Ann Arbor, Mich.: Servant Publications.

Mother Teresa. 1983. *Words to Love By.* Notre Dame, Ind.: Ave Maria Press.

———. 1985. *Total Surrender*, ed. Brother Angelo Devananda. Ann Arbor, Mich.: Servant Publications.

———. 1986. *Jesus: The Word to Be Spoken*, comp. Brother Angelo Devananda. Ann Arbor, Mich.: Servant Publications.

———. 1987. *Heart of Joy: The Transforming Power of Self-Giving*, comp. José Luis González-Balado. Ann Arbor, Mich.: Servant Publications.

———. 1991. *Loving Jesus*, comp. José González-Balado. Ann Arbor, Mich.: Servant Publications.

Muggeridge, Malcolm. 1977. *Something Beautiful for God.* New York: Ballentine Books.

Petrie, Ann and Jeanette. N.d. "Mother Teresa." Film. San Francisco: Dorsan Group (800–374–5505). (Narrated by Richard Attenborough.)

Poplin, Mary. 1996. "The Parallel Worlds of Social Work Versus Religious Work: Lessons from Mother Teresa." Unpublished paper. Claremont Graduate School.

Tanghe, Omer. 1989. "For the Least of My Brothers:" *The Spirituality of Mother Teresa and Catherine Doherty.* New York: Alba House.

Verkuyl, Johannes. 1978. *Contemporary Missiology: An Introduction.* Grand Rapids, Mich.: Eerdmans.

11

Who raises the child when there is no village?

Restoring Community in African Cities

STANLEY MUTUNGA

Nairobi, Kenya. Afternoon, March 1994. I had stopped at a grocery store on my way home from a meeting at the church where I served as associate pastor. As I came from the parking lot, a young boy in tattered clothes approached me and said, "Mdosi, we nenda tu nitakugaadia" (Kiswahili slang meaning "Boss, just go; I will guard your vehicle"). The boy was persistent, begging me to allow him to earn just 10 Kenyan shillings, barely enough for dinner that night. He told me he was eight years old and his name was Koi.[1] The fact that Koi was the same age as one of my own sons moved me greatly. But here he was, a "street boy," a statistic, one of 50,000 street children in Kenya.

After doing my shopping, I paid Koi his 10 shillings. I also took him to a nearby fast-food restaurant and bought him supper. He appreciated my gesture and began warming up to me. I invited him to meet me at the same restaurant in a week. Not yet sure whether I was truly what I had told him I was (and not an undercover policeman), Koi reluctantly agreed.

Stanley Mutuku Mutunga, a native of Kenya, has done pastoral work and Bible college teaching with the Africa Inland Church of Kenya. His Ph.D. research, completed in 1993, focused on rural-urban migration into Nairobi and its implications for leadership development for the church. Mutunga taught leadership development and missiology and served as dean of the Nairobi Evangelical Graduate School of Theology. He is currently dean of the School of Graduate Studies at Hope International University, California, U.S.A.

The following week we had coffee together and talked about life on the street. I asked him why he had to earn his living in this way, begging for work on the streets. He told me he had lost both parents and that it was hard taking care of himself and his four-year-old brother.

I felt bad that a child would be on the streets fending for himself. "Why does this happen?" I asked myself. "Where is this boy's family? What about the community he comes from?" I began to blame myself, my church and the churches in Nairobi. I lamented the fact that most churches continued with ministry-as-usual while children like Koi were begging on the streets. I became angry. Angry at myself. Angry at Koi's family. Angry at his larger family and the community. I was also angry at the city churches. And I was angry at God.

At home, my family prayed for Koi. We came up with some ideas for helping him. Meanwhile, I made another appointment to meet him. The day before the meeting, I happened to pass the parking lot where I had first met Koi. Suddenly I saw him. I noticed he was unusually happy. I also noticed he was not alone. He was walking with a woman and three other children, and as I drew closer, I noticed all the children looked alike. In fact, they looked like a big happy family. I greeted Koi, and the woman introduced herself as his mother. I learned that the other children were Koi's two brothers and a sister.

Koi was obviously embarrassed. He couldn't look me in the eye. I realized that not only had he been manipulating the people he begged work from, but he had also used and manipulated me. Although undoubtedly prompted by real economic need, Koi had deceived me, and this deception left me even more troubled than I had been before meeting his family.

I was not surprised when Koi did not show up for our next scheduled meeting. Since that day I have not seen him. However, my experience with this young boy rekindled my desire to search for responses to Africa's urban challenges, particularly in the wake of disintegrating community values.

The African urban context

Although I had encountered similar cases before meeting Koi, this particular incident touched me deeply. I asked myself, Why did Koi lie? What needs pushed Koi and his family to be involved in such unethical practices? What has happened to the Kenyan spirit of interdependence? Why isn't Koi's mother teaching her children the value of honest work?

My reflections broadened to include churches in the growing cities throughout Africa. Are Africa's city churches providing alternative communities where families migrating from villages can find spiritual and physical help? Do African urban churches understand the social ills that are plaguing families in the wake of unprecedented rural-to-urban migration?

Perhaps Koi's situation can best be appreciated by looking at the context of the urban centers of sub-Saharan Africa. My reflections identify broad factors that contribute to Koi's predicament. These factors are economic, political/tribal, educational and social.

The first factor is economics. Most African nations are poor (see Van Buren 1995, 928). Rapid population increase renders traditional subsistence farming insufficient to provide for basic needs (Mutunga 1993, 94–116). Thus, rural-to-urban migration is on the rise. In the cities, about two-thirds of the total labor force is either under-employed or unemployed (ibid.), and this situation forces many to find alternatives for survival. In the process, the rural concept of community gives way to "survival of the fittest," and desperate circumstances propel some to engage in traditionally questionable practices. Koi's family is a case in point.

Concerning political/tribal factors, Africa is going through a metamorphosis that is yet to be defined. Historically, the joining of tribes by colonial governments into artificial nations did not take into consideration traditional African boundaries.[2] Political independence did not change this "divide and rule" legacy, yet African tribalism remains a powerful force. With the introduction of Western democracy and the multiparty system in the 1990s, we are witnessing in the cities an emergence of political parties based on tribalism. This has created communities that are self-serving and exclusive. Only those tribes that are closest to the political leadership receive basic services.

Educational factors also contribute to the predicament of children like Koi who come to the city. The formal education introduced by missionaries and later by colonial governments has created the expectation of white-collar jobs that are available only in big cities. Of course, the jobs are not available to all, creating additional pressure on individuals and society. Since the majority of people in most African cities are competitive job seekers, it becomes impossible to live the traditional life of interdependence. Mutual economic help diminishes, and the supporting community becomes almost nonexistent.

All the above factors have a social dimension. The "bright lights" theory of a better life in the city is alive and well. Over 60 percent of young urbanites in Nairobi have come in hope of a better life (Mutunga 1993, 94ff.). With current economic hardships, new ideas for survival are developing, and village interdependence is fast disappearing.[3] As African novelist Chinua Achebe puts it, "Things fall apart."[4] Koi and his family are no longer constrained by traditional mores. They seem to have cut social ties with the village community. And they have not replaced traditional social bonds with any known acceptable community values in the city.

The African concept of community

Many writers have underscored the fact that in traditional Africa authentic living is found only in corporate connectedness.[5] This community bonding has a variety of expressions in different parts of the continent. In Kenya, the Kiswahili phrase *wa kwetu* means one who is from my home, family, tribe, nation or even continent. It may also include other social forms of belonging, such as that of a subculture group. The term carries the connotation of connectedness, however tenuous that relationship might be. To be an African is to be naturally connected to a community setting. *Wa kwetu* is the center around which members of a community find social identity, economic security, political stability and religious fulfillment. As Austin Echema puts it, "a person does not stand alone; one's first sense of personal identity is with the community" (1995, xxi).

Three levels of connectedness

African corporate connectedness can be analyzed on at least three levels: blood bond, social-fiction bond and subculture bond.

Blood connectedness refers to members in a set of concentric circles. At the center is the nuclear family with the husband, wife or wives, and children. Then comes the extended family—uncles, aunts, cousins, nephews and nieces, as well as in-laws. As we move outward through the circles we come to the clan or lineage. Finally, the tribe forms the outer layer of the concentric circles.

The second level of corporate connectedness is the social fiction bond. Among African societies, children address all adults as aunts and uncles, even when there is no blood relationship. As children grow, parents teach them respect for senior members of the community. In my community, for example, children were reprimanded if they ever called an adult by his or her first name. It is still difficult for even the most modern Africans to call people by their first names.

With increased rural-to-urban migration, a third category of relationship is emerging in African cities. These are the subcultures, consisting of people drawn together by similar interests.[6] They may be business associates, church affiliates, political allies, workmates or those interested in certain sports. Although this level of connectedness is less homogeneous than blood or social-fiction bonds, it is based on values its members hold in common.

The "bright" and "dark" sides of *wa kwetu*

To the extent that corporate connectedness gives communities social and economic security, identity and a sense of belonging, it is to be affirmed. To be human is to belong. This is the bright side of *wa kwetu*. In Africa, where people's identities are intricately connected to community, there can be no authentic living outside *wa kwetu*.

Sadly, *wa kwetu* has its dark side. This includes the tendency to exclude those who do not fall into one's *wa kwetu* categories. When preference is given to *wa kwetu*, to those who are closest to the center of the circle, excluding non-*wa kwetu*, the result is favoritism. In larger groups it becomes an issue of racism or tribalism. In these cases *wa kwetu* becomes divisive and can destroy corporate community structures.

For the church, it is important to engage in critical appraisal of corporate connectedness, particularly in dealing with the dark side of *wa kwetu*.. Why is tribal warfare on the increase while at the same time statistics indicate the African church is one of the faster-growing segments of world Christianity? How can we reconcile the two? Are churches different from politicians in their handling of tribalism? What biblical guidelines are there in handling *wa kwetu* issues?

The apostle Paul and community in urban mission

The apostle Paul serves as an example of a leader who intentionally sought to create communities of believers in the cities where he ministered. How did he manage to work with people of different religious, racial and educational backgrounds to form new communities of believers? To what can we attribute his success, given the racial tension between Jews and Gentiles, and even within various Jewish ethnic groups? (see John 4, Acts 6).

Paul was born in a particular sociocultural setting. He was raised within given blood bonds and educated with a certain worldview. When he converted to Christianity, he was brought into a new relationship, a spiritual bond, and he became a member of the family of God. How did Paul view these levels of relationships? How did he use them in fostering a biblical view of Christian community?

Blood bond

An examination of Acts and Paul's own testimony in his letters will show Paul mentioned his blood bond community only when provoked to do so. He did not boast about his biological background, but used it mainly to clarify a point or verify his identity (Acts 21:39, 22:3, 23:6). In defense against those who questioned his apostleship, Paul replies, "Are they Hebrews? So am I. Are they Israelites? So am I. Are they descendants of Abraham? So am I. Are they ministers of Christ? . . . I am a better one" (2 Cor. 11:22–23). Paul usually identified himself with the wider community of believers in Jesus Christ.

Writing to the Christians at Philippi, Paul again refers to his background credentials. He says in Philippians 3:4–5, "If anyone else has reason to be confident in the flesh, I have more: circumcised on the eighth day, a member of the people of Israel, of the tribe of Benjamin, a Hebrew born of Hebrews." In this passage, there are at least four important clauses that describe the privileges inherited by Paul through his blood bond (see Lightfoot 1975, 146–47). Gunther Bornkamm comments that

> the enumeration given in letters to Gentile Christians of the advantages he [Paul] once enjoyed is of more than biographical importance. It discloses that this was a form of introduction also used by his opponents on presenting themselves to the churches in order to make an impression. Their proud appeal to their descent was obviously intended to assume for themselves a higher authority and more likelihood of being listened to, and checkmate Paul. This sheds light on the high esteem in which Jews were then held even in an originally heathen milieu (1971, 4).

We get here the picture of a person who was highly privileged in terms of his blood community but does not appear ambitious to use his tribal connections to benefit himself. Rather, Paul states in Philippines 3:7, "Yet whatever gains I had, these I have come to regard as loss because of Christ." He had found a new identity in Christ. All Christians regardless of their racial background became Paul's primary community.

In Romans 11:1, Paul refers again to his background for the purpose of identifying with other Jews, and assuring them of their inclusion in God's plan of salvation. This is more of an encouragement to his fellow

Jews to stop feeling they had been left out of the salvation plan. He states emphatically, "I ask, then, has God rejected his people? By no means! I myself am an Israelite, a descendant of Abraham, a member of the tribe of Benjamin." Based on this passage, there is no solid ground for those who see Paul as anti-Semitic.[7] Paul did not disown his Jewish heritage when he became a Christian. Rather, he maintained his ties even as he embraced people of other heritages.

Religious/educational bond

We know a good deal of Paul's educational background from Luke's account in Acts and Paul's own testimony. Paul's citizenship is associated with Tarsus, the capital city of Cilicia, a province of the Roman empire. Despite this cosmopolitan setting, Paul's upbringing and education were deeply religious.

It is apparent from Paul's own testimony that he was brought to Jerusalem at an early age to study under the respected rabbi Gamaliel (Acts 22:3). William Barclay[8] and Joseph Grassi (1978, 4–5) analyze the educational stages Paul must have undergone before attaining the high status of a Pharisee. Barclay notes that of all Jewish religious groups, none were so respected as the Pharisees. They were the cream of the Jewish nation (1981, 20–23). And Grassi calls the Pharisees "a select fervent group within Judaism" (1978, 4). All of this would have placed Paul at the very peak of the Jewish social order. Paul himself, writing to the Philippians, testifies "as to righteousness under the law, [I was] blameless" (Phil. 3:6). And to the Galatian Judaizers he declared, "I advanced in Judaism beyond many among my people of the same age, for I was far more zealous for the traditions of my ancestors" (Gal. 1:14).

It is clear Paul attained the best education of the day. He probably learned the basics of Greek thought, while becoming an expert in traditional Jewish lore and Old Testament law. Because of his birth and education, he belonged to the upper stratum of society. Humanly speaking, he had reason to consider himself more important than others. However, his encounter with Jesus taught him love and acceptance for all peoples.

Spiritual bond

We can best understand the effect of Paul's conversion experience if we look at his pre-Christian life. His place as a Jewish leader and teacher would not have allowed him to mix with Gentiles. Grassi comments:

> Many of the regulations of the Torah concerned food, espe-
> cially the proper slaughtering of meat and preserving food
> from impurities and contact with Gentile hands. This meant
> that real fellowship with Gentiles was almost impossible, be-
> cause this would usually entail meals together. It meant that
> Jews had to live together in an enclave where they could be
> assured the support and atmosphere necessary for keeping
> the Torah (1978, 5).

After his dramatic conversion, however, Paul came out of that social
enclave and declared his newfound identity in Jesus and among people
of all colors and races. Writing to the Corinthians, he testifies that "to
the Jews I became as a Jew. . . . To those under the law I became as one
under the law. . . . To the weak I became weak. . . . I have become all
things to all people, that I might by all means save some" (1 Cor. 9:20,
22). As Grassi says, "For Paul, Christ was the great agent of oneness who
would cause people to discover their inner oneness-space and deepen it
to new dimensions made possible by the Spirit of God" (1978, 138).

Something transformational happened in Paul's life for him to de-
clare as "loss" his high social profile, and his religious and educational
background "for the sake of Christ" (Phil. 3:7, NIV). It no longer mat-
tered to Paul whether one was a *wa kwetu* racially, educationally or religiously. Paul learned to speak of "both Jews and Greeks" as those who
have been called (1 Cor. 1:24) and baptized (1 Cor. 12:13). He admonished the Corinthians to give no offense to Jews, Greeks or the church of
God (1 Cor. 10:32) (see Kummel 1975, 271).

We see Paul ministering in an urban cross-cultural situation. He embraced each race as a special people before God. Gentiles and Jews, circumcised and uncircumcised, former Pharisees, pagans and proselytes
worshiped together. Whereas his social, religious and educational upbringing had taught him to limit his contacts to Jews, the Spirit taught
him the principle of agape love that embraces all races as one in Christ.

Seeing Koi from a missiological perspective

The story of Koi illustrates a painful reality African urban churches must
face today. It reminds us that African community values are not being
experienced in urban centers. The story points out the cumulative effects of the economic hardships, political instability and social changes

sweeping the continent. In what ways, then, can churches help in forming new inclusive communities in the city? What can churches do to
enhance the bright side of *wa kwetu* ?

First, it would be unrealistic to ask Koi to go back to the village. Given
the economic realities, urban-to-rural migration is not an option. At any
rate, Koi's needs are deeper than the merely material. Koi represents the
new phenomenon of a "rootless generation" of people whose needs will
not be met by providing occasional hot meals and baths.

Churches need to intentionally seek out these people and create loving environments where children like Koi and their immediate families
will feel "at home," communities where they can be held accountable.
Such a church community would encourage Koi to ask "African questions," such as, "What would the community say if it caught me lying?
How can I do this bad thing to my community?"

It is gratifying to note that already there are more than 50 religious
organizations in Nairobi (Christian and Muslim) that are involved in
alleviating street children's needs. Most of these organizations, however,
do not provide comprehensive holistic help but primarily serve as centers of feeding, informal education, counseling and vocational skills training. A few of them provide alternative homes for street children, and
there are cases where rehabilitation has been achieved. Examples in
Nairobi include Ngong Hills Children's Home, Operation Save the
Children, Undugu Society of Kenya, and Mathare Children's Home.[9]
Involvement of local churches has, however, remained minimal. This
can partly be explained by the fact that most city churches (particularly
those comprised mainly of first-generation urbanites) perceive the city
in transitory terms. "Home" is always in the village and the city dwelling
is only a "house." This mentality, while understandable, has been a barrier to giving the challenge of street children the attention it deserves.

Christians need to rethink the whole issue of tribe or race. This factor
is not unrelated to the prevalence of children like Koi, particularly when
we think of the inseparable nature of politics and tribalism in Africa. If
there is anything to be learned from Paul, it is that while African Christians cannot abandon their blood *wa kwetu*, Christians' primary allegiance
should be to an inclusive *wa kwetu*, the larger Christian community. To
this end, churches in Africa's cities should encourage *subculture* churches,
as opposed to *tribal* churches. In subculture churches, members will not
seek to know Koi's tribe before they decide whether or not to help him.

Already we are witnessing faster growth in the newer racially and trib-
ally mixed congregations, compared to traditional denominations.
Nairobi Light House Church, Nairobi Pentecostal Church, Nairobi
Chapel and Nairobi Baptist Church are examples of growing subculture

churches. The interracial and intertribal composition of these churches creates a healthy environment for dealing with Koi as a person, not as a child from a particular tribe.

Churches must be critical of the notion that a political focus on changing the socioeconomic infrastructure is the answer to reducing the number of children on the streets. While it is true that some Christians may be called to serve in the political arena, if political activity is reduced to trading insults with other politicians, as has happened in some cases, it will yield little fruit for the gospel and do nothing to restore community. Politics is principally about power, while the church is about truth; mixing the two must be done under the guidance of the Holy Spirit and with the support of the church community.

I propose that Christians should pursue their prophetic call in credible ways. We must preach messages that have political, social and economic applications, thus addressing Koi's needs. However, we should be careful in our exegesis to consider the whole message of the Bible, not bending Scripture to support a particular political, social or economic agenda.

It has been said "it takes a village to raise a child." We need to ask ourselves, Who raises a child where there is no village? Who is responsible for Koi when there is no village in the city? City churches must rethink their identity and role so they can become relevant to the needs of people in the city. Paul provided us with an example by practicing an inclusive *wa kwetu* in the cities where he ministered. There are, as we have seen, examples of organizations and churches in Nairobi that are moving toward inclusive holistic ministries. More churches and Christian organizations must follow these examples, opening their arms and hearts to all the Kois in Africa's cities.

I still think of Koi and his family. I pray they will find a place of community and connectedness in the middle of Nairobi. I pray that there they will meet Jesus and his people.

Notes

[1] Not his real name.

[2] Faced with the practical problems of organizing people, colonial officials at times felt justified in forcing Africans into new locations. Benezet Bujo cites an interesting case in eastern Zaire, where a major misunderstanding between the European explorer and the local Africans led not only to the splitting of tribal groups, but also to giving misleading names to places and people groups.

[3] Robert Nisbert has identified four major processes of social change that I think aptly summarize Koi's situation. The first is individualization. This releases

individuals from the constraining ties and traditional social codes of authorities. The second is innovation. Third is the process of politicization, of which the assertion of power, whether individual or collective, succeeds the ordinary processes of customs and traditions. The fourth is secularization—the passage of sacred norms into secular, replaced by a social order largely governed by a worldview in which utilitarian or secular values dominate (1970, 370).

[4] The best-selling Nigerian author argues (*Things Fall Apart*, 1958) that the Westernization of Africa has led to major shifts in all areas of life to the point that "things have fallen apart"—that is, community living is no longer possible as the status quo.

[5] John Mbiti, for example, in *African Traditions and Philosophy*, compares African relationships to vast networks stretching horizontally in every direction to the point that "every body relates with every body else" (1970, 104).

[6] This category is similar to what Robert Bellah calls "lifestyle enclaves" in *Habits of Heart* (1985, 71–75, 335).

[7] Hyam Maccoby (1991, 180–84) points out that while Paul may appear to view the Jews as killers of Jesus (for instance in 1 Thess. 2:14–16), he is ultimately more concerned that Jews should eventually partake in the full pattern of salvation. He develops the idea that the "blindness" of the Jews is only temporary, and this temporary blindness is itself a necessary element in the total pattern of salvation.

[8] Barclay, in *Ambassador for Christ*, explains how a Jewish boy would start school at the age of six. At 12 or 13, a Jewish boy would be called "son of the law," and could read Scriptures in the synagogue. He then went on to study to become a rabbi. This would mainly involve reading the Old Testament. But Paul went even further to become a member of a professional religious sect, a Pharisee (1981, 18–20).

[9] For a complete list of organizations helping street children in Kenya see *Organizations and Individuals Working with Street Children in Nairobi* (Kamau and Shane 1995).

References

Achebe, Chinua. 1958. *Things Fall Apart*. Nairobi: East African Educational Publishers.

Barclay, William. 1981. *Ambassador for Christ: The Life and Teaching of Paul*. Valley Forge, Pa.: Judson Press.

Bellah, Robert, R. Madsen, W. Sullivan, A. Swidler and S. Tipton, eds. 1985. *Habits of the Heart: Individualism and Commitment in American Life*. New York: Harper Torchbooks.

Bornkamm, Gunther. 1971. *Paul Paulus*. New York: Harper & Row.

Bujo, Benezet. 1992. *African Theology in Its Social Context*. Maryknoll, N.Y.: Orbis Books.

Echema, Austin. 1995. *Corporate Personality in Traditional Igbo Society and the Sacrament of Reconciliation*. Frankfurt: Peter Lang.

Grassi, Joseph. 1978. *The Secret of Paul the Apostle.* Maryknoll, N.Y.: Orbis Books.

Kamau, Catherine W., and John J. Shane. 1995. *Organizations and Individuals Working with Street Children in Nairobi.* Nairobi: Urban Ministries Support Group.

Kummel, Georg. 1975. *Introduction to the New Testament.* Nashville, Tenn.: Abingdon Press.

Lightfoot, J. B. 1975. *Paul's Epistle to the Philippians.* Grand Rapids, Mich.: Zondervan.

Maccoby, Hyam. 1991. *Paul and Hellenism.* London: SCM Press; Philadelphia: Trinity Press.

Mbiti, John. 1970. *African Traditions and Philosophy.* New York: Doubleday/Anchor Books.

Mutunga, Stanley. 1993. "Contextual Leadership Development for the Church: An Investigation into Rural-urban Migration to Nairobi." Ph.D. dissertation. Fuller Theological Seminary, Pasadena, California.

Nisbert, Robert. 1970. *The Social Bond: An Introduction to the Study of Society.* New York: Knopf.

Van Buren, Linda, ed. 1995. *Africa South of Sahara.* London: Europa Publications Limited.

12

No longer aliens

A theology of mission
from the U.S. Hispanic periphery

DANIEL A. RODRIGUEZ

This chapter represents an effort to discover something more than the missiological perspective of Hispanic theologians.[1] It is an effort to re-discover my ethnic roots—roots that were lost during an acculturation and assimilation process that extended over three generations. Brought up in a heterogeneous environment in which the "American way of life" was embraced with few reservations, I became an anglicized Mexican. This process was reinforced by my grandparents, parents, teachers and church. Along with other upwardly mobile middle-class Mexican Ameri-cans,[2] I gradually lost touch with many of my sociocultural and ethnic roots. Like Moses, I was raised as an "Egyptian."

Then, like Moses, I received a call from the Lord to return to my people in the *barrio* with the good news that God is concerned about their suffering and has sent a Deliverer, Jesus of Nazareth! There was only one problem: three generations of acculturation and assimilation

Daniel A. Rodriguez, a native of California, has served the Churches of Christ as minister in Northern and Southern California since 1979, and as missionary in Puebla, Mexico (1985–94). In July 1988 he successfully defended his Ph.D. dissertation, "No Longer Foreigners and Aliens: Toward a Missiological Christology for Mexican Americans in Southern California," at Fuller Theo-logical Seminary's School of World Mission. He is assistant professor of religion and Hispanic studies at Pepperdine University in Malibu, California, and minis-ter for the Hollywood Church of Christ in Los Angeles. Daniel and his wife, Jeanette, have been married for 22 years and have four teenagers.

separated me from the majority of poorly educated, working-class Latinos, who are spiritual as well as socioeconomic prisoners in impoverished urban *barrios* on the periphery of U.S. society.

After receiving the "appropriate" theological training, the Lord led me to Puebla, Mexico, where I worked for nine years in church planting and leadership development as a minister for the Church of Christ. This experience allowed me not only to become bilingual and bicultural, but more important, to discover also my people's sociohistorical and spiritual legacy. In the summer of 1994 I returned to Southern California to teach at Pepperdine University and to pursue doctoral research.[3] My goal is to further prepare myself to facilitate Latino leaders to participate more effectively, and in culturally relevant ways, in the mission of God to reconcile all things to himself through the cross of our Lord and Savior Jesus Christ (Col. 1:19).

Throughout this chapter I focus on the writings of Virgilio P. Elizondo, a Mexican American priest in San Antonio, Texas.[4] I have made this decision for three reasons. Elizondo is considered the most prominent Hispanic Catholic theologian in the United States (Bañuelas 1995, 5). He is the only Latino theologian writing from the unique perspective of Mexican Americans. Finally, while I may disagree with him on a number of theological issues, his work represents theology done "from below," informed by and engaged in the sociohistorical challenges of the present. His responsibilities as rector of San Antonio's San Fernando Cathedral, as well as his duties as founder and first president of the Mexican American Cultural Center and of the Incarnate Word Pastoral Institute, make it possible for Elizondo, an academically trained theologian, to "do" theology *"desde el camino* (from the road), rather than *desde el balcon* (from the balcony) (Escobar 1987, 86).

Theology from a Latino perspective

Hispanic theology in the United States, like its predecessors in Latin America and other parts of the majority world, represents a shift in perspective that focuses on the role of the interpreter's context, as well as the essential nature of the gospel when developing or "doing theology" locally. This shift in perspective is elsewhere identified as contextualization (see Bevans 1994; Gilliland 1989; Hesselgrave and Rommen 1989; Schreiter 1985).

Since the late 1960s Hispanic theologians have been doing theology that reflects the unique social situation of Latinos in the United States. Hispanic Catholic theologians have been the most vocal in calling for and doing theology that is unashamedly contextual, assuming the sociohistorical situation of Latinos in the United States as a source for theological reflection (Romero 1992, 41). Latino theologians argue that theology from this perspective will help their people create a new knowledge about themselves, their social situation and their religious beliefs. It is a theology that is engaged in the sociohistorical challenges of the present. Fernando Segovia describes Hispanic theology as "a voice in search of freedom, independence, and autonomy; a voice that seeks to speak in its own terms and with its own visions in mind; a voice that wishes to lay claim to its own reality and experience, give expression to its own view of God and the world, and chart its own future" (1995, 35).

The influence of Latin American liberation theology

Latinos recognize the influence of Latin American liberation theology on Hispanic theology in the United States (see Gutiérrez 1973; Míguez Bonino 1975; Segundo 1979). For example, Elizondo acknowledges that from Gustavo Gutiérrez Latinos have learned "theology is so important that we cannot leave it to the theologians alone . . . and much less to theologians who are foreigners" (1995, 9). Latino theologians have also learned that theology is a corporate enterprise of the believing community, which is seeking the meaning and direction of its faith. Therefore Latino theologians reject the notion that theology can be imported or developed in isolation from the believing community. Hispanics are also indebted to Latin American theologians who, since the 1960s, have developed a methodology that promotes a reading of the Bible that seeks to recover its original sociopolitical and economic context, and then tries to come to grips with the biblical message in relation to the social, political, cultural and economic realities of our day (Castro 1985, 3).

The uniqueness of Hispanic theology

While Latino theology is informed by Latin American liberation theologies, it is not a stepchild of that movement. Liberation theology has focused on the greatest and most obvious need in Latin America: socioeconomic justice and revolutionary change. By contrast, Hispanic theology in the United States has been working out of a wider range of social, historical and cultural factors (Bañuelas 1995, 2–3).

That is why one of the most common starting points for Latino theological reflection has been *mestizaje* (that is, our unique sociohistorical perspective) (Deck 1994, 56). Traditionally and narrowly defined, *mestizaje* refers to "the birth of a new people from two preexistent peoples," such as resulted from the military conquest and colonization of the Mesoamerican peoples by the Spanish in the sixteenth century (Elizondo 1983, 10). For Latinos of Mexican descent, *mestizaje* suggests a dynamic reality, the creation of a new people who live in exile and ambiguity "as outsiders on the fringes of the dominant culture" (Bañuelas 1995, 1).

The sociohistorical context of Hispanic theology

Contemporary theology and biblical interpretation, especially in the majority world, focuses on the interpreter's social context. Following this trend, Hispanic theology emphasizes the sociohistorical and cultural context of Latinos in the United States as a source for theological reflection.

A conquered minority

Elizondo and other Latino theologians insist that in order to understand the sociohistorical and cultural status of Mexican Americans, one must understand a legacy that includes the effects of cultural conflict, segregation and discrimination. Elizondo claims that "since the late 1960s Mexican Americans have discovered that in order to affirm ourselves, we had to be able to retell our story—the story of the great pilgrimage of our ancestors that had led us to be who we are today" (1988, 39).

Social histories written by Hispanics have paid special attention to the impact of the conquest and colonization of the Southwest by the United States.[5] Unlike other immigrant groups from Europe and Asia, who entered the United States by leaving an "old country" and crossing oceans, Mexican Americans were not "voluntary immigrants." Rather, like Native Americans, Mexican Americans became an American ethnic minority through direct conquest of their homelands in what is now the American Southwest. Chicano historians argue convincingly that Mexican Americans "are not truly an immigrant group, for they are in their traditional home." They contend that this is of utmost importance in any effort to understand the contemporary status of Mexican Americans within U.S. society (McLemore and Romo 1985, 4).

A rejected minority

Two important consequences of the conquest and colonization of the American Southwest are frequently noted. First, the conquest set in motion a dominant-subordinate relationship between Anglo-Americans and Mexican Americans, contributing to the political, economic and social marginalization of the latter (Gómez-Quiñones 1971, 35). Second was the initiation of a process that has been described as the *barrioization* of the Mexican American community, "the formation of residentially and socially segregated Chicano barrios or neighborhoods" (Camarillo 1979, 53).

Latino historians and sociologists argue that the dominant society, profoundly racist, relegated Mexicans to a colonial status within the United States (Estrada et al. 1981, 109). Further, Anglo-Americans inherited a bias against things Spanish and Catholic from their British forefathers; this bias is referred to as the "Black Legend" (see Weber 1974; Sánchez 1990). E. C. Orozco insists "it did not matter that the Mexicans were not Spaniard, so long as they were Catholic and Spanish-speaking. . . . [Anglos] approached Mexican Catholics with a pre-existing hostility" (1980, 80). Two additional factors that contributed to the rejection of the Mexican-descent Latino by the dominant society include the ease and swiftness of the victory over the Mexicans in the war with the United States and the disdain with which early settlers (mostly from the slave states) looked upon the racially mixed Mexican (McWilliams 1968, 129; Weber 1974, 22–23).

Elizondo observes that "we have always been treated as foreigners in our own countryside—exiles who never felt at home. The Mexican Americans are a people twice conquered, twice colonized, twice mestized. This is our socio-historical reality!" (1995, 9). In another place he describes Mexican-descent Latinos as always "other," rejected in Mexico as *"pochos"* (Americanized) and rejected as "Mexican" in the United States (1988, 21).

Elizondo and others insist Mexican-descent Hispanics have also known rejection in their ancestral church (see Burns 1994; Deck 1994; Hinojosa 1994). Elizondo writes, "I had the experience of being an ignored and often despised minority within an Irish-German US Catholic Church and within the greater Protestant culture of the United States" (1995, 9). Elizondo insists that Mexican Americans and Hispanics in general are not accepted in the U.S. Catholic church (or Protestant churches) unless they cease to be Hispanic and conform to the way of Anglo-American institutions (1988, 53). The root of our oppression, according to Elizondo, is that "we were not allowed to be who we are" (1995, 9).

An impoverished minority

Recent demographic data indicate that as of the 1990 census Hispanics constitute the fastest-growing minority group in the United States. These figures also indicate this group has the nation's highest high-school dropout rate, the nation's highest unemployment rate and the nation's lowest median income for both men and women. Data also reveal that, with few exceptions, Latinos, especially Mexican-descent Latinos, are among the most likely U.S. Americans to live in poverty.[6]

The history and experience of Hispanics in the United States serve as important sources for doing theology. As Latino theologian Samuel Soliván-Roman has noted, "The experience of living in the 'belly of the beast,' of knowing hunger in the land of good and plenty, of being poor on the streets of gold provides a different perspective and a different set of questions about who God is and what God is doing in the world" (1995, 45).

The methodology of U.S. Hispanic theologians

Given the sociocultural for history outlined above, it is natural Latino theology to reflect critically and consciously from the perspective of *mestizaje*. It is not surprising that Latino theologians have opted for the methodology of liberation theology. Where traditional Euro-American theologies begin the theological enterprise with a received body of doctrines, traditions, and beliefs, Latino theologies start with the lived experiences of the community and a "preferential option for the poor and the oppressed" (Gutiérrez 1973, x). Allan Figueroa Deck observes that while mainline theologies purport to be "neutral and objective," they unconsciously take the middle-class, white, Anglo context as normative (1994, 57).

Another fundamental difference between the traditional Western theologian and the liberation theologian is that the latter feels compelled at every step to combine the disciplines that open up the past with the disciplines that help explain the present. Thus, another hallmark of Hispanic theology and its cousin in Latin America is its critical use of the social sciences. Through the social sciences theology gains a concrete understanding of the world in which faith is lived, and it is thus able to articulate the questions to which it must respond (Costas 1982, 127).

Mestizaje *theology*

Virgilio Elizondo is representative of Hispanic theologians. He has developed what he calls a theology of *mestizaje*, a theology of liberation for Mexican Americans characterized by a fundamental search for identity. He articulates this theology in *Galilean Journey* (1983) and *The Future Is Mestizo* (1988).

According to Elizondo, the dynamics of *mestizaje* describe the sociohistorical reality of Mexican Americans as "a violated people" (1988, 29). They are a people doubly marginalized by reason of their participation in two distinct cultural groups, and they are, thus, never fully accepted by either (see also Bañuelas 1995, 59). Also of major significance for Hispanic Catholic theology is Elizondo's description of the religiocultural symbols of identity and belonging, of struggle and suffering, and of new creation. These symbols include Ash Wednesday and the Posadas, the Cross and Good Friday, the Feast of Our Lady of Guadalupe and Baptism (1983, 32–48). He insists that "for a suffering and oppressed people, there is nothing more powerful than one's collective symbols" (1990, 16).

The Bible and Hispanic theology

Latino theologies opt for a new reading of the Bible similar to that of the Christian base communities of Latin America, a reading from the perspective of the oppressed. These theologies contend that both the Old and New Testaments illustrate God's preferential option for the poor, oppressed and rejected. This option figures prominently in the Exodus narrative and the prophetic tradition, and it lies at the very heart of Jesus' life, ministry and proclamation of the kingdom. Elizondo insists that the concrete sociocultural situation of Jesus as a rejected *mestizo* from the borderlands of Galilee and his message of universal inclusion anticipate the situation and liberation of Mexican Americans. Consequently, reading the Bible from the perspective of the marginalized constitutes a recovery of the fundamental message of the Bible (Segovia 1992, 35–37).

Hispanic theology from a missiological perspective

The missiological significance of Virgilio Elizondo's theology is that *mestizos*, rejected people living in exile and ambiguity, have a unique identity and mission, both of which are discovered when we recognize that God chooses what the world rejects to bring divine blessing to all.

From rejection to election

The *mestizo's* unique mission is made known in what Elizondo describes as "the Galilee principle" manifest in the incarnation, cross and resurrection of Jesus of Nazareth (1983, 91–102).

> God becomes not just a human being, but the marginated, shamed, the rejected of the world. . . . Because the world expected nothing good to come out of Galilee, God chose it to be the starting point of God's human presence among us. The principle behind the cultural image of the Galilean identity [of Jesus of Nazareth] is that God chooses what the world rejects (Elizondo 1995, 19).

Elizondo observes that Anglo-American Catholics and Protestants alike seem to be much more concerned with the Christ of glory who justifies the glories of the "American way of life" than with Jesus of Nazareth who lived and died as a despised Galilean *mestizo*. Elizondo insists that when God became a man, he became one of the rejected so that the rejected might in turn have new life as God's chosen ones (Isa. 53).

> He became a curse and a scandal for us so that we who are considered to be the curse and the scandal of this world might become the source of blessing and salvation for the world. He became the reject of the world so that in and through him the rejects of today's world might appear as what they really are: God's chosen and anointed ones (1990, 9–10).

The journey from rejection to election is a familiar theme in the Scriptures. Joseph is rejected by his brothers but chosen by God to be his instrument "to preserve a numerous people" (Gen. 50:19–20). Centuries later Moses is rejected by his people and later chosen by God to deliver the oppressed and "many other people" from bondage (Exod. 12:38, NIV). Israel, too, is described as despised and rejected from birth (Ezek. 16:1–14), but blessed and chosen by God to bring justice and righteousness to the nations (Isa. 5:7; 26:18). The same theme of rejection to election is evident in the life of many others, including Rahab, David, Mordecai and Daniel.

The theme of Jesus' rejection and election was also at the core of apostolic preaching. For example, to the Jews on Pentecost, and later in the Temple, Peter proclaimed that the despised Nazarene, whom they had rejected and crucified, had been made "both Lord and Messiah," the truth of which was manifest in the resurrection (Acts 2:22–36; 3:15–16). Before the Sanhedrin, Peter and John identify Jesus Christ of Nazareth as the rejected stone that had become the cornerstone (Acts 4:11–12).

In the home of Cornelius, a despised and rejected Gentile, Peter explained the significance of Jesus' ministry, which began on the periphery of respectable Jewish society in Galilee and came to an apparent end outside the gate of Jerusalem (Acts 10:37–40), "but God raised him on the third day." Thus, the rejected Jesus became the glorified Christ.

From election to mission

Mexican Americans and other *mestizo* peoples in the United States and around the globe will find not only their true identity in the Galilean experience of Jesus of Nazareth; they will also discover their mission in life. Elizondo observes that Hispanic and liberation theologies represent a rediscovery of a paradigm in mission in which the poor and oppressed themselves become "the active agents of the salvation of all" (1995, 7). Once again the Scriptures concur. For example, Paul reminds the Corinthians that when they were called to preach, few were wise by human standards, or influential or of noble birth.

> But God chose what is foolish in the world to shame the wise; God chose what is weak in the world to shame the strong; God chose what is low and despised in the world, things that are not, to reduce to nothing things that are (1 Cor. 1:27–28).

Paul reminds his despised and rejected readers that they were chosen to "speak wisdom . . . God's wisdom, secret and hidden" (1 Cor. 2:6–7). Similarly, Peter addresses his letters to "aliens and exiles" (1 Pet. 2:11) and reminds them of their true identity. He tells them that as they come to "a living stone, though rejected by mortals yet chosen and precious in God's sight," they too "like living stones, let yourselves be built into a spiritual house, to be a holy priesthood" (1 Pet. 2:4–5). Later he states emphatically, "But you are a chosen race, a royal priesthood, a holy nation, God's own people" (1 Pet. 2:5–9).

Paul also reminds his *mestizo* readers in Ephesus that God's intent in creating new humanity was "so that through the church the wisdom of God in its rich variety might now be made known to the rulers and authorities in the heavenly places" (Eph. 3:10). The church is the threshold to a new humanity Elizondo insists must "work not only for the salvation of individuals but for the salvation of peoples" (1990, 20). The church in its unity and maturity (Eph. 4:1–16), in its purity and love (Eph. 4:17–6:9), and in its moral and spiritual courage (Eph. 6:10–20) is a reminder to the world that the future is *mestizo*.

> The radical all-inclusive way of Christianity started among the rejected and the lowly of society. This is the ongoing starting

point. In the Spirit, they struggle to build new human alternatives so that others will not have to suffer what they have had to suffer (Elizondo 1995, 22).

Conclusion

Virgilio Elizondo has helped me rediscover my sociocultural and ethnic roots as a Mexican American. But more important, he has taught me I must not think only in terms of mission *to the barrio;* I must also think in terms of mission *from the barrio.* As foreigners and aliens in their own land, the vast majority of Mexican-descent Latinos have what can be described as an epistemological advantage over their middle-class Anglo-American brothers and sisters.

Paul indicates that through the blood of Christ "one new humanity" was created out of Jew and Gentile (Eph. 2:13–15). These words remind me that "the church is the *mestizo par excellence*" (Elizondo 1983, 107). Mexican Americans, who have been conquered, colonized and "mestized" twice since 1492, can appreciate the significance of this reality more fully than those whose *mestizaje* is less visible. Similarly, we are told that in the church we are "no longer strangers and aliens, but . . . are citizens with the saints and also members of the household of God" (Eph. 2:19). Once again, Mexican Americans and other *mestizos* of the world can more fully appreciate the importance of this citizenship since they have lived in ambiguity in a borderland between two cultures (Isa. 9:1–2; Matt. 4:12–16).

Hispanics experience the reality of being aliens in their native land. When told that proposed legislation will require them to show proof of citizenship in order to vote, receive medical assistance or enroll their children in public schools, they are reminded that they are outsiders. They are reminded of their alien status when they hear an angry motorist shout, "Why don't you go back where you came from, wetback?" or when someone comments, "For a Mexican you sure speak English well."

But the truth is we are "no longer strangers and aliens." In Christ we are God's elect, *La Raza Cósmica,* chosen to reflect the "light of the world" to those living in darkness (Matt. 4:15–16).

In order to communicate the gospel of God's all-inclusive kingdom it is imperative to heed Elizondo's advice: "We will no longer impoverish our understanding of God by limiting God to the knowledge of the Western World; we will come to the knowledge of a far greater God by knowing God also through the categories of thought of our own *mestizo* world of Iberoamerica" (1990, 19).

Hispanic theologians consciously resist doing theology that is solely theoretical and speculative. Rather than formulating abstract propositions, theologians like Virgilio Elizondo concur with Orlando Costas, who insists a person can only "do theology" as that person practices it (1982,2). This is the unique contribution and perspective of theology of mission from the U.S. Hispanic periphery.

Notes

[1] Throughout this chapter the terms *Hispanic* and *Latino* will be used interchangeably to refer to all individuals of Latin American ancestry who reside legally or illegally within the borders of the United States.

[2] In this chapter *Chicano* and *Mexican American* will be used interchangeably to designate Latinos of Mexican descent born in the United States.

[3] The contextual and Christological focus of my research is evident in the proposed title of my doctoral dissertation: "From Rejection to Election: A Missiological Christology from the Mexican American Periphery."

[4] I rely on the following writings by Virgilio Elizondo: *The Galilean Journey: The Mexican American Promise* (1983); *The Future Is Mestizo* (1988); "Foreword," in González 1990; "Mestizaje as a Locus of Theological Reflection," in Bañuelas 1995.

[5] Social histories from an emic perspective include, among others, Meier and Rivera 1989; Acuña 1988; Estrada et al. 1981; and Camarillo 1979 and 1984.

[6] The following sources provide data concerning median age, educational attainment, household size and income, employment and occupational trends among Latinos in the United States: Chapa and Valencia 1993; Ortíz 1993; Reddy 1993; de la Garza et al. 1992; Hispanic Policy Development Project 1987.

References

Acuña, Rodolfo. 1988. *Occupied America: A History of Chicanos.* Third edition. New York: Harper & Row.

Bañuelas, Arturo J., ed. 1995. *Mestizo Christianity: Theology from the Latino Perspective.* Maryknoll, N.Y.: Orbis Books.

Bevans, Stephen B. 1994. *Models of Contextual Theology.* Maryknoll, N.Y.: Orbis Books.

Burns, Jeffrey M. 1994. "The Mexican Catholic Community in California." In *Mexican American and the Catholic Church, 1900–1965*, ed. Jay P. Dolan and Gilberto M. Hinojosa, 129–236. Notre Dame, Ind.: University of Notre Dame Press.

Camarillo, Albert. 1979. *Chicanos in a Changing Society: From Mexican Pueblos to American Barrios in Santa Barbara and Southern California, 1848–1930.* Cambridge, Mass.: Harvard University Press.

————. 1984. *Chicanos in California: A History of Mexican Americans in California.* San Francisco, Calif.: Boyd and Fraser.

Castro, Emilio. 1985. *Sent Free: Mission and Unity in the perspective of the Kingdom.* Grand Rapids, Mich.: Eerdmans.

Chapa, Jorge, and Richard R. Valencia. 1993. "Latino Population Growth, Demographic Characteristics, and Educational Stagnation: An Examination of Recent Trends." *Hispanic Journal of Behavioral Sciences* 15, no. 2: 165–87.

Costas, Orlando E. 1982. *Christ Outside the Gate: Mission Beyond Christendom.* Maryknoll, N.Y.: Orbis Books.

Deck, Allan Figueroa. 1994. "Latino Theology: The Year of the 'Boom.'" *Journal of Hispanic/Latino Theology* 1, no. 2: 51–63.

de la Garza, Rodolfo O., L. DeSipio, F. Garcia, J. Garcia and A. Falcon. 1992. *Latino Voices: Mexican, Puerto Rican, and Cuban Perspectives on American Politics.* San Francisco: Westview Press.

Elizondo, Virgilio P. 1983. *The Galilean Journey: The Mexican American Promise.* Maryknoll, N.Y.: Orbis Books.

————. 1988. *The Future Is Mestizo.* New York: Meyer Stone.

————. 1990. "Foreword." In *Mañana: Christian Theology from a Hispanic Perspective*, ed. Justo L. González, 9–20. Nashville, Tenn.: Abingdon.

————. 1995. "*Mestizaje* as a Locus of Theological Reflection." In *Mestizo Christianity: Theology from a Latino Perspective*, ed. Arturo J. Bañuelas, 5–27. Maryknoll, N.Y.: Orbis Books.

Escobar, Samuel. 1987. *La Fe Evangélica y las Teologías de la Liberación.* El Paso, Tex.: Casa Bautista de Publicaciones.

Estrada, Leobardo F., F. C. García, R. F. Macías, and L. Maldonado. 1981. "Chicanos in the United States: A History of Exploitation and Resistance." *Daedalus* 110, no. 2: 103–31.

Gilliland, Dean S., ed. 1989. *The Word Among US: Contextualizing Theology for Mission Today.* Dallas, Tex.: Word.

Gómez-Quiñones, Juan. 1971. "Toward a Perspective on Chicano History." *Aztlán* 2, no. 2: 1–49.

González, Justo L. 1990. *Mañana: Christian Theology from a Hispanic Perspective.* Nashville, Tenn.: Abingdon.

Gutiérrez, Gustavo. 1973. *A Theology of Liberation.* Maryknoll, N.Y.: Orbis Books.

Hesselgrave, David J.. and Edward Rommen. 1989. *Contextualization: Meanings, Methods, and Models.* Grand Rapids, Mich.: Baker Book House.

Hinojosa, Gilberto M. 1994. "Mexican American Faith Communities in the Southwest." In *Mexican Americans and the Catholic Church, 1900–1965*, ed. Jay P. Dolan and Gilberto M. Hinojosa, 11–125. Notre Dame, Ind.: University of Notre Dame Press.

Hispanic Policy Development Project. 1987. *The Hispanic Almanac.* New York: Hispanic Policy Development Project.

McLemore, S. Dale, and Ricardo Romo. 1985. "The Origins and Development of the Mexican American People." In *The Mexican American Experience: An Interdisciplinary Anthology*, ed. Rodolfo O. de la Garza, F. D. Bean, C. M.

Bobjean, R. Romo, and R. Alvarez, 3–32. Austin, Tex.: University of Texas Press.

McWilliams, Carey. 1968. *North from Mexico: The Spanish Speaking People of the United States.* New York: Greenwood Press.

Meier, Matt S., and Feliciano Rivera. 1989. *The Chicanos: A History of the Mexican Americans.* New York: Hill and Wang.

Míguez Bonino, José. 1975. *Doing Theology in a Revolutionary Situation.* Philadelphia: Fortress.

Orozco, E. C. 1980. *Republican Protestantism in Aztlán: The Encounter Between Mexicanism and Anglo-Saxon Secular Humanism in the United States Southwest.* New York: Petereins.

Ortíz, Manuel. 1993. *The Hispanic Challenge: Opportunities Confronting the Church.* Downers Grove, Ill.: InterVarsity Press.

Reddy, Marlita A., ed. 1993. *Statistical Record of Hispanic Americans.* Detroit, Mich.: Gale Research Inc.

Romero, C. Gilbert. 1992. "Tradition and Symbol as Biblical Keys for a United States Hispanic Theology." In *Frontiers of Hispanic Theology in the United States,* ed. Allan Figueroa Deck, 41–61. Maryknoll, N.Y.: Orbis Books.

Sánchez, Joseph P. 1990. *The Spanish Black Legend: Origin of Anti-Hispanic Stereotypes.* Albuquerque, N.M.: National Park Service, Spanish Colonial Research Center.

Segovia, Fernando F. 1992. "Hispanic American Theology and the Bible: Effective Weapon and Faithful Ally." In *We Are a People! Initiative in Hispanic American Theology,* ed. Roberto S. Goizueta, 21–49. Minneapolis: Fortress.

———. 1995. "Two Places and No Place on Which to Stand." In *Mestizo Christianity: Theology from a Latino Perspective,* ed. Arturo J. Bañuelas, 29–43. Maryknoll, N.Y.: Orbis Books.

Segundo, Juan Luis. 1979. *The Liberation of Theology.* Second edition. Maryknoll, N.Y.: Orbis Books.

Schreiter, Robert J. 1985. *Constructing Local Theologies.* Maryknoll, N.Y.: Orbis Books.

Soliván-Román, Samuel. 1995. "The Need for a North American Hispanic Theology." In *Mestizo Christianity: Theology from a Latino Perspective,* ed. Arturo J. Bañuelas, 45–52. Maryknoll, N.Y.: Orbis Books.

Weber, David J. 1974. *Foreigners in Their Native Land: Historical Roots of the Mexican American.* Second edition. Albuquerque, N.M.: University of New Mexico Press.

Part III

MISSION *ON* THE WAY

The third section of this book presents mission as a process on the move. Mission journeys forward over time in the faith-pilgrimage of God's people as they anticipate Christ's present and coming kingdom. Kingdom mission is pilgrim mission, as we proclaim the Good News to challenge people to become disciples of Jesus Christ and members of his church. Biblical theology of mission needs to be kingdom-directed missional action. The connection of reflection with action is essential for missiology directed by the already-not-yet kingdom of God. The following chapters depict mission *on* the way, as the writers search for avenues for the present kingdom of God to move toward the coming kingdom.

As director for the Overseas Ministries of Overseas Missionary Fellowship International, Ian Prescott has a strong interest in learning about missiology from a mission executive's perspective. Prescott considers fellow Englishman, Max Warren, whose life bears an uncanny similarity to the author's. Considered a leading British missiologist of this century, Warren, as general secretary of the Church Missionary Society (Church of England) for over 20 years, became an interpreter of world events and a strategizer of mission trends. His clear vision of mission as a committed community with a task to perform, not a structure to maintain, and his responsiveness to the unpredictability of the Holy Spirit, remains a legacy for mission *on* the way.

Chinese-Filipino theologian Santos Yao examines his friend David Lim's missiology of transformation, noting its contribution to Asian missiology. Lim's transformational missiology, while recognizing the theological primacy of evangelism, emphasizes the contextual nature of mission and its practical outworking among the poor of Asia. The resulting "church" is a decentralized network of small groups that plan and work together for the evangelization and transformation of their community. In contrast to the Christendom model of ecclesiology, Lim favors the servant-church model as pictured in the New Testament, which can readily embark on this holistic task of mission. Although Yao notes a number of weaknesses in Lim's missiology, he greatly respects his friend's solidarity with the poor of Asia.

Japanese missiologist Yoshiyuki Billy Nishioka faces the lack of church growth in his nation. He suggests that the issue is not that the Japanese are not open to Christianity, but that the church culture excludes non-Christians. In order to offer new directions for Japanese church leaders,

Nishioka compares the respective approaches of Charles Kraft and Paul Hiebert to worldview studies. This leads Nishioka to a deeper understanding of his culture and a stronger realization of the need for contextualizing the biblical message without compromising the integrity of the Scriptures.

Bokyoung Park's evaluation of Christian feminism is seen through the eyes of a woman whose Korean culture embraces a traditional view of women as subordinate to men. Park classifies Christian feminism into three major groups. While acknowledging that all three make positive contributions toward equal opportunities for women in God's mission, she disagrees with the revisionist's selective use of Scripture and the revolutionist's total rejection of the Christian church. As a person called by God to ministry, she finds hope in evangelical feminism that believes that the Bible teaches equality and mutuality between male and female. Park continues her search for a biblical missiological feminism that will provide opportunities for Korean women to fulfill God's mission call.

Concerned with the thinness of Australian Pentecostal pneumatology, Robert Gallagher's quest for further understanding of the work of the Holy Spirit and mission yielded disappointing results. Extensive research of prominent Protestant missiological writers during the last 50 years led to the discovery of a neglect of this important subject. Gallagher, a former Australian Pentecostal pastor, classifies his findings under five functions of the Spirit and provides a review of trends in pneumatology. The survey challenges the student of mission to a deeper understanding of the activity of the Spirit in our world.

In speaking of the new culture of virtual reality Shawn Redford predicts that we are on the threshold of a new faceless frontier in mission, where cyberspace redefines human interaction. There is a relaxing of normal social restraints in these virtual worlds—especially in the area of human sexuality—that may eventually lead to the blurring of reality and virtuality for those involved. Redford challenges Christian mission to use computer-mediated communication effectively to proclaim the gospel, with the possibility of planting churches on the Internet. However, as a missiologist preparing to face the needs of future generations, Redford is also sensitive to the Western technological danger of losing what he experienced among the Maasai peoples of Africa—physical human community in a real world. This is a cutting edge of mission *on* the way.

ROBERT L. GALLAGHER

13

Max Warren

The mission executive as missiologist

IAN C. H. PRESCOTT

Max Warren was a fascinating character–whether lecturing to an American audience on a theology of imperialism (Warren 1955, 10–41), arguing about economics and race relations with four trade unionists in the belly of a troop-carrier in the Atlantic (Warren 1974, 111), or trying to fathom the purposes of God in the expulsion of missionaries from China.

My intention is not to give an authoritative overview of Max Warren's life or missiology–a task others have already done (e.g., Dillistone 1980; Yates 1985). Instead, I come to this topic as one who has just taken up an executive position in a large historic missionary society. I want to learn from Max Warren what it meant for him to do missiology from his position as mission executive.

Previously I had only known of Warren as a name vaguely linked with the Church Missionary Society (CMS), which is the official mission board of the Church of England. I was surprised to find that, although we are divided by a time span of more than 50 years, we have much in common. We spent some of our formative younger years overseas, he in India and I in Argentina. For both of us the Christian faith came alive around the age of 16, and, in both our lives, that was soon followed by a clear call to service overseas. We were both scholars at Cambridge, he in history and

Ian Prescott is International Director for Evangelization of Overseas Missionary Fellowship (OMF) International, based in Singapore. Prior to this he served for nine years with OMF in the Philippines as a church planter and regional director. His doctoral research deals with strategies for evangelization in restricted access situations. He is married, with three children.

I in engineering, and there we both served as missionary secretaries concerned to challenge our fellow students to serve Christ overseas. We are both ordained but see our primary calling as a missionary one. And we were both asked at a similar age to take up an executive role in a historic mission at a time of great change in the world.

Brief biography: Max Alexander Cunningham Warren (1904–77)

Max Warren was born in Ireland of Irish parents, but he never lived there long. His parents were CMS missionaries, and Warren was born on one of their furloughs. Three months later they took their son back to India, where he lived until he was eight. At that point his mother's poor health forced them to return to England, and Warren was sent to boarding school at Marlborough while his father served on the home staff of CMS. He describes himself in this period as intensely shy but an avid reader with a vivid imagination. His father was an important figure to him in his early teens, but when Warren was sixteen his father returned alone to India to resume his missionary service there and died six months later.

Warren inherited a clear evangelical faith from his parents, but in his own words it lacked "the warmth of desire" (1974, 29). It was only as he joined his brother at a beach mission to young children and enjoyed the enthusiastic fellowship of other young people dedicated to Jesus Christ that his own faith came alive. His too became a "religion of enthusiasm," based on the "unwavering assurance of the utter trustworthiness of Jesus" (ibid., 33).

He won a scholarship to Cambridge to read history, a subject in which he won the highest honors. However, academic achievement was always secondary to his calling to serve Christ. Within a few weeks of his arrival at college, he felt a clear call to take the gospel to the Muslim Hausa of northern Nigeria. "To get so clear a directive about the future within a few weeks of going up to Cambridge was breathtaking" (ibid., 35). He was soon part of a group of six men who were preparing to make up a new team to reach the Hausa.

Warren straddled the breadth of evangelicalism, joining and holding office in both the Cambridge Inter Collegiate Christian Union (CICCU)[1] and the Student Christian Movement (SCM). At that time the SCM's Student Volunteer Missionary Union (SVMU) was still strong, and he became its secretary, organizing missionary breakfasts and other activities to challenge his fellow students toward missionary commitment.[2]

After graduating, Warren took a year of theology and then his ordination exams. However, his sense of vocation was that of a missionary and ordination was his goal only as it served that vocation. Thus at the age of 23 he was accepted by the CMS as a layman and sent to Nigeria. His task was "to learn the Hausa language, to teach six senior boys the rudiments of English history, and to help in the dispensary" (Warren 1974, 58). He only preached one sermon in Hausa, for within a year his health collapsed and he was sent back to England critically ill with bovine tuberculosis. For three years he struggled with the disease and almost died. He lost an eye to the infection and was left with poor health for the rest of his life.

That period of recovery was critical spiritually. For a long time he felt he was descending into a bottomless well and only began to ascend again when he realized that God was at the bottom of the well. Looking back on that time he writes, "It was . . . a personal encounter of a kind which meant that someone I had always known had revealed himself to me as being of necessity 'the Great Unknown' and *only then* to be for ever afterwards in a quite indefinable way 'well-known'" (ibid., 65–68).

Upon his recovery he was married and ordained, and he spent a few years organizing diocesan youth work before accepting an unexpected invitation to the charge of Holy Trinity, Cambridge.[3] It was 1936, and Warren soon realized that war was on its way. He determined to prepare his congregation for it and particularly found inspiration for this in the Old Testament prophets. One of his delights was the way the evening service became a joint congregation with that of a predominantly Jewish-German congregation the very week before war was declared in September 1939.

Warren had begun to serve on the executive committee of CMS in 1938. In 1942, at the age of 37, he was asked to become its general secretary, a position he held for 22 years. It was a difficult period—it was the middle of the war and CMS had a thousand missionaries scattered around the world, some of them interned, many unable to come home. When eventually they could return, most were exhausted by their long service in trying conditions. Following the war the world would never be the same—the large umbrella of the British Empire, under which so much had been established, was steadily being replaced by a host of newly independent countries struggling to work out what their new identity meant.

With his academic ability, Warren's life could have taken many directions. At different times he was offered other roles: a chaplaincy at Queens College, Cambridge, which would have led to a deanship and a fellowship

(Kings 1993, 55); an appointment as a British diocesan bishop at the age of 42 (Warren 1974, 129; Dillistone 1980, 109–10), an Australian archbishopric (Dillistone 1980, 111); even a teaching position in America (Warren 1974, 226). However, he always felt called first and foremost to mission. In later life he wrote to the archbishop of Canterbury, saying, "Ever since I was a school boy at the age of sixteen I have been totally committed to the missionary enterprise. . . . From the evangelistic task of the Church in loyalty to the Church's Lord there can be no retreat" (ibid., 226).[4]

He made no apologies for the word *missionary*, and once described himself as "the son of missionaries, for a short time a missionary myself, the father of one missionary, the uncle of another" (1974, 132). His biographer, Dillistone, writes, "To the end he gloried in the term *missionary*. It was a noun which exactly expressed the concept of sent-ness . . . and this sent-ness was primarily . . . concerned with cross-cultural, cross-national, cross-ideological adventures with the purpose of making Christ known in circles hitherto ignorant of his name" (1980, 122). When Ramsey, then archbishop of Canterbury, suggested at the Anglican Congress in 1963 that the words *mission* and *missionary* were not New Testament terms and should be "debunked," Warren asked to speak and, in his own words, "went straight into attack . . . convinced that there was no other word which would succinctly express what we meant . . . and pleaded for us to redeem the word" rather than abandon it (Dillistone 1980, 123–25).

By training Warren was a historian. However, in theological approach he saw himself as a biblical theologian, for "the Bible is the place where I find God speaking to me" (Yates 1985, 234). It was from this perspective that he did his theology of mission. He saw this theologizing as vital, without which the only alternative was "sheer opportunism of the kind that wastes resources, damps enthusiasm and finally fails for lack of recruits" (Warren 1974, 154).

The mission executive as missiologist

Doing serious missiological reflection in the midst of the demands of an executive position is easier said than done. The administrative challenges facing Warren were enormous, and he also had a wife and two daughters whom he did not neglect. Yet he achieved a rare quality of reflection that has led others to cite him as one of the leading British missiological thinkers of this century.[5] How did he manage that?

Warren's role as he saw it

As Dillistone notes, Warren "might surely have been justified in concluding that he could give little time to wide reading and deep thinking. On the contrary however, this was the part of his ministry that he regarded as so important that only by paying constant attention to it could he adequately fulfill his other duties" (1981, 116).

The key is how he saw his role as the chief executive of CMS. He had to grasp the larger story of God's work in the world. Warren wrote, "As General Secretary I was often abroad. But at all times it was my responsibility to be scanning the horizon, marking the direction of events in the world and their bearing on our enterprise, and in broad outline indicating what it must mean for the Society" (1974, 121).

And he had to communicate what he meant to the different constituencies of CMS:

> Somehow, as I saw it, I had to share my understanding of the context in which the modern missionary had to work, help the missionary to understand it, and go on to better understanding myself. At the same time I had to try, as far as possible, to help the devoted and dedicated members of the Society at home to welcome the brave and strange new world in which the Gospel had to be interpreted (ibid., 114).

Opportunities he used

But still the question remains: How, among the demands of leadership and the business of essential administration, did he find the time for the reading, reflection and writing that this "scanning the horizon" required? The answer, I believe, lies in the way that he seized his opportunities and responsibilities and turned them into ways to achieve this end. Thus he achieved this goal without succumbing to the fruitless passion he increasingly observed to try and fill "the unforgiving minute with five minutes' worth of distance run" (Warren 1974, 174).

He inherited the job of writing a monthly newsletter that had been launched by the previous general secretary. This went to the society's missionaries and supporters. He quickly saw the newsletter's potential and turned it into a major instrument in his strategy of reflection and communication about mission. Dillistone notes:

> It was not enough for the *News-Letter* to record statistics of conversions or stories of the successful establishment of new

missionary institutions. Rather, it was of the first importance that those concerned with the missionary enterprise should come to realise what great changes were taking place in the world, the emergent problems of race, the burgeoning of nationalistic aspirations, the decline of European influence, the resurgence of non-Christian faiths–in short, the wholly new context in which the missionary enterprise must be carried out (1981, 115).

In his first newsletter Warren wrote that he wanted to "consider the meaning of the things which are happening," which was "no small part of what the Bible means by a prophet."[6] To achieve this, each issue of the newsletter was planned several months in advance. A research assistant collected and organized the mass of information he needed. However, it was his work, and it was his absolute rule that he never recommend a book he had not first read himself (Warren 1974, 112). In his time the CMS Newsletter reached a circulation of 14,000. Johannes Verkuyl called it "one of the richest sources of missionary information ever written" (1978, 55).

The second opportunity Warren seized was that of his travels. Dillistone tells of how this was also turned into an instrument of missiological reflection and communication:

> On each of his journeys he kept a careful and yet lively travel diary. However exhausted he might be at the end of each day, he still found strength to write down his impressions, his memories of significant interviews, his comments on important issues raised. When he returned to London, the whole diary for the particular trip was typed and circulated to his fellow secretaries for information and ultimately all the diaries were bound in separate volumes. There are nearly forty of these volumes in existence and in some respects they constitute Max's most distinctive legacy. I do not know of any comparable record of developments international, political, ecclesiastical, and missiological between the years 1944 and 1970 (1981, 115).

The final opportunity was his lectures. A careful examination of his publications during his time as CMS general secretary reveals that they were nearly all first prepared as series of lectures, then afterward reproduced in print. His disciplined habit of doing his thinking on paper meant that rather than hastily prepared talks he had careful and serious thinking to offer, which was often worth publishing afterward for the benefit of a wider audience.

Warren's longer works–his autobiography, *Crowded Canvas*, and his magnum opus, *I Believe in the Great Commission*–were not written in the midst of his executive responsibilities but afterward, when his retirement from the CMS gave him more time.

Warren's concept of the voluntary principle

Warren's missiological thinking was broad in scope and made a significant contribution in many areas, including discussions on the uniqueness of Christ and the place of God in history. Here I want to focus only on a contribution that was unique to Warren in his double role as missiologist and mission executive–his concept of the voluntary principle in mission.

A key concern relating to the practice of mission was the principles of what he called the voluntary society. He drew a careful distinction between organs of coordination and organs of voluntary action. He saw both as necessary for Christian witness and activity. By *organs of coordination* Warren meant ecclesiastical structures and church organizations that would give institutional permanence to mission endeavors. By *voluntary action* he meant loose networks of like-minded persons committed to working together in mission, their cooperation based on their dedication to the task rather than their ecclesial position.

Organs of coordination were necessary, for "without them no community can exist beyond the smallest unit." However, "the desire to coordination almost inevitably leads to the pursuit of power," and that quickly stifles the "spiritual experimentation and initiative" that are needed for mission. That is why the "organs of voluntary action" are needed. "But they serve each other best by being in tension" (Warren 1974, 157). He asked:

> How best can we secure an abiding place for a spiritual initiative, which will at the same time be itself safeguarded from degenerating into anarchy? Here . . . is the role of the voluntary organization. . . . [It] is not an end in itself. It exists to be a channel for the initiative of those who compose it. If it ceases to express that initiative it will die. . . .

> If one believes this with all one's heart, one is of necessity
> opposed to the creation of monolithic structures (ibid., 158).[7]

He fought for this principle in two places. First, in the Anglican church,
where there was a strong movement to bring together the various Anglican missionary societies into a single department under the guidance,
and possibly the governance, of the Church Assembly. In response he
wrote a pamphlet called Iona and Rome, in which he drew attention to
the two strands of mission that had brought Christianity to Britain.
Dillistone writes:

> There was the Celtic strand, the result of heroic efforts by
> bands of monastic missionaries from Ireland, held together
> by a common loyalty; there was the Roman strand, the result
> of the extension of Roman Christianity by more authoritar-
> ian means. Max did not deny there was the possibility of both
> concepts of mission but deplored the possibility of the first
> being nullified by being swallowed up in the second (1981,
> 116).

In the Anglican context his argument is summed up well by Sir Kenneth Grubb, an Anglican layman, and president of the CMS for most of
Warren's time.[8] Grubb noted that while the Church of England might
be a "nice" body, "it does not strike me with irresistible force as an enter-
prising or enthusiastic one, ready to spend and be spent in the worldwide extension of the kingdom of God" (Yates 1988, 13). The proposed
merger never happened.

Warren also fought for this principle in the World Council of Churches
(WCC), when it was proposed that the International Missionary Council (IMC) should be integrated with the WCC. "The great hope being
that this would inject an evangelistic urgency into an organisation which
seemed over-preoccupied with ecclesiastical structures" (Warren 1976,
125).[9] This time he fought and lost. The integration of the two took
place in New Delhi in 1961.

At the time, Warren confided to Donald McGavran his fear that evangelization would disappear in the broader concerns of the WCC. Writing to McGavran some years later, Warren said, "I thought it would be
disastrous and events have fully justified my fears" (1975, 520).[10]

One of the last things Warren wrote was a reflection on this fusion of
the WCC and the IMC.[11] His language is kinder and his assessment
more tempered, but his fundamental concern for maximum flexibility
for the missionary task in a world of change still shines through. He

justifies this flexibility theologically by the need to be responsive to the uncontrollable Holy Spirit, who "in his operation in history is strictly incalculable. He is as uncontrollable as the wind. And his fire falls in very unexpected places and upon the most unlikely people. Unless the missionary movement can be responsive to the unpredictability of the Holy Spirit, it will cease to be a movement" (1978, 194).

Warren's opposition to integration, whether in the Anglican church or the WCC, was never based on a desire to protect his power and influence. His concern was always to protect the Christian mission from structures that would stifle its freedom to respond creatively to the new challenges it faced. He had a healthy disrespect for tidy organization, quoting Abbé Michonneau approvingly when "he bids us scrutinize the values that we set on organization, lest we find that having organized everything tidily we have left no room for the operation of the Holy Ghost" (1951, 77). In a new situation he saw that the maximum of initiative and experiment is needed. Mobility becomes "an essential attribute of the Christian Mission, a mobility which must be freely acknowledged and gladly granted to individuals and the group in the work of exploration" (ibid.). At all times "Christian strategic thinking [must be] flexible . . . and never, never, never trying to be tidy!"[12]

Conclusion

My encounter with Max Warren as a mission executive doing missiology encourages and challenges me.

I am challenged by the vision he had for his task of leadership. Executive leadership demands looking with discernment at what is happening in the world, and in depth at the Scriptures, and trying to bring the two together in a missiology that informs and directs. This is not a fascinating sideline for those with time to spare but an essential activity for those entrusted with leadership in God's mission.

I am also challenged by the vision Warren had for a mission organization as an organ of voluntary action. All structures have a way of developing a life of their own and taking over. Administrators can easily become preoccupied with structures. The establishment and maintenance of an organization becomes the measure of success instead of the completion of the task for which the organization was formed. Warren's vision of a mission as a community of the committed for whom the mission's structure is "a channel for the initiative of those who compose it" is an antidote to this. Today we may use different terminology, such as *empowerment*, but the goal is the same—to enable our members to take initiative and experiment as they seek to work out the Great Commission calling. Warren wrote, "For effective obedience to the great commission the one thing supremely needed in every age is a lively response of Spirit-inspired opportunism, ever alert to the certainty that God will provide different opportunities in different circumstances" (1976, 92).

Max Warren challenges me to be a person of vision and depth, a leader who uses structure as a servant, an enabler committed to the growth of the members who make up the mission community—as together we seek to carry the gospel of God's love to the world.

Notes

[1] From which InterVarsity Christian Fellowship had sprung.

[2] Throughout his life he was happy to be identified as an evangelical (Yates 1985, 233–34) but, as he liked to say, an unhyphenated one. His was an inclusive evangelicalism, always with "an openminded attitude to the discovery of truth" (ibid., 234). This was a position that sometimes brought him the censure of more conservative evangelicals but to which he held tenaciously. He set out his own understanding of what it meant to be an evangelical in the context of the Church of England in two small booklets, *What Is an Evangelical?* (1944) and *The Seven-Fold Secret* (1962).

[3] This is Charles Simeon's church, with a unique history and situation in the center of the life of Cambridge and its university.

[4] Even when he stepped down as general secretary, at which point he was offered a number of posts (both in the UK and America), the key consideration for him was which one gave most opportunity for "wider service of the Church as a whole," in particular "the Church overseas" (Warren 1974, 226). In his case that was a ministry that he exercised from the role of a canon at Canterbury.

[5] Yates calls him one who "raked the horizons for signposts to the Christian future with great discernment" (Yates 1994, 143).

[6] CMS Newsletter no. 31 (July 1942). Quoted in Yates 1994, 138.

[7] His view of "organs of coordination and organs of voluntary action has similarities to Ralph Winter's sodalities and modalities (Winter 1974), but it also has significant differences. Not least is the fact that Winter works so strongly from the model of the Roman Catholic orders but, because Protestantism has no pope, Winter's sodalities end up being missionary structures with little or no relation to modalities. In contrast, Warren's "voluntary societies" were always part of Anglicanism. Charles Mellis draws heavily from Warren in developing his ideas of "Committed Communities" as against "Nurture Structures" or "Congregations" (Mellis 1976).

[8] Grubb was president of the CMS from 1944 to 1969. He was also chairman of the Commission of the Churches on International Affairs of the WCC (Warren 1974, 152).

[9] He later referred to a "preoccupation with structures [which] . . . has over the years become dangerously neurotic" (Warren 1978, 191).

[10]Warren wrote to McGavran, "To the second question, 'why was it made?' the answer is very complicated. At the grave risk of over-simplification, I would say it was due to a neurotic over-simplification with structures born out of a Church Unity Movement which had lost its way theologically" (Warren 1975, 521).

[11]This was published posthumously as part of a *festschrift* for Johannes Verkuyl.

[12]CMS Newsletter no. 256 (1963), quoted in Yates 1985, 243.

References

Dillistone, F. W. 1980. *Into All the World: A Biography of Max Warren.* London: Hodder and Stoughton.

———. 1981. "The Legacy of Max Warren." *International Bulletin of Missionary Research* 5, no. 3: 114–17.

Kings, Graham. 1993. "Max Warren: Candid Comments on Mission from His Personal Letters." *International Bulletin of Missionary Research* 17, no. 2: 54–58.

Mellis, Charles J. 1976. *Committed Communities: Fresh Streams for World Missions.* Pasadena, Calif.: William Carey Library.

Verkuyl, Johannes. 1978. *Contemporary Missiology: An Introduction.* Grand Rapids, Mich.: Eerdmans.

Warren, Max A. 1944. *What Is an Evangelical?* London: Church Book Room Press.

———. 1951. *The Christian Mission.* London: SCM.

———. 1955. *Caesar, the Beloved Enemy: Three Studies in the Relation of Church and State.* The Reinecker Lectures at the Virginia Theological Seminary, Alexandria, Virginia. Chicago, Ill.: Alec R. Allenson.

———. 1962. *The Seven-Fold Secret: A Study of the Evangelical Contribution in a World of Change.* London: SPCK.

———. 1964. *Perspective in Mission.* London: Hodder and Stoughton.

———. 1974. *Crowded Canvas: Some Experiences of a Life-time.* London: Hodder and Stoughton.

———. 1975. "The Warren-McGavran Letters on World Evangelization." *Church Growth Bulletin* 11(6).

———. 1976. *I Believe in the Great Commission.* Grand Rapids, Mich.: Eerdmans.

———. 1978. "The Fusion of I.M.C. and W.C.C. at New Delhi: Retrospective Thoughts After a Decade and a Half." In *Zending op weg Naar de Toekomst.* Kampen, Netherlands: Uuitgeversmaatchappij J. H. Kok.

Winter, Ralph D. 1974. "The Two Structures of God's Redemptive Mission." *Missiology* (January): 121–39.

Yates, Timothy E. 1985. "Evangelicalism Without Hyphens: Max Warren, the Tradition and Theology of Mission." *Anvil* 2, no. 3: 231–45.

———. 1988."Newsletter Theology: CMS Newsletters Since Max Warren 1963–1985." *International Bulletin of Missionary Research* 12, no. 1: 11–15.

———. 1994. *Christian Mission in the Twentieth Century.* Cambridge, England: Cambridge University Press. 138–43.

14

David Lim

A transformation missiology
for Asian contexts

SANTOS YAO

David Lim and I became friends in 1974, when we were students at Asian Theological Seminary in Manila. Both of us are of Chinese descent, and our spiritual roots can be traced to the Reformed Church in America. We have worked together in many parachurch organizations. Both of us are likewise imbued with the rich heritage of Fuller Theological Seminary. Having known Lim for almost a quarter of a century, I have found him to be a person with a deep passion for the poor and evangelization of the world. He has become a significant voice in the theological and missiological arena of Southeast Asia.

In this chapter I explore Lim's missiology of transformation, noting its contributions to a missiology for Asia.

Biographical profile

David Sun Lim was born in Bacolod City in the Philippines on September 9, 1953. He is the eldest of the three children of Lim Eng Pang and Rosario Sun Lim, lay leaders in their local Filipino-Chinese church.

Santos Yao is of Chinese origin but was born and raised in Manila, Philippines. He traces his spiritual roots to the Reformed Church of America. He has been involved with theological education for many years and currently works among Filipinos in the Los Angeles area. His Ph.D. research, completed in 1997, centered on a theology of table fellowship in mission.

From his youth, Lim was an avid reader. He would skip meals and read late into the night until his parents had to prod him to eat and get more sleep. He earned the master of divinity from the Asian Theological Seminary in Quezon City in 1977 and immediately began serving on the faculty of that institution, teaching Greek and New Testament. He earned the master of theology degree at the Asian Center for Theological Studies and Mission in Seoul, Korea, in 1981, and in 1987 completed his doctorate at Fuller Theological Seminary, doing research under Ralph P. Martin on the servant church in Paul's writings.

Between 1978 and 1992, Lim served as professor of New Testament and Contextual Theology at Asian Theological Seminary, where he was also dean of Academic Affairs. Simultaneously, he was involved as a youth pastor in the United Evangelical Church of the Philippines. He has co-founded and served in many parachurch organizations that specialize in holistic ministry development, evangelization of the Filipino Chinese, and international partnership. By 1989 he was actively involved in at least 23 organizations.

Lim resigned from Asian Theological Seminary in 1992 to become director of training at the Center for Community Transformation, which he had co-founded. After eight months, he moved to Oxford to serve as associate dean and chaplain at the Oxford Centre for Mission Studies.

Lim joined China Ministries International in 1994, where he serves as executive director of its Philippine Office. This move has furthered the realization of one of his lifelong dreams—the evangelization of China. Aside from his administrative responsibilities, Lim also acts as the organization's researcher in Chinese mission theology.

Lim is married to Racquel Ortega. They have two children, Jefferson and Tsina Grace.

The missiology of David S. Lim

In his personal correspondence with me David Lim labels his mission theology "transformation missiology" (Lim 1997b).[1] Such a missiology, he contends, differs in basic ways from the "evangelization missiology" expressed in the Lausanne Covenant (1974) and the Manila Manifesto (1989).[2] As he observes, evangelization missiology affirms "the theological (and logical) priority of evangelism over social concern; after all, evangelism has to do with the salvation of souls, and one soul is more valuable than the whole world" (1997a, 1). Such a theological priority, moreover, extends also to the "practical or strategic aspects in mission" as evangelism demands priority "in the allocation of resources (personnel, time/efforts, and budget)" (ibid.).

Transformation missiology, on the other hand, seeks

> to bring about shalom (OT) or the Kingdom of God (NT) in obedience to Christ's Great Commission. Historically, this has developed into a strategy that aims to facilitate the discipling process of empowerment of the members of a community or people-group from being passive recipients to becoming active participants in tackling issues (both local and global, as well as physical, social, or religious) that affect their lives, primarily through the "community development–community organization" approach (1996c, 1).

Although transformation missiology "recognizes the theological primacy of evangelism," it nevertheless "emphasizes the contextual nature (with sensitivity to differences in local situations) of the practical outworking of mission" (1992b, 29). In contrast to other missiologies that tend to stress either the evangelistic or cultural mandate,[3] transformation missiology is "the most biblical and balanced view (and the truly holistic paradigm of the Church's mission)" (1997b).

Moreover, Lim's transformation missiology is ecclesiologically oriented. It is "premised on the conviction that the basic unit of God's Kingdom is the Church, which is found primarily in small groups (servant church structures like house churches, Bible study groups, Basic Christian Communities, etc.) not the local church (Christendom structures)" (ibid.).[4]

The "community development–community organization" approach of transformation missiology, according to Lim, is "the most consistent with the missionary strategy of Jesus Christ, Paul, and the New Testament Church" (1996c, 1). It is the best way

> to attain the goal of transforming an entire people-group into Christ-worshipping and Bible-studying communities of love, justice and peace. The evangelization process is (a) led by a team of committed Christian professionals who (b) start with "immersion," which is to incarnationally "live among the people" so as (c) to contextually "serve them." They also (d) try to discover (by doing field research) and (e) then address the key needs, longings and aspirations of the people. There is also (f) a phase-out plan, so that the missionaries can leave as soon as possible, (g) after having formed a core-group of

trained Christian disciples who can confidently serve as leaders in the church and in the community, and mobilize their members to serve and witness in other communities and networks. Thus, as much as possible, the missionaries should have secular degrees and professional identity, so as to better relate to community leaders and government officials (ibid.).

Mission, Lim maintains, includes both evangelism and social action:

Social action includes works of mercy (medical, relief, educational, etc.) and works of justice (economic development, ecological concern, and political involvement). . . . The objective is community transformation (not just individual conversions), so that Christian witness is really as "a city on a hill" (Mt. 5:13–16). The resulting "church" is a decentralized network of small discipleship groups (kingdom cell-units) that are each self-governing, self-supporting, and self-propagating. Their leaders gather regularly (at least once a month) as "elders of the community/city" to pray, plan and work together for the evangelization and transformation of their community (ibid., 2).

Missiological contributions

Emerging from that part of the world where poverty is widespread and oppression is rampant, Lim has developed his transformation missiology as the biblical response to the social realities of Southeast Asia.

The emphasis on biblical theology

In contrast to many evangelical missiologists who are inclined to be sociological or anthropological in their critique of missions and missionary practice, Lim opts to discuss missiological issues strictly from a biblical-theological framework.[5] He insists that mission must not succumb to the pragmatism offered by the social sciences at the expense of its anchorage within Scripture. Just because something works does not mean it is the best method to use.

The "servant-church" ecclesiology

There exists, Lim claims, a diametric contrast between the Christendom model of ecclesiology that many contemporary churches subscribe to and the servant-church model pictured in the New Testament. This contrast is clearly observed in the diverse mission emphases and practices, church planting activities and leadership/church development strategies.

The Christendom model, as Lim points out, reflects the vestiges of the "hierarchical, paternalistic, clergy-centered 'heresy' of the medieval Church" (1989c, 87) and is "the major cause of stagnation in most of modern Christianity" (ibid., 89). The servant-church model, on the other hand, is the vibrant church we see in the New Testament. It is composed of

> a loose network of small communities/churches organized as simple Christ-worshipping Bible study groups which live out the radical demands of the gospel in non-hierarchical, non-paternalistic and non-clerical ways in . . . worship, fellowship, and community service (*leitourgia, koinonia,* and *diakonia*).
> . . . Each small group will have a local locus (working for contextualized witness) and global vision (working for transformation) (ibid., 88).

Due to its simplicity and flexibility, the decentralized and democratic servant-church model can easily embark on the holistic task of mission—the transformation of communities.

A concrete program of mission practice

Lim advocates a specific approach to doing mission. He calls this method "spiritual reproduction through small groups" (1990f, 1). He argues that the best context for evangelism and outreach, discipleship and spiritual growth is the small group, where the priesthood of all believers can be realized. The small group is the locus where the servant-church model is put into practice. It is the best method for fulfilling the Great Commission and also for the mobilization of the whole church for world evangelization. As Lim defines it,

> Christian mission should primarily be seen as a few disciples (be they students, professionals, business people, housewives or farmers), each in their own natural settings, sharing God's love spontaneously, even without the presence of "fulltime" missionaries or church leaders. The "fulltimers" are to serve as models, trainers, and coordinators—as "equippers" of all the saints to do the work of ministry (Eph. 4:11–12) (ibid.).[6]

Small groups, as the embodiment of the servant-church model, have for their objective the transformation of their communities. In order to restore shalom, they must use the "community development–community organizing" approach to evangelism and church planting. Such an approach is truly holistic because it is concerned "for the total welfare of the people—religious, social, economic, political, educational, physical, etc. (Mt. 9:3538; cf. 25:3146; Lk. 2:52; 10:30–37)" (1996b, 3).

The goal of the community development–community organizing approach is that people become empowered.

> Whether the whole community turns to Christ or not (most probably a majority will become at least sympathetic to the gospel), we hope that the target people will have been enabled to become mature and responsible (not dependent) adults who can make dignified and wise decisions for their individual and communal life–as active participants (not passive onlookers) in tackling issues that affect their lives and destinies (ibid.).

The explicit strategy of the community development–community organizing approach is the contextualization of the gospel in every facet of life within specific communities.[7] A corollary to this strategy is "the call to transform or 'Christianize' the culture of a nation or people group (where a significant number in the community works out their faith in Christ in the world marketplace culture)" (1997b).[8] At the same time, it also entails political action in doing mission, particularly in ministries among the poor (ibid.).[9]

Lim also calls for mutual respect and acceptance among all Christians (1983a, 57–73; 1984, 34–73), and for interfaith dialogue that seeks common ground (1996b; 1983b, 175–203). The intent is to look for entry points for meaningful dialogue and to allow the convicting power of the Holy Spirit to move among the hearts of people of different faiths.

Concluding observations

Coming from a land where nominalism characterizes the religious life of the majority of believers, it is laudable to see my friend and colleague develop an action-oriented missiology of transformation. There are, however, two mitigating factors that work against the goal of transformation—

human sinfulness and the problem of maturity. Despite the claims to conversion and the many training programs for church growth and community development, the reality of human depravity and indifference has taken its toll upon the churches. Many Christians are like the Ephesian believers—they have "lost their first love" amid their hectic programs and ecclesiastical activities (Rev. 2:2–4). Some can be compared to the church in Sardis—they have a reputation for being alive and active, yet they are dead (Rev. 3:1–2). The basic issue appears to be spirituality. Transformation will be handicapped if not preceded by an emphasis on the spiritual development of Christians within their communities.

Moreover, Christians in developing countries like the Philippines usually espouse a "split-level Christianity" (Bulatao 1966), seeking to ignore the supernatural powers and beliefs that affect the daily lives of people in favor of a more intellectual faith.[10] The task of transformation will fail without a prior change in the worldview system of believers.

While it is noteworthy to stress contextual issues (e.g., politics, economics, ecology) in the task of community development–community organizing, the issues of spirituality and worldview change should take precedence. Reality dictates that unless a person is changed from within, there will be no real change without. In this sense, transformation missiology would be akin to evangelization missiology. It will have to subscribe to the logical and theological priority of spiritual and worldview issues over other issues at hand.

A doubt persists in relation to the "smallness" of the servant-church structure. Is the smallness of the churches among the Pauline communities meant to be normative for every church worldwide in all generations? Are there variations of ecclesiastical structures found in the New Testament that would warrant the existence of larger churches? Is the size of the church structure culture-specific or biblically mandated? These questions are crucial to insistence on the small house churches or Bible study groups as the biblical model for the transformation of communities.

I believe that the strength of simple and flexible structures is at the same time their area of weakness. Small structures are always inadequate in their resources, whether personnel, material, space, time or energy. While Lim would propose a loose network of these small groups, the network itself still needs clarification. The fine line between control and autonomy needs further definition. Without a clear picture of this "loose network," cell groups can easily degenerate into competing units or, in some cases, alliances that swallow up smaller units to become monoliths.

Nevertheless, Lim remains a positive influence in the shaping of my own mission theology. I am deeply impressed by his zeal for the poor and by his penetrating insights into our Philippine society. He brings to mind the Old Testament prophets who burned with zeal for Yahweh and Yahweh's covenant people. Like the whirlwind, Lim stirs and uproots many of us young ministers and pushes us to work in the areas of marginality and liminality.

When I am tempted to look at our churches and communities pessimistically, Lim infects me with his optimism and idealism. His is an optimism, I believe, undergirded by one crucial trait—authenticity. Lim models his teachings. I recall many instances when he would bring street people to the Asian Theological Seminary in order to help them. I remember the worn-out clothes and shoes he wore, and the frugal meals he ate in keeping with his simple lifestyle. Despite his affluent background, Lim continues to opt for a simple life in order to express his solidarity with the poor.

I deeply respect this man of God, my esteemed friend and colleague. Whatever the weaknesses of his transformation missiology, I am sure of this one thing—that it reverberates with authenticity. It originates from his heart and from his passion for the poor.

Lim is a significant voice in the theological and missiological arena of Southeast Asia. As focus is shifting to "doing theology" and "doing missiology" in the majority world, Lim's concept of transformation missiology will remain an important agenda in the missiological discussion.

Notes

[1] With his letter he mailed copies of his published and unpublished materials. Lim also graciously included some jottings on his missiological viewpoints and his contributions to missiological discussions.

[2] Lim has detailed the differences between evangelization missiology and transformation missiology in "A Comparison of Two Evangelical Missiologies" (1997a).

[3] Lim has classified all other missiologies into the following types: (1) "humanization" missiology, which upholds "social action as the only agendum in the Church's witness to the world"; (2) "liberation" missiology, which "prioritizes social action, but does not neglect the importance of evangelism"; (3) "evangelization" missiology of the Church Growth School, which stresses evangelism and considers "social concern as a partner of evangelism"; and (4) "salvation" missiology, which "views evangelism to be the only strategy, and social action to be unimportant, if not detrimental, to the Church's mission" (1992b, 29).

[4] For a detailed discussion on the servant-church structures and the Christendom structures, see Lim 1989c, 87–90; 1996a. See also Lim 1988c, 67; 1989b, 27–33.

⁵ See also Lim 1987a, 47; 1987b, 318–58; 1988b, 36–39; 1989b, 20–41; 1990e, 45; 1991a, 16–20; 1991b, (143) 45–47, (144) 52–55, (145) 40–42; 1992b, 16–20.

⁶ See also Lim 1988a, 292–306; 1988c, 1–7; 1989b, 20–41; 1990c, 5, 8–9; 1990d, 2–4, 6.

⁷ For details on Lim's views of contextualization, see Lim 1983b, 175–203; 1983c, 95–104; 1988a, 292–306; 1992a, 16; and 1994, 17–19.

⁸ See also Lim 1989a, 27–32.

⁹ See also Lim 1985, 12–14; 1987a, 47; 1988b, 36–39; 1996b, 34; 1993.

¹⁰ See Paul Hiebert's explanation of the "excluded middle" concept (1982).

References

Bulatao, Jaime. 1966. *Split-Level Christianity.* Quezon City: Ateneo de Manila University.

Hiebert, Paul G. 1982. "The Flaw of the Excluded Middle." *Missiology* 10, no. 1: 35–47.

Lim, David Sun. 1983a. "Baptism and the Church." *Christian Forum* 6: 57–73.

———. 1983b. "Biblical Christianity in the Context of Buddhism." In *Sharing Jesus in the Two-Thirds World*, ed. V. Samuel and C. Sugden, 175–203. Grand Rapids, Mich.: Eerdmans.

———. 1983c. "Of Filipinos and Fiestas." *Christian Forum* 6: 95–104.

———. 1984. "Speaking in Tongues." *Christian Forum* 7: 34–73.

———. 1985. "Towards a Christian Response to Communism." *Evangelical Thrust* 12: 12–14.

———. 1987a. "A Biblical Theology of Christian Patriotism, Part I." *Evangelical Thrust* 14: 4–7.

———. 1987b. "The Servant Nature of the Church in the Pauline Corpus." Ph.D. dissertation. Fuller Theological Seminary, Pasadena, California.

———. 1988a. "Asian Churches as Servants of God." *Evangelical Review of Theology* 12, no. 4: 292–306.

———. 1988b. "A Biblical Theology of Christian Patriotism, Part II." *Evangelical Thrust* 15: 36–39.

———. 1988c. "The Living God in the Structures of Philippine Reality." *Transformation* 5: 1–7.

———. 1989a. "Church and State in the Philippines, 1980–1988." *Transformation* 6, no. 3: 27–32.

———. 1989b. "The City in the Bible." In *Urban Ministry in Asia*, ed. Bong Rin Ro, 20–41. Taichung: Asia Theological Association.

———. 1989c. "The Servant Church." *Evangelical Review of Theology* 13, no. 1: 87–90.

———. 1990a. "Biblical Basis for National Sovereignty." *Isip Isak* 3, no. 3: 4–5.

———. 1990b. "The Doctrine of Creation and Some Implications for Modern Economics." *Transformation* 7, no. 2: 28–32 and 7, no. 3: 21–23.

————. 1990c. "Doing Christ's Mission in Christ's Way." *Asian Center for World Mission Newsletter* 3: 5, 8–9.

————. 1990d. "Holy Church in the Secular World." *Koinonians* 1, no. 2: 2–4, 6.

————. 1990e. "The New Testament Teaching on Jesus in Relation to the Jews." Paper presented at the Consultation on Conversion and World Evangelization, January 1988, Hong Kong.

————. 1990f. "Reaching the World Through Discipleship Groups." *Asian Center for World Mission Newsletter* 4: 1–2, 4.

————. 1991a. "Born to Debt? Reflections on the Debt Crisis." *Patmos* 7, no. 2: 16–20.

————. 1991b. "Understanding Poverty from the Doctrine of Creation." *Chinese Churches Today* 143: 45–47; 144: 52–55; 145: 40–42.

————. 1992a. "Reaching the Diaspora Chinese: New Testament Insights for the Contemporary Situation." *Chinese Around the World* (October): 1–6.

————. 1992b. *Transforming Communities: Biblical Concepts on Poverty and Social Justice.* Metro-Manila: OMF Literature, Inc.

————. 1993. "The Maturation of Social Ministry in Local Churches." In *Abundance and Maturity*, ed. First Evangelical Church Editorial Committee. Hong Kong: Christian Communications.

————. 1994. "Theological Trends in Asia." *Themelios* 26, no. 2: 17–19.

————. 1996a. "Advancing the Servant Church Model." Unpublished manuscript.

————. 1996b. "How To Really Help the Poor." *Koinonians* 2, no. 1: 3–4, 8.

————. 1996c. "What Is Wholistic Mission?" Unpublished manuscript.

————. 1997a. "A Comparison of Two Evangelical Missiologies." Unpublished manuscript.

————. 1997b. Personal correspondence. February 14, 1997.

15

Charles Kraft's and Paul Hiebert's approaches to worldview

"Why don't you build a Christian shrine?"

Yoshiyuki Billy Nishioka

I come from Japan, where Christian churches have not grown since the revival movement that arose after World War II in spite of the fact that most Japanese Christians are committed and pastors are striving to stimulate church growth. The problem is not that the Japanese are not open to Christianity, but rather that the culture of the church in Japan unconsciously excludes outsiders—"non-Christian" Japanese. A major task of missiology in this situation is to analyze the approaches of the church and to suggest new directions for Japanese Christian leaders.

This issue has challenged me to study missiology in the United States, where I took a class from missiologist Charles H. Kraft. I often asked what seemed to be unanswerable questions, both in the class and in Kraft's office. One day he said to me, "Why don't you build a Christian shrine?" He was challenging me to use a Japanese cultural form to communicate the gospel.

Another missiologist important to my study is Paul G. Hiebert. Though I have never met him, through his writing he has joined the

Yoshiyuki Billy Nishioka completed the Ph.D. in 1997; his research focused on worldview theory and metaphor. He served as a church planter for three years in Japan and as assistant pastor in Los Angeles (OMS Holiness) for nine years. He is currently a pastor, adjunct professor of Tokyo Biblical Seminary, and research director of Tokyo Mission Research Institute. Nishioka is married, with three daughters. He has published *The Time to Think of God* (in Japanese) and is editing and translating David Bosch's *Transforming Mission* into Japanese.

conversation I am having with Kraft. Hiebert's writings tell me to be critical when using cultural forms.

How can I reconcile their suggestions? This chapter addresses this issue. I describe and compare the respective approaches of Kraft and Hiebert to worldview studies. This type of research leads to a deeper understanding of culture and is crucial for learning how to contextualize the biblical message while maintaining faithfulness to the Scriptures.

Kraft and Hiebert on worldview

Charles H. Kraft and Paul G. Hiebert are anthropologists whose insights have received wide recognition in the discipline of missiology. Kraft was a missionary in Nigeria before coming to Fuller Theological Seminary's School of World Mission, where he currently serves as professor of anthropology and intercultural communication.[1] Hiebert has worked as a missionary in India and has served on the faculty of the School of World Mission; currently he is professor of mission and anthropology and chair of the department of mission and evangelism at Trinity Evangelical Divinity School.

Although Hiebert and Kraft hold worldview theories that seem to share common philosophical ground and definitions, their basic approaches are quite different. Before comparing these views, I will discuss their definitions of worldview.

The study of worldview is grounded in the question, What is reality? Both these scholars develop worldview theory on the basis of a position known as critical realism. The distinction between objective reality (with capital letters) and subjective reality (with small letters) is of utmost importance. There are three positions in the relation of reality and reality: (1) "naive realism" (objective reality only); (2) "relativism" (subjective reality only); and (3) "critical realism" (integration of reality/reality).[2]

Naive realism affirms that reality exists in the world, knowledge can be totally objective, and subjective dependence on the knowing process is not important.[3] On the other hand, relativism holds that there is no objective knowledge "out there." Those who espouse relativism negate any rational basis for arriving at objective or absolute knowledge. Rather, they stress subjective dimensions of knowledge and hold that interpretations or theories should not be judged as to whether they are true or false, but by their usefulness. Critical realism insists that both objective reality and subjectively perceived reality exist. Ultimate reality, once it is interpreted or understood, becomes perceived reality. This critical assessment at the deeper assumption levels is what worldview study is all about. Both Kraft and Hiebert hold the position of critical realism as a valid way of describing cultural knowledge.

Generally, Hiebert and Kraft agree on their definition of worldview. According to Hiebert, worldview is the set of "basic assumptions about reality which lie behind the beliefs and behavior of a culture" (1985, 45). Elsewhere he states that "they [basic assumptions] are taken for granted and never questioned. Together, they form a more or less consistent worldview that orders people's experience and gives meaning to their lives" (1983, 369). Kraft defines worldview in a similar way as "the totality of the culturally structured assumptions, values and commitments (allegiances) underlying both a people's perception of reality and their responses to those perceptions" (1994b, 2).

Both Hiebert and Kraft suggest that worldview exists at the core of culture. Any culture can be viewed from at least two levels: the surface level and the deep level. Aspects of culture touching various areas of experiences (for example, kinship, social structure, economics, political organization, religion, language, education, art) are integrated in terms of complex cultural patterns. These cultural patterns can be classified according to visible surface patterns in behaviors and deeper invisible patterns of assumptions. The latter type of patterning is what is identified with worldview.

Whereas both Hiebert and Kraft agree that worldview exists at the core of culture and observation can point to the "invisible," they differ in their analysis of worldview.

Theoretical Backgrounds and Frameworks

Hiebert and Kraft differ most markedly in the philosophies and theories that undergird worldview studies.

Kraft's fourfold matrix and worldview universals

Kraft's theory of worldview is highly interdisciplinary, drawing from insights developed in linguistics, communication studies and anthropology. The most important theoretical tradition for his approach to worldview is the work of Robert Redfield and Michael Kearney.[4] Following their perspectives, Kraft uses two major frameworks: a fourfold matrix and worldview universals.

Kraft's first basic framework for analyzing worldview is the fourfold matrix (Figure 15–1), which has two dimensions: surface/deep and person/structure. Kraft explains the importance of the surface/deep distinction in describing the relationship among culture, religion and worldview. According to the traditional anthropological approach, religion was once considered to be the core of culture. Kraft, however, suggests that religion is not the core of culture but one of the cultural subsystems, along with other subsystems of economics, politics, social relationships, material culture and language. The core of culture is, instead, worldview, "the culturally patterned basic understandings (assumptions, presuppositions, beliefs) of Reality in terms of which the members of a society organize and live their lives" (1986c, 53).[5] By distinguishing the deep assumption level (worldview) from the surface level (cultural subsystems), a systematic, consistent and comprehensive approach to culture is possible.

	Person	Structure (cultural system)
Surface	**Behavior** Habitual behavior Overt/covert Creative behavior Overt/covert	**Cultural patterns for behaving** Overt customs that pattern doing and speaking Covert customs that pattern thinking
Deep	**Assumptions** Assigning meaning Responding to assigned meanings Underlying personal— willing, emoting, reasoning, motivations, predispositions	**Worldview assumptions** Patterns for assigning meaning Patterns for responding to meaning Patterns for— willing, emoting, reasoning, deciding, motivation, being predisposed

Figure 15—1: Kraft's fourfold matrix (1994a, 85)

The other important distinction in the fourfold matrix is that of person/structure. Even though a person lives within a cultural context, the person is different from the cultural system (for example, any pattern or structure of that system). Kraft argues that the lack of a person/structure distinction ends in a deterministic understanding of culture, which has little room for explaining personal will, intention, motivation, freedom and choice. Kraft insists that "culture is not a person. It does not 'do' anything. Only people do things. The fact that people ordinarily do what they do by following the cultural 'track' laid down for them should not lead us to treat culture itself as something possessing a life of its own" (1989, 56).

Culture does not have personality, Kraft claims, nor are human beings robots of cultural structures. There is always "room to wiggle" (ibid.,
60). A person's actual behavior, consequently, can never be fully understood only in terms of cultural or habitual behavior, without dealing with
creativity in the person.

Kraft also uses Michael Kearney's concept of worldview universals.[6]
Kraft, however, modifies Kearney's number of universals from six to five,
using the following terms: (1) categorization (classification or logic); (2)
person-group; (3) causality; (4) time-event; and (5) space-material. For
Kraft, categorization is the backbone for all other universals. Kraft omits
Kearney's category of self-other from worldview universals,because of
the distinction Kraft makes between person and structure. For Kraft,
self should be understood as a person who interacts with structure.

Hiebert's triads

Like Kraft, Hiebert also takes an interdisciplinary approach, incorporat-
ing the following schools of the discipline: structural anthropology, symbolic anthropology, cognitive anthropology and sociology of knowledge.
Using the insights of these disciplines, two triadic frameworks are piv-
otal in Hiebert's worldview analysis: surface/assumption/deep levels in
human experience and cognitive/affective/evaluative aspects of human
experience.

The first triad provides a perspective that classifies human experiences on three levels.[7] The surface level is the explicit and visible aspect
of culture (for example, social events, behaviors, institutions, processes).
The assumption level refers to the explanatory systems by which people
meaningfully structure their lives. Here Hiebert follows Clifford Geertz's
approach, which sees a "web of significance" that renders visible culture
intelligible (Geertz 1973, 5, 14). Hiebert sees this tendency of human
beings to seek meaning and structure as a way of overcoming the dread
of chaos caused by death and suffering.

The final level in the first triad is the deep level. At this level major
concerns are the cognitive structuring of knowledge, classifying processes
and taxonomic systems.[8] Hiebert does not identify this deep level with
the worldview system itself, but with orientations or processes by which
worldview is formed.

The second triadic framework (see Figure 15–2) distinguishes three
dimensions of human experience: cognitive, affective and evaluative.[9] The
cognitive dimension includes knowledge, categories, logic and wisdom;
the affective dimension consists of feelings and aesthetics; and the evaluative dimension involves values and allegiances. People commit to a certain

belief with both an affective appreciation and a cognitive understanding. This framework is useful to explain the relationship between observable human behaviors and unseen factors (for example, beliefs, emotions and value orientations).

A Model of Worldview

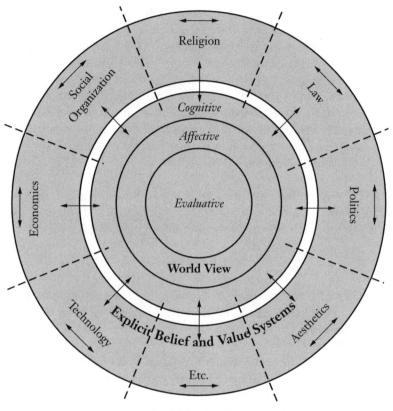

Social Institutions

Figure 15—2: Hiebert's model of worldview (1985a, 46)

Assumptions and approaches to worldview

Let us now focus on Kraft's and Hiebert's assumptions in order to clarify their differences. A comparison of their approaches will involve three major issues: (1) the concept of culture; (2) the form-meaning issues; and (3) the orientation of their approaches to culture.

Concepts of culture

The fact that Kraft and Hiebert draw from different schools in the discipline results in the divergence in their views of culture. According to Kraft, culture (as well as worldview) is a "complex set of patterns in terms of which people think and behave" (1989, 54). Culture in this perspective can be seen primarily as a neutral vehicle for producing and responding to assigned meanings (1979, 90–95; 1985, 397).[10] For Hiebert, in contrast, culture consists of both patterns and ideas. He defines culture as "the integrated system of learned patterns of behavior, ideas, and products characteristic of a society" (1983, 25).[11] Hiebert states,

> In addition to patterns of behavior, culture is made up of a system of shared *concepts* by which people carve up their worlds, of *beliefs* by which they organize these concepts into rational schemes, and of *values* by which they set their goals and judge their actions (1983, 28).

For Hiebert, culture is not just a process, but also content and meaning, while Kraft claims that meaning is always in people, and culture is pattern, system or structure, and should be distinguished from person.

Form and meaning

This difference in the concept of culture is deeply related to the issue of form and meaning. Hiebert and Kraft differ considerably on the issue. As Kraft states:

> *Meanings lie in people*, not in the external world nor language, gesture, writing, or any of the other symbols we use to describe and discuss our perceptions of that world. Neither the external world nor the elements of life interpret themselves. *People interpret and assign meaning to the world in which they are involved*. They are, however, guided in this process by the "tracks" of the worldviews they are taught (1989, 191).

This clear distinction between form and meaning is associated with Kraft's distinction between person and structure. For Kraft, culture is a tool, a means, a vehicle, a map or framework for the process of meaning construction in thinking, behaving, expressing and responding. Unless a person assigns meanings to form (for example, behavior, symbols, materials, languages), no communication occurs. Form and meaning should not be confused in analysis. It is likely that since one of Kraft's major tasks in his mission work was Bible translation, in his view meaning should be transcendent with respect to cultural or linguistic forms. Hence the meaning presented in certain forms can be transferred to other forms through an encoding/decoding process. The distinction itself is a practical prerequisite for a translator. Therefore, his approach is more cross-cultural and comparative.

Hiebert, on the other hand, disagrees with such a strong separation of form and meaning. Following insights developed in symbolic anthropology, Hiebert maintains various linkages between form and meaning. He does not deny the importance of a distinction between form and meaning but emphasizes the danger of equation and/or separation. Examples for equation can be seen when missionaries reject certain local symbols that were previously equated with idol worship.

Hiebert suggests a rigid separation of form and meaning that results in: (1) a simplistic view of culture; (2) a de-contextual view of symbol that ignores a symbol's inseparable association with social experience and history; and (3) a denial of the validity of truth-claims in favor of relativism and pragmatism. He maintains the importance of critical realism, in which researchers see various relationships between form and meaning, rejecting both the extreme positions of a positivistic form-meaning equation and a relativistic form-meaning separation (1989, 102–7; 1995).[12]

Orientations to culture

Kraft and Hiebert also have different orientations as they approach culture. Kraft's approach is primarily etic, looking at culture from the outside's perspective,[13] using universal categories for analyzing worldview assumptions and making cross-cultural comparisons. With the etic framework, the actual content of the discovery is emic, looking at culture from the insiders' perspective. Kraft's approach thus begins with etic tools and ends with discovery of emic cultural assumptions.

Hiebert's approach to worldview, on the other hand, is primarily emic (the insider's view), in that he focuses on particular meaning systems that are culturally idiosyncratic and integrated with symbols. The meaning system is symbolically represented in a particular domain of cultural phenomena (for example, ritual, myth, social structure or political system). He takes a domain-specific descriptive approach to worldview,[14] aiming at the discovery of meaning systems from particular cultural symbols in the selected domain. He then tries to compare such systems of meaning with a larger cross-cultural framework (etic).

Implications for mission theology and practice

Charles Kraft and Paul Hiebert agree that worldview methodology is an anthropological tool for mission theology. The differences in their approaches are seen in their respective goals and are related to issues developed in their mission experiences. For Kraft, the major goal for using worldview methodology is achieving meaning equivalence in cross-cultural communication.[15] One of his mission assignments was Scripture translation, a task that emphasizes the decoding and encoding process with its distinction between form and meaning. He struggled with the confusion caused by the intrusion of foreign forms in communicating the gospel in Nigeria and came to believe any culture can be used for communicating the gospel to the people in that culture. For him, the primary task of mission is not changing culture but using culture to communicate the gospel and change people's allegiance (1989, 80, 187). Initial acceptance of the receptor culture is a key task of mission. If cultural change is necessary, it should be initiated by indigenous persons who are changed by Christ (1979, chap. 19; 1989, chaps. 7–8; 1994a, chaps. 23–28).

Hiebert, however, struggled with syncretism in the Indian context, where the pluralistic concept of divinity is contradictory to biblical teaching. He aims at critical assessment of meaning systems and worldviews to avoid a distortion of truth (syncretism) in transmitting the biblical message.[16] For him, certain cultural forms deviate from biblical truth. Therefore, certain elements within cultural systems need to be changed or rejected at the beginning point of the mission practice. The major missiological task is to identify, on the basis of critical assessment, forms that may distort biblical truth. This is why he strongly maintains critical realism (1984; 1989; 1995; Hiebert and Shaw 1993, chap. 12).

Kraft would affirm the importance of using a "Christian shrine" in the Japanese context, letting persons filled with the Holy Spirit pour new meanings into this cultural form. For me, this signifies building a receptor-oriented church that is sensitive not only to visible forms but also to invisible features (worldview) in terms of time, space, relationships and other patterns common to Japanese religious life.

If I follow Hiebert's perspective, on the other hand, it would be difficult to build a "Christian shrine." In analogically oriented Japanese minds, the shrine form seems deeply associated with religious beliefs and practices incompatible with biblical truth. Leaders in Christian churches in Japan would feel acceptance of this form might cause syncretism.

In summary, Kraft stresses the importance of using indigenous cultural forms in communicating the gospel, while Hiebert sees the difficulty in creating appropriate new meanings out of forms in which old meanings are deeply embedded. To what degree can we create new meanings with old forms and avoid syncretism? Would non-Christian Japanese feel less excluded if the church had Christian shrines? Where is the line between dynamic equivalence and over-contextualization?

I hesitate to put the approaches of Kraft and Hiebert into an either-or category, choosing one and rejecting the other. Yet, although they may be complementary at the practical and application levels, theoretical synthesis may not be possible. Further investigation is needed to clarify the nature of culture and the relationship between forms and meanings. It may be necessary to create a completely new paradigm.

The younger generation in Japanese society does not hold strongly to the linkage between traditional cultural forms and traditional meanings. It might be possible in the future to use these forms for creating new meanings. Or perhaps the church will discover culturally appropriate forms we haven't yet considered.

At any rate we need forms that will clearly and with a welcoming spirit say to the non-Christian people surrounding us, "Yes, we are Christian. We are also Japanese."

Notes

[1] For more biographical information on Kraft, see the article by Levi De Carvalho in this volume.

[2] See Kraft 1979, 24–31; 1986a, 27ff.; 1989, 11–22; 1994a, 42–55; 1994b, chap. 2. Hiebert explains the epistemological issue in a slightly different manner (1994, chaps.1–2). He compares five different philosophical positions in terms of the nature of knowledge: (1) idealism (including absolute idealism, critical idealism); (2) naive realism; (3) critical realism; (4) instrumentalism; and (5) determinism (1994, 40, cf. 21–26).

[3] Because of such overemphasis on attainability of objective reality, naive realism is close to positivism. Positivists, as Barbour states, hold that "theories can be inferred directly from observations by a process of inductive generalization" (1974, 36). Positivists overlook the fact that such theories themselves are paradigm-dependent (mediated).

[4] Redfield (1953) and Kearney (1975, 1984) provide comprehensive and cross-culturally comparable approaches to the study of deeper levels of cultural knowledge. Cf. Grant (1986, 125–26) and Bensley (1982).

[5] Here Kraft follows Redfield's (1953) view.

[6] See Kearney 1984, chap. 3. Worldview universal is also explained in various sections of Kraft's work (1986b, 41–42; 1986c, 61–62; 1989, 195–205; 1994b, chaps. 11–15).

[7] This section depends largely on Clinton's analysis of Hiebert's theories (see Clinton 1986).

[8] For further discussion, see Hiebert 1994, chaps. 1–2, 6. See also Clinton 1986, 68–70.

[9] Hiebert 1985, 30–34, 45. This triadic framework was originally developed by Parsons and Shills (1962 [1951]). This framework also appeared in Geertz's definition of religion (1973, chap. 4) and other various materials (see also Hall 1959, chap. 4).

[10] This view of cultural (not ethical) relativism is slightly modified in recent work (1994a, 161–77) in which Kraft stresses the importance of evaluating cultures.

[11] His definition is analogous to Geertz's symbolic view (Geertz 1973).

[12] For Hiebert, a form-meaning demarcation accords with a dualistic mode of thinking inherited from and biased by Western culture. Recently, following C. S. Pierce's triad, Hiebert (1994, 64ff.; 1995, chap. 3) introduces a triadic model for his new view of meaning: (1) forms (signs or symbolic representations); (2) mental image, maps, categories these signs stimulate (*subjective* realities); and (3) externally existing objects (*objective* realities). For example, (1) the sign "dog," which evokes (2) a mental image or a category of what is called dog, points out (3) the external object, the dog on a street. He sees symbols "as the links between that world [a real world with a real history] and our mental maps of it" (1994, 67). "Symbols, therefore, have both objective and subjective dimensions. Truth and meaning lie not in mind alone, but in the correspondence between our mental maps or models, and the reality represented. This means we must test our interior view of the symbol (and all knowledge comprises symbols) against the external reality by careful examination and independent verification" (1994, 67).

[13] In the etic approach cultural phenomena are analyzed by means of outsiders' analytical methods, for the purpose of cross-cultural comparison. In the emic approach a culturally specific system is described from insiders' perspectives (Lett 1990, 130–31).

[14] Domain specific and dimension specific are two different foci in selecting scope for studying culture(s). By *dimension*, I refer to particular aspects of human experience (time, space, classification, and the like) that permeate multiple domains of experience (economics, rituals, politics, and social relations). *Dimension specific* refers to the primacy of a specific dimension in cultural analysis. *Domain* is associated with a certain area of experience (e.g., ancestor worship, rice-cultivation, marriage, education and so on) in which multiple dimensions of human life are integrated.. *Domain specific* indicates the primacy of a particular domain (e.g., wedding) in describing cultural phenomena and knowledge.

[15] Kraft calls this receptor oriented process "dynamic-equivalence" translation or communication (1979, see also 1991).

[16] The concept of excluded middle is one famous example (Hiebert 1982).

References

Barbour, Ian G. 1974. *Myths, Models, and Paradigms: A Comparative Study in Science and Religion*. San Francisco: Harper & Row.

Bensley, Ross Edward. 1982. "Toward a Paradigm Shift in World View Theory: The Contribution of a Modified Piagetian Model." Ph.D. dissertation. Fuller Theological Seminary, School of World Mission, Pasadena, California.

Clinton, J. Robert. 1986. "A Comparison of Some Worldview Models." In *Worldview Source Book: The School of World Mission Models*, ed. Ian Ludbrook Grant, 65–92. M.A. thesis. Fuller Theological Seminary, School of World Mission, Pasadena, California.

Geertz, Clifford. 1973. *The Interpretation of Cultures*. New York: Basic Books.

Grant, Ian Ludbrook. 1986. "Worldview Source Book: The School of World Mission Models." M.A. thesis. Fuller Theological Seminary, School of World Mission, Pasadena, California.

Hall, Edward T. 1959. *The Silent Language*. Garden City, N.Y.: Doubleday.

Hiebert, Paul G. 1976. "Traffic Patterns in Seattle and Hyderabad." *Journal of Anthropological Research* 32: 326–36.

——. 1982. "The Flaw of the Excluded Middle." *Missiology* 10, no. 1: 35–47 (reissued in 1994).

——. 1984. "Critical Contextualization." *Missiology* 12, no. 3: 287–96 (reissued in 1985, *International Bulletin of Mission Research* 8, no. 4: 104–12).

——. 1983. *Cultural Anthropology*. Second ed. Grand Rapids, Mich.: Baker Book House.

——. 1985. *Anthropological Insights for Missionaries*. Grand Rapids, Mich.: Baker Book House.

——. 1989. "Form and Meaning in Contextualization of the Gospel." In *The Word Among Us*, ed. Dean S. Gilliland, 101–20. Dallas, Tex.: Word Publishing.

——. 1994. *Anthropological Reflection on Missiological Issues*. Grand Rapids, Mich.: Baker Book House.

——. 1995. *Missiological Implications of Epistemological Shifts*. Unpublished manuscript.

Hiebert, Paul G. and R. Daniel Shaw. 1993. *The Power and the Glory: Missiological Approach to the Study of Religion*. Unpublished manuscript.

Kearney, Michael. 1975. "World View Theory and Study." *Annual Review of Anthropology* 4: 247–70.

——. 1984. *World View*. Navato, Calif.: Shandler and Sharp.

Kraft, Charles H. 1979. *Christianity in Culture*. Maryknoll, N.Y.: Orbis Books.

——. 1986a. "Reality, Perception, and Mental Mapping." In *Worldview Sourcebook: The School of World Mission Models*, ed. Ian Ludbrook Grant, 20–33. M.A. thesis. Fuller Theological Seminary, School of World Mission, Pasadena, California.

——. 1986b. "Worldview, A Society's Map of Reality." In *Worldview Sourcebook: The School of World Mission Models*, ed. Ian Ludbrook Grant, 34–50. M.A. thesis, Fuller Theological Seminary, School of World Mission, Pasadena, California.

——. 1986c. "Worldview, Paradigms, Power and Bible Translation." In *Worldview Sourcebook: The School of World Mission Models*, ed. Ian Ludbrook Grant, 51–73. M.A. thesis, Fuller Theological Seminary, School of World Mission, Pasadena, California.

——. 1985. "Cultural Anthropology: Its Meaning for Christian Theology." *Theology Today* 41, no. 4: 390–400.

——. 1989. *Christianity with Power*. Ann Arbor, Mich.: Servant.

——. 1991. *Communication Theory for Christian Witness*. Revised ed. Maryknoll, N.Y.: Orbis Books.

——. 1994a. *Anthropology for Christian Witness*. Unpublished manuscript, Fuller Theological Seminary, School of World Mission, Pasadena, California.

——. 1994b. *Worldview for Christian Witness*. Unpublished manuscript.

Lett, James. 1990. "Emics and Etics: Notes on the Epistemology of Anthropology." In *Emics and Etics: The Insider/Outsider Debate*, ed, Thomas N. Headland, Kenneth L. Pike and Marvin Harris, 127–42. Newbury Park, Calif.: Sage.

Parsons, Talcot, and Edward A. Shils. 1962. "Values, Motives, and System of Action." In *Toward a General Theory of Action*, ed. Talcott Parsons and Edward A. Shils, 45–275. New York: Harper & Row (originally published in 1951).

Redfield, Robert. 1953. *The Primitive World and Its Transformations*. Ithaca, N.Y.: Cornell University Press.

16

Feminism and missiology

A Korean woman's perspective

BOKYOUNG PARK

For more than a hundred years the feminist movement has been active in Western society. During this time the movement has changed in various ways. One key change occurred during the 1960s with the emergence of Christian feminism.[1] Since then, contemporary Christian feminism has influenced almost every aspect of traditional Christian theology and produced a large international body of literature that reaches across all theological domains.

However, in spite of the powerful influence of Christian feminism in the church, the feminist issue remains a neglected area in missiological studies. Feminist studies have been stigmatized as unbiblical, liberal and dangerous, certainly not an area evangelical missiology should consider.

When I express my interest in feminist studies in missiology, both mission scholars and practitioners respond with skepticism. Many seem to feel Christian feminism belongs in the realm of theology, not missiology. Some advise me that the issue is too controversial for mission-minded people. Others comment that my concern would better suit a liberal Christian.

Bokyoung Park received the Ph.D. from Fuller Theological Seminary's School of World Mission on Korean women's issues from a missiological perspective. Previously, she studied at the Wartburg Lutheran Seminary in Iowa after completing her M.Div. in Seoul, Korea. Park has been serving in child evangelism in Korean churches for several years. Currently she teaches on the subject of women in ministry at World Mission University, Los Angeles. Park and her husband, Rev. Yohan Jang, have one daughter.

Even in the face of such doubts and suspicion, I can't give up this subject as a missiological concern. What makes this issue so important to missiology? I will attempt to answer that question in this chapter, giving first an overview of the present state of Christian feminism and then reflecting on its potential contributions to missiology. Because current Christian feminism around the world has been influenced mainly by Western feminism, I will limit my overview to Western Christian feminists, focusing on North America. However, I do this from the unique perspective of a Korean woman dedicated to the cause of Christ's mission in the world. I will conclude by reflecting on how a missiological Christian feminism might affect the Korean mission enterprise.

Traditional view

The traditional Korean view of women as subordinate creatures has touched my life profoundly. I grew up in a family of seven girls. Not having a son or a brother was a source of frustration for our family. The experience of female discrimination intensified after my father's death. We all felt ashamed of not having any males in the family. During important family events, no one could represent us to the community, a role reserved only to male members of a Korean family. We had lost our public voice. In a sense we had become invisible as a family.

Discrimination against females extends to the Korean church. The most difficult obstacle to my entering the seminary was my gender. Although people agreed about my gift of leadership and my strong sense of calling for ministry, everyone, in both my family and church, tried to persuade me to give up my dream of going to the seminary. "Women are not suitable for professional Christian ministry," they told me. I became confused. I wondered, Am I not called by God for ministry? Is God's call false and my response unreal? As I struggled with these questions, I realized the traditional view of women could not fully support a woman's call to ministry or encourage women to be active participants in God's mission in the world.

A view of women as subordinate to men has appeared in many cultures throughout history. Each gender is seen as created for a specific role, with women being assigned to the private sphere, where they have a supportive function. Men are frequently assigned to the more public sectors of society, where they take on leadership roles. A woman who questions her place and seeks change in the status of women in home, church or society is often viewed in Christian circles as rebellious toward God (Scanzoni and Hardesty 1974, 333).

In 1987 the formation of the Council on Biblical Manhood and Womanhood reaffirmed this view for modern conservative Christian churches. These conservative Christians reject all aspects of the feminist movement, believing that the Bible teaches subordination of women to men. This important reaffirmation of the traditional view of women has been called traditionalist. The most widely known representatives of this view include Susan H. Foh, W. A. Visser 't Hooft, and Donald G. Bloesch.

Missiologically, this traditional view of women has been a major factor in discouraging women's active participation in God's mission. At the heart of this perspective is the assumption that God would limit a person's opportunities to participate in God's mission because that person is a woman. This view runs counter to Galatians 3:28, which affirms that the church is a community in which "there is no longer male and female; for all of you are one in Christ Jesus." As a person called by God to ministry, I could not remain satisfied with a traditional view of women as inferior and subordinate. Christian feminism provided another perspective, one that gave me hope.

The state of contemporary Christian feminism

I would classify contemporary Christian feminism in three major groups: revisionist, revolutionist and evangelical.

Prevailing position: Revisionist feminism

Among contemporary Christian feminists, revisionists are the most representative group and the most prolific in terms of literature. They accept only those parts of Scripture that are free from sexism as authentic revelation. Therefore, in order to define a nonsexist vision for Christianity, the sexist elements of Scripture must be rejected (Groothius 1994; Young 1990). Accordingly, Christian tradition is a source of the theologizing process for revisionist feminists, but is not seen as normative.

Revisionists believe that theology should grow out of the experience of the community. They claim that traditional Christianity reflects only half of the human community, because traditional Christianity has been written and interpreted by men. Therefore, for revisionists, women's experience should be the only norm as well as the source of their theology.

In order to understand the revisionist view, I have chosen three representatives whose works are accessible and widely known: Letty Russell, Rosemary Radford Ruether and Elisabeth Schussler Fiorenza.[2]

Letty Russell begins her feminist discussion in the light of her eschatological message of the Bible (Russell 1979, 173). Her vision for utopia distinguishes her from other present or past-oriented feminist theologians. From this future aspect of her theology she develops the concept of the shared community of partnership (Russell 1979, 19; 1985, 144), the community of Christ, where faith connects faith in action / reflection, where justice works in solidarity with those at the margins of society, and where everyone is welcomed as a partner in God's world house (Russell 1993, 12). Russell recognizes the importance of the biblical tradition as usable past (Russell 1985, 138).

From a more liberal position, Rosemary Radford Ruether advocates a critical principle of feminist theology that keenly analyzes past and present male-centered Christianity (Ruether 1983, 18). Her goal is "the promotion of the full humanity of women" (ibid.). During her early period Ruether found her feminist motive in the prophetic-liberating tradition of Christianity.[3] She saw the prophetic-messianic tradition of Judeo-Christianity as the central norm for evaluating all sources, including Scripture and tradition (Ruether 1983, 23–24).[4] Where this prophetic-liberating tradition is exercised, there is true church. However, at least since her *Sexism and God-Talk* (1983), she has begun to move toward a post-Christian feminist stance (ibid, 22).

Elisabeth Schussler Fiorenza represents the left wing of revisionists. Her well-known book *In Memory of Her* (1983) is a major contribution to Christian feminism. For her, Jesus' vision of *basileia* and the early Christian movement included women's leadership (Schussler Fiorenza 1983, 140). Jesus and early Christians recognized the feminine aspect of God as divine *sophia* (ibid., 132). However, although Fiorenza draws upon biblical sources for her feminist theology, the Bible is not her main source. She sees biblical traditions as thoroughly patriarchal. Therefore, Fiorenza suggests the prototypical use of Scripture as opening from the past into the present, observing a continuity between past and present revelation (Young 1990, 27). But the chief means of divine revelation and grace are not in the Bible or in the tradition of a patriarchal church; rather, it is found in the *ekklesia* of women (Schussler Fiorenza 1985, 128).

Anne Carr, a Roman Catholic feminist, cites the following as beneficial contributions of revisionist feminism to the church: a critique of the past, especially those Christian teachings and traditions that have belittled women; a recovery of the lost history of women in the Christian tradition; and a revisitation of Christian messages that give serious attention to women's equality and experience (Carr 1988, 7–8).

In agreement with Carr and with the addition of a missiological perspective, I find the major contribution of revisionist feminism to the

Christian church in its attention to women's lost heritage in the Christian tradition. Through the efforts of these feminist theologians, Christian women are discovering and giving voice to their own experience of God and their yearning for mission.

Moreover, this concern for women's experience provides a message that is relevant to contemporary Christian women. As Charles Van Engen states, "The *Missio Dei* happens in specific places and times in our contexts. Its content, validity, and meaning are derived from Scripture; yet its action, significance, and transforming power happen in our midst" (Van Engen 1993a, 29). In that sense these efforts to respond to women's life experiences have been missiological. Moreover, the constant challenge to correct abusive relationships between men and women, both in the church and in society, should be interpreted as a remarkable contribution in realizing God's mission.

However, in spite of constant interaction with Scripture, for revisionists biblical tradition serves only as one of many sources, and then only because it is part of their own historical context, not because it is normative.

The basic frame of most of revisionist approach is that of liberation theology (Groothius 1994), with discrimination against women viewed as one form of oppression. Therefore, revisionist feminism does not see the central message of Christianity as repentance and forgiveness of sin through the grace of God in Christ. Rather, these women superimpose their own agenda on the Scriptures (Van Engen 1993b, 58). Revisionist feminism seems to use the biblical text only as a source for the struggle toward women's liberation.

Extreme position: Revolutionist feminism

Whereas many liberal feminists agree on selective use of biblical tradition, some feminists reject the entire Christian tradition. These women are called revolutionists or post-Christian feminists. Declaring that Christianity in its images, concepts and stories is hopelessly sexist, revolutionists propose to do away with the symbol of God as male. Revolutionist feminism sees women's experience as the only norm for and source of its theology.

An early proponent of this view, former Catholic nun Mary Daly, became its best-known representative when her book *The Church and the Second Sex* was published in 1968. A few years later, with *Beyond God the Father*, Daly finally separated herself from Christianity.

According to Daly, Christian religion at its core is incurably patriarchal, and the only solution for women is to leave Christianity in order to build a new community of sisterhood.[5] She states, "The entire conceptual systems of theology and ethics, developed under the conditions of patriarchy, have been the products of males and tend to serve the interests of sexist society" (Daly 1973, 4).

Many revolutionists agree with Daly that in order to develop a theology of women's liberation, women should reject the Bible. Moreover, these women seek to reconstruct the feminist church through rituals that incorporate the worship of an immanent goddess as the personification of true femaleness. Contemporary goddess worship symbolizes the emerging power of women and celebration of the powers of the female body (Christ 1983, 249). Revolutionists' emphasis on goddess religion is also related to their concern for ecology. According to these women's ecofeminism, whereas traditional religions failed to recognize our profound interconnection with all beings in the web of life, recovery of the goddess religion appreciates this connection (Christ 1985, 121; Ruether 1992).

The adoption of goddess religion in feminist theology and the new emphasis on a feminine God spread rapidly during the 1980s, encouraged by the leadership of theologians such as Carol Christ, Naomi Goldenberg, Merlin Stone, Christian Downing, Starhawk and Z. Budapest. During the 1990s many liberal feminists who once criticized the revolutionists' radical departure from Christian tradition found themselves drawn to this position. After the publication of *Sexism and God-Talk*, Ruether gradually stopped dealing with feminist issues in Christianity and began to concentrate on women's spirituality as reflected in goddess religions. These views are crystallized in her 1992 work, *Gaia and God*. Schussler Fiorenza also demonstrated a similar shift in *Jesus: Miriam's Child, Sophia's Prophet* (1995), in which she develops the divine *sophia* as the goddess symbol.

These women reacted to abusive hierarchical church structures by taking an extreme position, and in so doing provided a spiritual release for the deep rage of women who had reached the limit of their tolerance for patriarchy. They strongly affirmed women and women's role in a creative theology with an impressive literary output. Their strong emphasis on ecology and their acknowledgment of human life as part of the larger creation have provided a more holistic perspective of the human situation.

However, the revolutionist feminist position has serious weaknesses. First is its ahistorical and apolitical approach (Ruether 1983; Fiorenza 1983). A cultural and social feminist transformation of Western society must take into account the biblical story and the historical impact of the biblical tradition. Revolutionists' enemy-making approaches should be criticized. Making enemies of men would ultimately subvert the dream of a women's culture based on mutuality and altruism (Ruether 1983, 23). Their separatism sets up women as normative humanity, while regarding men as defective members of the human species (ibid.). Actually, the underlying assumption of women's superiority to men is no better than a male-oriented patriarchal understanding of women.

From an evangelical and missiological perspective, rejection of the Bible as God's Word precludes revolutionist feminism from being regarded as Christian. If the biblical text is given up, the fundamental motivation of mission practice for Christian women is at stake. As Van Engen states, missiology attempts "to allow Scripture to not only provide the foundational motivations for mission, but also to question, shape, guide and evaluate the missionary enterprise" (Van Engen 1996, 220). Therefore, a feminism that rejects a biblical basis conflicts with missiology at a fundamental level.

Another option: Evangelical feminism

Despite my identification with the desperate yearning for equal opportunities in Korean churches and society, I could not agree with the revisionist or revolutionist branches of Christian feminism. While both make positive contributions toward equal opportunities for women in God's mission I could not agree with revisionists' selective usage of the Scripture for their feminist vision, or with the revolutionists' total rejection of the Christian church. Indeed, as evangelical feminist Rebecca G. Groothius says, many conservative Korean women have been caught in the conflict between the feminist and the traditional views of women (Groothius 1994). However, when I first came in contact with the evangelical feminist position, it was like a light shining through thick, black clouds.

Evangelical feminism emerged during the 1970s at the same time the liberal feminists were experiencing tremendous growth. Letha Scanzoni and Nancy Hardesty's book, *All We're Meant to Be*, initiated evangelical participation in the women's movement (Scanzoni and Hardesty 1974; Conn 1984, 104). However, the major development of evangelical feminism has occurred since 1986, when evangelical feminists resigned from the Evangelical Women's Caucus International (EWCI), in protest against EWCI's affirmation of civil rights for gays and lesbians, and formed another biblical feminist group, Christians for Biblical Equality (CBE). The emerging CBE marks the major launching point of evangelical feminism, which stands against both liberal feminism and traditionalism. After formation of the CBE, liberal feminists moved rapidly to a post-Christian position, and one result of the extremes to which they have gone has been a backlash against liberal Christian feminism during the 1990s.

Another impulse toward the formation of the CBE was as a response to growing extremes of the traditionalist approach.

Presently, the CBE is the most representative body of the evangelical feminist position. This group includes people such as Catherine Kroeger, Aida B. Spencer, Gilbert Bilezikian, Ruth Tucker, David Scholer, Millard Erickson, Richard Mouw, Mary S. Van Leeuwen, Kari T. Malcolm, Leonard Swindler and Rebecca Groothuis.

Unlike other feminists and traditionalists who insist on the patriarchal nature of the Bible, evangelical feminists believe the Bible teaches equality between men and women. They believe that the Scripture teaches that the purpose of both women and men is to live to their full human potential for the glory of God. In this view there are no assigned places or prescribed roles for men or women, but persons of either gender are to be guided by their talents and interests in determining what they should do with their lives (Groothius 1994).

Evangelical feminists' most distinctive difference from liberal feminists (of either the revisionist or revolutionist persuasions) is in their use of the Scriptures. Whereas liberal feminists either reject the Bible entirely or seek to interpret it selectively from the perspective of women's experience, evangelical feminists hold to its divine inspiration and regard the Bible as normative (ibid.; Scanzoni and Hardesty 1974, 5). They are convinced that sexism in the church derived from the traditional practice of interpreting Scripture through the patriarchal lens of "men's experience," not directly from the Word of God. Moreover, the inequalities of societal and cultural institutions are the result of human sin (Groothius 1994, 109). Therefore, for evangelical feminists, the Bible teaches equality and mutual submission between male and female (ibid.).

According to feminist Elaine Storkey, evangelical feminism's emphasis on male-female equality springs from a concern for ministry rather than for self-assertion and self-fulfillment. In other words, the purpose of freeing women is to maximize a person's opportunities to serve God and to increase partnership in ministry. It is an other-centered focus, in contrast to the self-fulfillment focus of liberal feminism. Evangelical feminism works for the benefit of those who are most in need of liberation from inequality and injustice (Storkey 1985, 178).

Another important difference between evangelical feminism and liberal feminism is evident in the use of liberation theology. Whereas liberal feminists believe the central theme of the biblical message is found in the principles of social equality and liberation, evangelical feminists understand that the heart of the gospel is repentance and forgiveness of sin through the grace of God in Christ. Issues of social equality and liberation are implications of the gospel message but not its heart.

Evangelical feminism is still developing. However, it is influencing evangelical women who are seeking fuller participation in Christian ministry and in God's mission in the world. From a missiological perspective, I see evangelical feminism offering a biblical understanding of women's issues. This evangelical feminism must continue to be developed and supported by theologians. Furthermore, the work of evangelical feminism needs to extend beyond the academic realm and find its expression at the concrete ministry level. In this way a genuinely Christian sense of women's liberation will be actualized through women's participation in God's mission.

The search for a missiological feminism

As a Korean woman I am still searching for a missiological feminism. I am looking for a feminism that does not abandon the significance of the Bible as the Word of God or the lordship of Jesus Christ. At the same time, I seek a feminism that provides a framework for the fuller participation of women in God's mission, a feminism that will benefit the whole church and the whole mission of God. I envision a missiological feminism that will not abuse committed Christian women by demanding that they relinquish their desire to work in God's mission.

This missiological feminism needs to consider the issue of horizontal relationships between human beings and their connection to a vertical relationship with God. Missiologist Lesslie Newbigin claims that "neither freedom nor equality is fundamental; what is fundamental is relatedness. . . . The breakdown of relationships will destroy freedom and will destroy equality, but neither of these will be achieved by being sought for itself " (Newbigin 1986, 118–19).

Therefore, in missiological feminism we should accept that without genuine reconciliation with God we cannot anticipate any kind of reconciliation between human beings. A missiological feminism would acknowledge that the real transforming power of social justice and of solidarity with the oppressed comes from a genuine encounter with Jesus Christ. Moreover, missiological feminism must acknowledge that without a "oneness" in Christ between male and female, and without endeavors for regaining the image of God in human community, we cannot fully participate in God's mission in the world.

Finally, I seek a biblical missiological feminism that can be expressed and lived out in our Korean churches and mission organizations. It might look different from Western evangelical feminism, in that it must continually interact with our background of poverty and our heritage of Confucianism. Yet the gender issue is universal, and I believe a Korean feminist missiology would have much in common with its Western counterpart.

In spite of discouragement from my family and friends, I enrolled in a Korean seminary. As I had halfway expected, female students at the seminary experienced considerable discrimination. At the time, women in my denomination could not be ordained,[6] so even with a theological degree our options were limited. I remember the warning of a senior female colleague: "If you cannot survive here in the seminary, you will not be able to endure what you find in the real field of ministry."

She was right. Connected with the seminary, I worked as an intern for three years in a local church. There were several of us interns who were in the same seminary class. We were at the same level in our education and spiritual development, and we all felt called to active leadership in the church. Yet the members of the church treated us differently, granting male interns the respect they felt due a future minister. My male colleagues were even allowed to preach occasionally, an opportunity I never had in that church.

Yet I could not deny my call. It was from a sense of obedience that I went to seminary in Korea and that I am furthering my studies abroad. My faith in God's call gives me strength to persevere. I take courage from the stories of my sisters in the West and their search to fulfill their God-given ministries in the church. I sense that God is calling me to encourage other Korean women who have experienced the same struggles. I know God wants to use us in God's mission, and I know God will make a way.

Notes

[1] Valerie Saiving's now classic article, "The Human Situation: A Feminine View" (1960), was one of the first expressions of Christian feminism.

[2] Young also suggests these three persons for the most influential liberal feminists in her analysis of contemporary feminist literature (1990).

[3] Ruether uses "prophetic-messianic tradition" and "prophetic-liberating tradition" interchangeably.

[4] For her understanding of prophetic-messianic tradition, see also Ruether 1985, 117.

[5] For Daly, the community of sisterhood is the alternative structure of Christian church for women's liberation movement. This community is the generator

and life-center of feminist reality construction. This community becomes an exodus community, a sacred place, the bonding of the Be-ing, and the friendship of self-centering women opposing patriarch. It serves as an anti-church, cosmic covenant, and final cause (1978, 12).

⁶ That situation has since changed, and the denomination now ordains Korean women as ministers of the gospel.

References

Carr, Anne. 1988. *Transforming Grace*, San Francisco: Harper & Row.

Christ, Carol P. 1983. "Symbol of Goddess and God in Feminist Theology." *The Book of the Goddess Past the Present: An Introduction to Her Religion*, ed. Carl Olson. New York: Crossroad.

———. 1985. "Roundtable Discussion: What Are the Sources of My Theology?" *Journal of Feminist Studies in Religion* (Spring): 120–23.

Conn, Harvie M. 1984. "Evangelical Feminism: Some Bibliographical Reflections on the Contemporary State of the Union." *Westminster Theological Journal* 46: 104–24.

Daly, Mary. 1968. *The Church and the Second Sex*. New York: Harper & Row.

———. 1973. *Beyond God the Father: Toward a Philosophy of Women's Liberation*. Boston; Beacon.

———. 1978. *Gyn/ecology: The Metaethics of Radical Feminism*. Boston: Beacon.

Groothius, Rebecca Merrill. 1994. *Women Caught in the Conflict: The Culture War Between Traditionalism and Feminism*. Grand Rapids, Mich.: Baker Book House.

Newbigin, Lesslie. 1986. *Foolishness to the Greeks: The Gospel and Western Culture*. Grand Rapids, Mich.: Eerdmans.

Ruether, Rosemary Radford. 1983. *Sexism and God-Talk: Toward a Feminist Theology*. Boston: Beacon.

———. 1985. "Feminist Interpretation: A Method of Correlation." *Feminist Interpretation of the Bible*, ed. Letty Russell. Philadelphia: Westminster.

———. 1992. *Gaia and God: An Ecofeminist Theology of Earth Healing*. San Francisco: Harper Collins.

Russell, Letty. 1979. *The Future of Partnership*. Philadelphia: Westminster.

———. 1985. "Authority and the Challenge of Feminism Interpretation," *Feminist Interpretation of the Bible*, ed. Letty M. Russell, 137–46. Philadelphia: Westminster.

———. 1993. *Church in the Round: Feminist Interpretation of the Church*. Louisville, Ky.: John Knox/Westminster.

Saiving, Valerie. 1960. "The Human Situation: A Feminine View." *The Journal of Religions*, 40: 100–112.

Scanzoni, Dawson Letha, and Nancy Hardesty. 1974. *All We're Meant to Be: Biblical Feminism for Today*. Grand Rapids, Mich.: Eerdmans.

Schussler Fiorenza, Elisabeth. 1983. *In Memory of Her: A Feminist Theological Reconstruction of Christian Origins*. New York: Crossroad.

Storkey, Elaine. 1985. *What's Right with Feminism*. Grand Rapids, Mich.: Eerdmans.

Van Engen, Charles. 1993a. "The Relation of Bible and Mission in Mission Theology." *The Good News of the Kingdom: Mission Theology for the Third Millennium*, ed. Charles Van Engen, Dean Gilliland and Paul Pierson. Maryknoll, N.Y.: Orbis Books.

——. 1993b. "What Is Mission Theology?" Syllabus of "Biblical Foundations of Mission." Fuller Theological Seminary, Pasadena, California.

——. 1996. "Specialization/Integration in Mission Education." *Missiological Education for the Twenty-First Century: The Book, The Circle and the Sandals*, ed. J. Dudley Woodberry, Charles Van Engen and Edgar J. Elliston. Maryknoll, N.Y.: Orbis Books.

Young, Pamela Dickey. 1990. *Feminist Theology, Christian Theology: In Search of Method*. Minneapolis: Fortress Press.

17

The forgotten factor

The Holy Spirit and mission in Protestant missiological writings from 1945—95

ROBERT L. GALLAGHER

It was my first occasion to be with a particular small group of Christians, and I could not stop crying. I was fresh out of high school and was very aware that Australian men do not cry. After years of attending church I was listening for the first time to the mission story about God's love for me through Jesus Christ. As the leader shared from the Bible, I could feel the presence of God. The Spirit was in the room speaking to me. From that night I became aware of the Holy Spirit in mission.

During the next 20 years that house group grew into a thriving Pentecostal church. During that time I observed and experienced many aspects of the work of the Holy Spirit. However, I struggled with some of the pneumatology in Australian Pentecostal churches. It seemed to me that the emphasis in many churches was too self-centered and not kingdom-centered. Their interest was in the Spirit blessing their world and receiving what they could. There was little or no interest in how we might cooperate with the Spirit in what the Spirit was doing beyond the walls of our churches. There seemed to be little understanding of the work of the Holy Spirit in mission. My study of the Book of Acts showed

Robert L. Gallagher, a former Pentecostal executive pastor in Australia (1970–90) and theological educator in Papua New Guinea and the Solomon Islands, teaches theology, history and leadership studies in the Missions and Intercultural Studies program at Wheaton College Graduate School, Illinois. His doctoral work focused on Luke, the Holy Spirit and mission, an integrative analysis of selected Protestant writings in theology, mission and Lukan studies.

me that Luke stressed the work of the Holy Spirit as the key to the successful growth of Christianity. If the Spirit was so vital to the mission of the early church, then why was there so little understanding of this relationship among Australian Pentecostals?

My studies at Fuller Theological Seminary provided an opportunity to continue my quest for an understanding of the relationship of the Spirit and mission. One of the projects I undertook was to survey the ways missiologists have understood the work of the Holy Spirit and mission. First, let me explain the boundaries of what I did in the survey. I chose to study the English writings of the 70 most influential Protestant missiologists between 1945 and 1995. For my selection of missiologists I used the opinions of Gerald H. Anderson (1991, 165–72), David J. Bosch (1980, 29), Samuel Escobar (1991, 328), Wilbert R. Shenk (1987, 426–27) and Johannes Verkuyl (1987, 26–88) (see appendix of missiologists at the end of this chapter). Altogether, I read 59 books, 113 chapters in books and 295 journal articles from the selected missiologists, and recorded any mention they made of the Holy Spirit.

The summary of the trends observed in my survey are as follows. The 1950s saw little or no interest in the Holy Spirit. During the 1960s evangelicals considered the work of the Spirit in conversion. The next decade saw the influence of the Pentecostals. Their focus was on the gifts of the Spirit and church growth. Also in the 1970s liberation theology brought an awareness of the work of the Spirit in social change. In the 1980s the Charismatic focus on signs and wonders was prominent in the literature. In the 1990s the interest has been in spiritual warfare, a spin-off from this former trend.

Having completed the survey I felt disappointed. The 70 most influential missiologists in the last 50 years have largely neglected the work of the Holy Spirit. The Holy Spirit is a forgotten factor in mission. My questions on the relationship between mission and the Spirit's work are only partially answered. I believe missiologists need to consider seriously the relationship between the Holy Spirit and mission. Much yet remains to be done.

The work of the Holy Spirit

I have chosen to approach this survey by categorizing five functions of the Spirit's work observed in missiological writings. Following are my findings.

The Spirit and the world

There are three aspects used to distinguish the Spirit's working in the non-Christian world. These aspects are pre-conversion, conversion and post-conversion.

In pre-conversion the Holy Spirit is at work preparing people for the gospel. The Spirit is indispensable in missionary witness since the Spirit alone prepares the world to receive the church's message and "opens the hearts of hearers" (Boer 1961, 60, 205). In the view of D. T. Niles, the Spirit goes ahead of the church, "preparing a response to the Gospel," and then leads the church to those people and places already prepared (1962, 64). In a similar fashion, David J. Hesselgrave suggests that persuasion, to be genuine and effective, must be the work of the Spirit. "It is the Holy Spirit who takes the Word and makes it understandable and operative in the hearer" (1991, 89). The Dutch missionary and theologian Johan H. Bavinck says that the Holy Spirit first convicts the individual of their sins. Then, through that repentant person, the Spirit convicts the world by revealing the world's unwillingness to follow God (1960, 272).

A second way to distinguish the work of the Spirit in the world focuses on how people come to God. Latin American missiologist Orlando E. Costas refers to this work of the Holy Spirit as "transformation." The power of the Spirit works to transform persons and communities (1981, 7). As Alan R. Tippett puts it: "When the Holy Spirit falls on a group, that group becomes transformed. It is this new dynamic that gives the group outreach and makes it witness and leads to what Roland Allen called 'spontaneous expansion'" (1972, 95).

Lesslie Newbigin and Walter Holsten prefer the term *conversion* to *transformation*. They insist that only the Spirit can convert people (Newbigin 1979, 307; Holsten 1966, 456). It is "His work (only His) of bringing men and women to conversion and faith in Christ" (Newbigin 1982, 154). However, the work of the Spirit brings human beings to conversion through the action of the church—the faithful believers who are "partners in his tribulation" (Newbigin 1981, 255).[1]

A third group of missiologists concentrates on the fruits of conversion. Here the relationship between the world and the Spirit deals with people being filled with the Spirit,[2] thereby receiving freedom[3] and new life in the Spirit of God.[4] Such life in Christ can only be possible through the power of the Spirit.[5] Donald A. McGavran, for instance, says, "God wants all people to believe in Jesus Christ, become members of his body, be filled with the Holy Spirit and live in him. The Holy Spirit leads

Christians everywhere in this direction. Anything less than this is not biblical" (1986, 58).

The three aspects of the Spirit's working in the world showed that ecumenical and evangelical missiologists wrote on pre-conversion in the early 1960s. In the early 1980s evangelicals wrote on the Spirit and conversion, while writing on the post-conversion results of the work of the Holy Spirit occurred in the late 1980s, also by ecumenicals and evangelicals.

The Spirit and the church

Similarly, missiologists have developed different approaches in perceiving the function of the Spirit and the church. The first thing missiologists recognize is that the Spirit is the gift of God to the church.[6] At Pentecost, God gave the gift of the Spirit to communicate the gospel to all peoples. Newbigin puts it this way: "The gift of the Spirit is always for mission, is always the equipping of God's people for their witness to the world, exactly as the gift of the Spirit to Jesus at his baptism was his anointing for his mission as the Messiah" (1972, 46).

The next item is the various gifts that come from the Holy Spirit. For missiologists, manifestations of the Spirit center on evangelism. It is in the witness of the church that the gifts of the Spirit are prominent (Hodges 1977, 50; McGee 1988, 60). These gifts of witness are a promise to the church (Newbigin 1979, 308). To make disciples in the world, the church needs to discover the different gifts the Spirit has given and seek the Spirit's guidance how best to use these resources for evangelism (Costas 1976, 156). According to Arthur F. Glasser, this will allow the church to be obedient to cultural and redemptive mandates (1985b, 12).[7]

What are some of these gifts? Let us consider these gifts bestowed to the church by the Holy Spirit under three expressions—the initiation, nature and renewal of the church.

At Pentecost the church came into existence as a gift of the Spirit through the resurrected Lord Jesus (Gort 1980, 159). As a direct result of this visitation, the church became the dwelling place of the Holy Spirit, and was "continuously aware of the presence of the Spirit in her midst" (Boer 1961, 74).

The Spirit also imparts to the church the gifts of God's nature, namely, understanding, wisdom and power. If the church has an understanding of the signs of the kingdom of God, then it is only possible by the Spirit. Niles maintains these are the signs that need proclaiming to the world (1962, 63).[8]

A second gift of the nature of God to the church is wisdom. The church needs the wisdom of the Spirit to allow the presence and action of the Holy Spirit to do God's mission in our world. This is the prayerful call of Emilio Castro to the World Council of Churches (1990, 148).

Then there is the gift of power to the church. Missiologists mention this gift more than any other,[9] but usually within the context of witnessing.[10] The Spirit gives power to proclaim Jesus Christ "under all circumstances" (Niles 1962, 69). "It was for this task and privilege that the power of the Holy Spirit was promised and given" (Beaver 1961, 258).[11]

Harry R. Boer, in his book *Pentecost and Missions*, addressed himself to this issue (1961, 74, 109, 161). At Pentecost, he says, the Holy Spirit indwelt the church and became universal in operating power. The disciples did not carry out the Great Commission out of obedience but by the guidance and power of the Spirit. Boer argues that the dominant motif of Acts is the expansion of the faith. This occurs through missionary witness in the power of the Spirit.

Pentecostals refer to this gift of the Spirit's power as "the baptism of the Spirit." They believe it enables a person to do missionary work[12] as they are Spirit-directed and empowered (Hodges 1977, 38–39; 1972, 142). Walter J. Hollenweger comments on the baptism in the Spirit: "It is meant for the church on earth . . . without it . . . the church cannot be a missionary church" (1972, 332, 334).

The last gift of the Spirit for the church observed in this survey is that of renewal (McGavran 1972a, 18; Newbigin 1979, 307). Taylor speaks of the church being constantly renewed in its relationship with God as an activity of the Spirit (1980, 296). This renewal of the church's life is a gift of the Spirit and a vital component of our missionary proclamation. The Spirit brings renewal, which in turn brings missionary commitment (Castro 1981, 115). Evidence is in the emergence of new Christian communities "that claim a new awareness and a new presence of the Holy Spirit" (Castro 1990, 148–49).

The influence of the Pentecostal movement is evident in this function of the work of the Spirit. Writings on the gifts of the Spirit to the church span the 1970s. These include Pentecostal missiologists such as Melvin Hodges and his book *A Theology of the Church and Its Mission—A Pentecostal Perspective*, and Swiss missiologist Walter J. Hollenweger and his work *The Pentecostals*. In comparison, ecumenicals tended to write on the gift of renewal for the church in the 1980s.

The church and the Spirit

The Holy Spirit's work as observed in missiological writings is that between the church and the Spirit of God. It is the task of the Spirit to strengthen this relationship in obedience, righteousness and devotion.[13]

The Holy Spirit creates "the spirit of missionary devotion, perseverance and self-sacrifice" (Boer 1961, 205), and directs the Christian's life in willing obedience to God, rather than through religious observance (Niles 1962, 64).

By prayer the church expresses its dependence on the Spirit as it seeks God's guidance and will (Costas 1979, 34). This submission to the Spirit leads to worship, and it is through worship that the Holy Spirit meets with the church (Aagaard et al. 1979, 80–81). In the words of John V. Taylor, "It is through worship that we constantly renew, by the activity of the Holy Spirit, our Abba, relationship with the God of Jesus Christ" (1980, 296). Christian worship is to God through Christ in the Holy Spirit (Boer 1961, 61), and keeps the church in close relationship to God.[14] Costas puts it in the following words: "Mission is a comprehensive and dynamic process. It involves the missional action of the Spirit, moving to-and-fro in the world, pointing to the Lamb and eliciting responses of faith and adoration from the human family (1979, 89–90).

Prayer as an expression of our dependence on the Spirit for mission became prominent in the late 1970s and early 1980s. However, the function of the Spirit's work between the church and the Trinity is a neglected area, and the relationship between spirituality and mission deserves further study.

The church and the demonic

The fourth area of the work of the Spirit is action against demonic forces. Newbigin maintains that the effectiveness of "the communication of the Good News of the reign of God" depends on a number of factors. He mentions the sovereign work of the Holy Spirit and the church bearing "the scars of the conflict between the reign of God and the usurped power of Satan" (1981, 255). In the view of Costas, "The battle against the principalities and powers requires not technological know-how and speculative knowledge, but commitment to God's truth and righteousness, obedience to God's Word and sensitivity to God's Spirit" (1980, 403).

Two missiologists who have done the most writing in this area are C. Peter Wagner and Charles H. Kraft. It is Wagner's opinion that the Holy Spirit enabled Jesus to defeat demonic powers. Jesus cast out demons by "the finger of God" that is a metaphor for the Holy Spirit (cf. Matt. 12:28 and Luke 11:20). In turn, Jesus taught his disciples to do the same, relying on the same power of the Spirit (Wagner 1996, 134). Wagner then suggests that with the Holy Spirit, the Christian can do the same power ministry as Jesus and his disciples. Commenting on this "strategic-level spiritual warfare," Wagner writes:

Only the Holy Spirit can overcome the territorial spirits, destroy their armor and release the captives under their wicked control. Where is the Holy Spirit today? He is in us who have been born again and have asked God to fill us with the Holy Spirit. . . . One high-priority use of the Holy Spirit power by those who wish to serve Jesus in evangelism is to overcome whatever strongman may be holding a particular neighborhood or city or people group in spiritual captivity. Nothing I know of could be more important for winning the lost (1996, 152).

In a similar vein, Kraft believes that Jesus gave believers authority to minister in the power of the Holy Spirit. This involves not only preaching the gospel, but also demonstrating the Good News through healing and demon deliverance. Jesus did not use his divine attributes on earth, but relied on the insight of the Spirit. This is also the way Christ wants his followers to continue his ministry on earth today. As Kraft puts it:

He [Jesus] did his works as a human being empowered by the Holy Spirit. When Jesus left, then, he promised the same Holy Spirit to his followers to enable us to do the same and greater works than he did. As with Jesus, then, the Holy Spirit is our Source of power and Jesus himself our Authority-giver and our model (1995, 96).

The 1990s have seen a number of evangelicals focus on the church and the demonic. This area reminds us that the ministry of the Spirit is one of personal sovereignty. The Spirit's mission is to glorify Christ, to make Christ known and to bring people into fellowship with Christ. The Holy Spirit is not a reservoir of power on which we may draw. We cannot control the Spirit.

The church and the world

Through my survey I discovered three positions in considering the function of the Holy Spirit's working in the church to reach the world. First, I will discuss different terms missiologists employ to describe the works of the Holy Spirit in mission. Next, I will consider the importance of the guidance of the Spirit in missions. Finally, I will consider the results of missions in the world, such as church growth and social change.

Some terms used by missiologists to describe the works of the Spirit of God in sharing the gospel with the world are *communication*,[15] *evangelism*[16] and *mission*.[17] However, the most common term used is *witness*.[18] The Spirit witnesses through the gospel that in Christ, God has reconciled the world to himself.[19] The church acts as a witness only because the Spirit is present with it. Witness is not so much an activity of the church as it is an activity of the Spirit.

Missiologists who use the word *witness* tend to have different definitions for the word. Newbigin defines witness to mean the church's identification with the suffering of the world that occurs when "the church is being faithful under pressure" (1979, 308).[20] This action of the Spirit causes change in both the church and the world. Costas understands witness to be God's people trusting in the transforming action of the Spirit in the world (1981, 7), whereas Boer sees the witness of the Spirit as the verbal proclamation of the church (1961, 59, 63). It is the Spirit that "must establish the spoken word" (ibid., 205).

Many missiologists recognize that the guidance of the Holy Spirit is essential for the church to do Christ's mission in the world (Orchard 1965, 87; McClung 1986, 161). The Spirit "is seeking to lead the church in its mission" (Niles 1962, 64), and the Christian community needs to seek the Spirit's leadership if there is to be any success in the church's mission (Hodges 1977, 142). Mission is foremost a work of the Holy Spirit. At the same time, it is a work requiring participation of the people of God.[21] Mission depends upon the integrity of the witness of the church and its faithfulness. As Wilhelm Andersen puts it, "Mission is at the same time the work of God in the world which he shares with men as his instruments . . . bestowing upon them and honoring them with his Spirit to be his fellow workers" (1961, 304).

Newbigin sees in the Acts of the Apostles a model for the church of today. The Spirit always led and the early church followed. In this way the church "confesses that the Spirit is the sovereign, the only true controller and strategist of the mission of the church" (1962, 8). Newbigin compares the church of today with the church of Acts and suggests our priorities need adjusting. He asks: "Why is it we have created in so many situations a picture of the work of missions which seems to be centered more in the office than in the sanctuary, more in the program than in prayer, more in administering than in ministering?" (ibid.).

Costas believes that through prayer the church obtains the guidance of the Spirit in preaching and teaching. This motivates believers for witness (1979, 34). Also, through prayer, the church discovers the most effective way to use the gifts of the church for evangelism (1976, 156). Costas uses the occasion of the separation of Saul and Barnabas from the Antioch church in Acts 13 to reinforce the importance of prayer to reveal the plans of the Spirit (1986, 466).

Two results of the work of the Spirit in the world are church growth and social change. Some missiologists focus on the fact that the Holy Spirit causes church growth (see Glasser 1973, 453). The Pentecostal mission historian Gary McGee attributes the mission success of the Assemblies of God to the work of the Spirit in church growth: "It [the Assemblies of God] has successfully demonstrated that the pneumatological dynamic of its mission theology is relevant for twentieth-century church planting" (1986, 169; also 1988, 60). In a similar vein McGavran of the Church Growth movement acknowledges that the Spirit grants growth, yet recognizes that the Spirit uses the complex world of our society to achieve God's will (1972b, 459–60).

One cause for the growth of the church is the Holy Spirit's demonstration of healing power. Missiologists who believe in divine healing for today operate under the theological assumption that Jesus performed miracles through the Holy Spirit. In his book *How to Have a Healing Ministry*, Wagner states his theological premise: "The Holy Spirit was the source of all of Jesus' power during his earthly ministry. Jesus exercised no power of or by himself. We today can expect to do the same or greater things than Jesus did because we have been given access to the same power source" (1988, 114).

For this group of missiologists, doing the work of Jesus in today's world involves healing the sick through the supernatural power of the Holy Spirit. In the 1980s Wagner studied how signs and wonders related to the growth of the church in the past and how they would likely affect the church in the future. He examined various models of power and came to the conclusion that, overall, power evangelism resulted in the most vigorous growth for the church (1986b, 36–37).

Another group of missiologists views mission as causing political and economical change. This, they believe, will not come from radical preaching, but rather from the Spirit's involvement with the faithful poor (Taylor 1971, 338). The people of God, filled with the Holy Spirit, will cause transformation in their society. Peter Beyerhaus comments on this approach: "People truly indwelt by the Spirit of the gospel of liberty work for the elimination of inhuman structures and principles and for a reconstruction of society which does justice to the dignity of humanity for which Christ sacrificed His life" (1972, 56).

The guidance of the Spirit in mission is important throughout the writings of Protestant missiologists. Different groups maintain different perspectives on the Spirit's leading. Ecumenicals wrote on social change in the early 1970s while evangelicals in the same decade studied church growth. In the 1980s, Charismatics concentrated on signs and wonders as a means to church growth.

The missiology of the Holy Spirit

My survey of missiological writing on the Spirit over the past 50 years reveals that, apart from Boer and Taylor, little significant work has been done. The statement of the Ephesian disciples to Paul echoes throughout this study: "We have not even heard that there is a Holy Spirit" (Acts 19:2).

Why the silence? It could be argued that the selected missiologists have focused their energy on other important areas. This may be so, but many of the authors do not even mention the Holy Spirit. Perhaps this surprising dearth in missiology comes from an attitude that relegates the responsibility for the study of the Spirit to systematic theologians. Indeed, for the last 30 years the study of mission has centered on anthropology and the social sciences, to the neglect of mission theology (see Hiebert 1994, 9–10).

Another possibility is that Western missiologists have had a hermeneutic of cynicism toward issues of the Spirit. If it is not in prepositional form in the Bible, then it is not considered a genuine work of the Spirit. Narrative theology from the Scripture and life's experiences are of little importance. Our appreciation of the work of the Spirit may change as more and more majority-world missiologists enter the academic arena. Perhaps the appearance of this new era in mission, with the majority-world church leading the way, will produce a missiology more aware of the work of the Holy Spirit. Even more surprising is the lack of Pentecostal writing on the Spirit. Being too busy in doing mission is a poor excuse for not being in reflection, for in reflection comes a greater understanding and the accompanying power of the Spirit to do the Spirit's mission. It seems that Australian Pentecostals are not the only Pentecostals struggling to articulate their pneumatology.

There are many areas that need further study in the missiology of the Spirit. A reading of the book of Acts reveals two main categories. The Holy Spirit worked in the disciples of the early church to bring: joy in the midst of persecution (5:41), paradigm shifts from monocultural to cross-cultural perspective,[22] boldness in preaching (4:29–31), contextualization of the message,[23] selection and training of leadership (6:1–7; 13:1–4; 20:28), planning and development of the church (15:28; 16:6–7) and deep spirituality (Acts 1:14; 3:1; 4:31; 6:4; 8:15; 10:1; 13:3). On the other hand, the Spirit also worked in non-Christians through the gifts of the Spirit (1 Cor. 12:1–11) to empower the weak and lowly (Acts 1:13–14; 2:17–18; 9:32–42; 16:14–15, 25–34) as well as to create a sense of awe and wonder (Acts 2:6–7, 12; 3:10–11) through the fear of God

(Acts 5:5, 11) and the joy of the gospel (Acts 8:8). These are some areas that Protestant missiology has not considered seriously as works of the Spirit in mission. It is time for missiologists to fill in the hole.

It has been more than 25 years since I experienced the initial mission of the Holy Spirit in my life. My understanding of the blessed Spirit has grown yet is no more precious than my first experience of the Spirit's presence sitting in the lounge room of the home group with tears flowing down my face. My desire is to see people experience the eternal presence of the Spirit in their lives. How can we intentionally foster the influence of the Holy Spirit to mobilize the churches in mission in the world? To do this, the discipline of missiology and the people of the church need to grow in their understanding of the person and work of the Holy Spirit. In this way we can better recognize and cooperate with what the Spirit of Jesus is already doing in his kingdom.

Appendix of missiologists

Aagaard, Johannes
Andersen, Wilhelm
Anderson, Gerald H.
Arias, Mortimer
Bavinck, Johan H.
Beaver, R. Pierce
Beyerhaus, Peter
Blauw, Johannes
Boer, Harry R.
Bosch, David, J.
Castro, Emilio
Costas, Orlando E.
Davies, John Gordon
De Santa Ana, Julio
Devanandan, Paul David
Escobar, Samuel
Forman, Charles W.
Freytag, Walter
Gensichen, Hans-Werner
Glasser, Arthur F.
Gort, Jerald D.
Hallencreutz, Carl F.
Hayward, Victor E. W.
Hesselgrave, David J.
Hodges, Melvin L.
Hoekendijk, Johannes C.
Hogg, William Richey

Hollenweger, Walter J.
Holsten, Walter
Horner, Norman A.
Ilogue, Edmund
Johnston, Arthur P.
Kane, J. Herbert
Koyama, Kosuke
Kraemer, Hendrik
Kraft, Charles H.
Latourette, Kenneth Scott
Margull, Hans-Jochen
Mbiti, John S.
McClung, L. Grant Jr.
McGavran, Donald A.
McGee, Gary B.
Miguez Bonino, Jose
Mott, John
Myklebust, Olav Guttorm
Neill, Stephen C.
Newbigin, Lesslie
Nida, Eugene A.
Niles, Daniel T.
Orchard, Ronald K.
Padilla, C. Rene
Rossel, Jacques
Samartha, Stanley J.
Sawyerr, Harry

Scherer, James A.

Shenk, Wilbert R.

Song, Choan-Seng

Spindler, Marc R.

Stott, John R. W.

Sundkler, Bengt G. M.

Taylor, John V.

Thomas, M. M.

Tippett, Alan R.

Van Engen, Charles E.

Verkuyl, Johannes

Visser 't Hooft, W. A.

Wagner, C. Peter

Walls, Andrew F.

Warren, Max A. C.

Winter, Ralph D.

Notes

[1] See also Newbigin 1979, 307: "It is the Spirit who converts, not the Church. Where, then, does the Church come into the picture? . . . At the point where it is on trial for its faith, at the point where it confesses the sole Lordship of Jesus in the face of the overwhelming power of that which denies it, at the point—therefore—where it bears the marks of the cross."

[2] Tippett 1972, 99–100; also see Boer 1961, 96–97; and Glasser 1985a, 12.

[3] Castro 1990, 149 and Aagaard 1982, 276.

[4] See Newbigin 1970, 72; Niles 1962, 69; McGavran 1965, 459; and Boer 1961, 96–97.

[5] Bosch 1987, 100; also see Ilogu 1964, 276.

[6] See Aagaard et al. 1979, 80–81; Castro 1990, 148–49; Beaver 1968, 43; and Tippett 1972, 91–100.

[7] According to Niles, the Holy Spirit then gives to people the gifts of repentance and faith to believe what they have heard proclaimed (1962, 69).

[8] Aagaard calls this an "eschatological and pneumatological urgency" and adds: "Most of us do agree that missiology is a part of eschatology and that missions are pneumatological realities and therefore that missions have a peculiar urgency as their nature" (1974, 20).

[9] Castro 1990, 148; see Escobar 1987, 534–535; Beaver 1961, 265; McGavran 1972b, 106; and Boer 1961, 59.

[10] See Newbigin, who says that there "is a life in the fellowship of the Father and the Son through the power of the Spirit" (1970, 72). Furthermore, Costas suggests that to motivate the church for this evangelism there needs to be a dynamic presence of the Holy Spirit. It is this empowering presence of the Spirit in the preaching and teaching of the churches' leadership that will motivate believers for witness (1979, 34).

[11] Also see Beaver 1968, 43, and 1979, 95–96; Boer 1961, 59, 61, 205; and Glasser 1974, 8.

[12] See McGee 1988, 58 and Hodges (1977, 19), where he writes, "The Holy Spirit dwells in the Church and becomes the source of power and equipment for missions as believers receive His fullness."

[13] McGavran describes what he sees as "the rising tide of revival and renewal." He states, "In answer to earnest prayer for in-filling, the Holy Spirit is descend-

ing on His church and empowering it to be righteous, do justice and rejoice in the Lord" (1972a, 18).

[14] Beaver 1961, 265; also see Glasser 1985a, vii, and McClung 1990, 153. Both observe that the Pentecostals believe that the presence of the Spirit moves the church closer to Christ.

[15] See Newbigin 1972, 46; 1979, 312; 1981, 255; and Boer 1961, 96–97.

[16] See Costas 1979, 34, and McGee 1986, 169.

[17] Bosch 1993, 184–185; McGee 1986, 166; Hodges 1977, 35.

[18] See Costas 1979, 34 and Tippett 1972, 95.

[19] See Newbigin 1979, 308 and 1980, 158; Beaver 1961, 258 and 1979, 95–96.

[20] Also see Newbigin 1980, 159–160 and 1981, 255. Cf. Beaver 1953b, 2.

[21] Hesselgrave writes: "The Holy Spirit works in and through the missionary to bring unbelievers to repentance and faith" (1991, 638). Cf. Wagner 1986a, 64. Also see Beaver 1968, 31–32, and 1953a, 1; McGavran 1986, 58; and Hodges 1972, 142–43. The Spirit "directs the campaign in which the Christian is a participant," writes Niles (1962, 64). Further, McClung discusses a person in prayer hearing "the Holy Spirit whisper to his heart," the exact location of the place he is to share the gospel (1988, 2–6).

[22] Acts 1:6–8; 2:21; 3:25; 4:24; 8:14–25; 9:43; 10:44–48; 11:15–18; 15:6–11; Gal. 2:11–21.

[23] See Peter's speeches in Acts 2:14–40; 3:12–26 and Paul's speeches in Acts 13:16–41; 14:15–17; 17:22–31.

References

Aagaard, Johannes. 1974. "Mission After Uppsala 1968." In *Mission Trends No. 1*, ed. Gerald H. Anderson and Thomas F. Stransky, 13–21. Grand Rapids, Mich.: Eerdmans; New York: Paulist Press.

———. 1982. "The Soft Age Has Come." *Missiology: An International Review* 10, no. 3: 263–77.

Aagard, Johannes, D. P. Niles, and Mark Albrecht. 1979. "New Religious Movements." *Missiology: An International Review* 7, no. 1: 77–81.

Andersen, Wilhelm. 1961. "Further Toward a Theology of Mission." In *The Theology of the Christian Mission*, ed. G. H. Anderson, 300–313. New York: McGraw Hill.

Anderson, Gerald. 1991. "Mission Research, Writing and Publishing: 1971–1991." *International Bulletin of Missionary Research* 15, no. 4: 165–72.

Bavinck, J. H. 1960. *An Introduction to the Science of Missions*, trans. David Hugh Freeman. Philadelphia: Presbyterian and Reformed Publishing.

Beaver, R. Pierce. 1953a. "Race and Nationality in North American Foreign Missions." *Occasional Bulletin* 4, no. 11: 1–5.

———. 1953b. "The Worldwide Christian Community in 1952." *Occasional Bulletin* 4, no. 4: 1–4.

————. 1961. "The Apostolate of the Church." In *The Theology of the Christian Mission*, ed. Gerald H. Anderson, 258–68. New York: McGraw-Hill.

————. 1968. *The Missionary Between the Times*. Garden City, N.Y.: Doubleday.

————. 1979. "The Legacy of Rufus Anderson." *Occasional Bulletin* 3, no. 3: 94–97.

Beyerhaus, Peter. 1972. "Mission, Humanization and the Kingdom." *Crucial Issues in Missions Tomorrow*, ed. D. A. McGavran, 54–76. Chicago: Moody Press.

Boer, Harry R. 1961. *Pentecost and Missions*. Grand Rapids, Mich.: Eerdmans.

Bosch, David. 1980. *Witness to the World*. Atlanta, Ga.: John Knox Press.

————. 1987. "Evangelism: Theological Currents and Cross-currents Today." *International Bulletin of Missionary Research* 11, no. 3: 98–103.

————. 1993. "Reflections on Biblical Models of Mission." In *Towards the Twenty-first Century in Christian Mission*, ed. J. M. Phillips and R. T. Coote, 175–92. Grand Rapids, Mich.: Eerdmans.

Castro, Emilio. 1981. "The Bible in the Mission of the Church." *International Review of Mission* 70, no. 279: 113–18.

————. 1990. "Mission in the 1990s." *International Bulletin of Missionary Research* 14, no. 4: 146–49.

Costas, Orlando E. 1976. "Churches in Evangelistic Partnership." In *The New Face of Evangelicalism: An International Symposium on the Lausanne Covenant*, ed. C. Rene Padilla, 143–61. Downers Grove, Ill.: InterVarsity Press.

————. 1979. *The Integrity of Mission: The Inner Life and Outreach of the Church*. San Francisco: Harper & Row.

————. 1980. "The Whole World for the Whole Gospel." *Missiology: An International Review* 8, no. 4: 395–405.

————. 1981. "Church Growth as a Multidimensional Phenomena: Some Lessons from Chile." *International Bulletin of Missionary Research* 5, no. 1: 2–8.

————. 1986. "The Mission of Ministry." *Missiology: An International Review* 14, no. 4: 463–72.

Escobar, Samuel. 1987. "Recruitment of Students for Mission." *Missiology: An International Review* 15, no. 4: 529–45.

————. 1991. "Evangelical Theology in Latin America: The Development of a Missiological Christology." *Missiology: An International Review* 19, no. 3: 313–32.

Glasser, Arthur F. 1973. "Timeless Lessons from the Western Missionary Penetration of China." *Missiology: An International Review* 1, no. 4: 443–64.

————. 1974. "What Is 'Mission' Today?" In *Mission Trends No. 1*, ed. G. A. Anderson and T. F. Stransky, 5–8. Grand Rapids, Mich.: Eerdmans; New York: Paulist Press.

————. 1985a. "Foreword." In *The Third Force in Missions: A Pentecostal Contribution to Contemporary Mission Theology*, ed. Paul A. Pomerville. Peabody, Mass.: Hendrickson.

————. 1985b. "The Evolution of Evangelical Mission Theology Since World War II." *International Bulletin of Missionary Research* 9, no. 1: 9–13.

Gort, Jerald D. 1980. "Contours of the Reformed Understanding of a Christian Mission: An Attempt at Delineation." *Occasional Bulletin* 4, no. 4: 156–60.

Hesselgrave, David. 1991. *Communicating Christ Cross-Culturally: An Introduction to Missionary Communication.* Second edition. Grand Rapids, Mich.: Zondervan.

Hiebert, Paul G. 1994. *Anthropological Reflections on Missiological Issues.* Grand Rapids, Mich.: Baker Books.

Hodges, Melvin L. 1972. "A Pentecostal's View of Mission Strategy." In *The Eye of the Storm: The Great Debate in Mission,* ed. D. A. McGavran, 142–49. Waco, Tex.: Word.

———. 1977. *A Theology of the Church and Its Mission: A Pentecostal Perspective.* Springfield, Mo.: Gospel Publishing House.

Hollenweger, Walter J. 1972. *The Pentecostals: The Charismatic Movement in the Churches,* trans. R. A. Wilson. Minneapolis: Augsburg.

Holsten, Walter. 1966. "The Muslim Presence in the West." *International Review of Mission* 55: 448–56.

Ilogu, Edmund. 1964. "The Contribution of the Church to National Unity in Nigeria." *International Review of Mission* 53: 272–80.

Kraft, Charles H. 1995. "'Christian Animism' or God-Given Authority?" In *Spiritual Power and Missions: Raising the Issues,* ed. E. Rommen, 88–136. Pasadena, Calif.: Wm. Carey Library.

McClung, Grant. 1986. "Explosion, Motivation and Consolidation: The Historical Anatomy of the Pentecostal Missionary Movement." *Missiology: An International Review* 14, no. 2: 159–72.

———. 1988. "Theology and Strategy of Pentecostal Missions." *International Bulletin of Missionary Research* 12, no. 1: 2–6.

———. 1990. "Mission in the 1990s." *International Bulletin of Missionary Research* 14, no. 4: 152–57.

McGavran, Donald A. 1965. "Wrong Strategy, the Real Crisis in Missions." *International Review of Mission* 54: 451–61.

———. 1972a. "Introduction." In *Crucial Issues in Missions Tomorrow,* ed. D. A. McGavran, 5–29. Chicago: Moody Press.

———. 1972b. "Wrong Strategy: The Real Crisis in Mission." In *The Eye of the Storm: The Great Debate in Mission,* ed. D. A. McGavran, 97–107. Waco, Tex.: Word.

———. 1986. "My Pilgrimage in Mission." *International Bulletin of Missionary Research* 10, no. 2: 53–58.

McGee, Gary B. 1986. "Assemblies of God Mission Theology: A Historical Perspective." *International Bulletin of Missionary Research* 10, no. 4: 166–70.

———. 1988. "The Azusa Street Revival and Twentieth-Century Missions." *International Bulletin of Missionary Research* 12, no. 2: 58–61.

Newbigin, Lesslie. 1962. "Bringing Our Missionary Methods Under the Word of God." *Occasional Bulletin* 13, no. 11: 1–9.

———. 1970. "Co-operation and Unity." *International Review of Mission* 59, no. 233: 67–71.

———. 1972. *Journey into Joy.* Madras: Christian Literature Society and the Indian Society for Promoting Christian Knowledge.

———. 1979. "Context and Conversion." *International Review of Mission* 68, no. 271: 301–12.

———. 1980. "Common Witness and Unity." *International Review of Mission* 69, no. 274: 158–60.

———. 1981. "Integration–Some Reflections 1981." *International Review of Mission* 70, no. 280: 247–55.

———. 1982. "Lesslie Newbigin Replies." *International Bulletin of Missionary Research* 6, no. 4: 154–55.

Niles, Daniel T. 1962. *Upon the Earth: The Mission of God and the Missionary Enterprise of the Churches.* New York: McGraw-Hill.

Orchard, Ronald K. 1965. "Joint Action for Mission: Its Aim, Implications and Method." *International Review of Mission* 54: 81–94.

Shenk, Wilbert R. 1987. "Mission in Transition: 1972–1987." *Missiology: An International Review* 15, no. 4: 419–30.

Taylor, John V. 1971. "Small Is Beautiful." *International Review of Mission* 60, no. 239: 328–38.

———. 1980. "The Lord's Prayer: The Church Witnesses to the Kingdom." *International Review of Mission* 69, no. 275: 295–97.

Tippett, Alan R. 1972. "The Holy Spirit and Responsive Populations." In *Crucial Issues in Missions Tomorrow*, ed. Donald A. McGavran, 77–101. Chicago: Moody Press.

Verkuyl, Johannes. 1987. *Contemporary Missiology: An Introduction*, trans. Dale Cooper. Grand Rapids, Mich.: Eerdmans.

Wagner, C. Peter. 1986a. "A Vision for Evangelizing the Real America." *International Bulletin of Missionary Research* 10, no. 2: 59–64.

———. 1986b. "The Church Growth Movement After Thirty Years." In *Church Growth: State of the Art*, ed. C. P. Wagner, 21–39. Wheaton, Ill.: Tyndale House.

———. 1988. *How To Have a Healing Ministry Without Making Your Church Sick.* Ventura, Calif.: Regal Books.

———. 1996. *Confronting the Powers: How the New Testament Church Experienced the Power of Strategic-Level Spiritual Warfare.* Ventura, Calif.: Regal Books.

18

Missiology and the Internet

Facing the faceless frontier

SHAWN B. REDFORD

My first "computer" had no electronic parts. It was a simple adding machine that used mechanical gearing to come up with the correct value. It even had a "10s" button so that it could add two-digit numbers! This toy was made obsolete by a US$45 calculator that had less functionality than today's US$5 models. Eventually I had the chance to program a computer that had an unprecedented 16 kilobytes of memory and used a standard audio cassette tape to store the program. I write this chapter on a computer that has 1,000 times more memory, with a tape drive that acts as the backup system for 1.5 gigabytes of hard-drive storage. No doubt some readers will find even this obsolete.

I contrast this with my experience among the Maasai people of central Africa. Western technology was largely absent from the village where I lived as a short-term missionary for two years. Flies hovered everywhere except inside the mud huts where smoke from a continuously smoldering fire drove them away.

In spite of their living conditions, there was one thing I could not help but envy in the Maasai way of life. These people had a level of relational interaction unlike anything I had ever experienced in the United

---

Shawn Redford has worked in engineering and computer consulting for more than eight years. He has cross-cultural mission experience in tribal ministry in Africa. Redford received his B.A. in mechanical engineering from Purdue University and his M.A. in intercultural studies from Fuller Theological Seminary's School of World Mission. He is currently involved in the Ph.D. program in Fuller's School of World Mission.

States. They spent their days in community living, forming relational bonds. Every evening, when enough firewood had been gathered and the cows had come back from grazing, the village's gates closed and everyone was part of a community.

Recently a television advertisement for a telecommunications company showed a small group of Maasai men huddled around a computer. One of them was surfing the Internet, and my two worlds came together.

But the spheres of technology and interpersonal relationships are coming together in more profound ways as computers are becoming more relational, providing a place where people interact with one another through the medium of the machine. I am speaking of the new culture of virtual reality. We stand at the threshold of a new frontier in mission—a "place" where human interaction is electronically simulated and physical proximity has little bearing. Now we must consider the implications of witnessing within technology, rather than merely using technology for witness.

The Christian community must approach this new frontier missiologically, applying what we have learned in the past from experiences in new cultures and in new eras. At the same time, we know that this new frontier will redefine our perception of "reality," and in doing so it will test and stretch the foundations of missiological theory and practice.

Facing the reality of virtual contexts

With conventional cable television and Internet services being combined in add-on units, and monthly rates equal to current cable television rates, computer technology is becoming a standard part of middle-class North America, as well as expanding around the world.[1] Today's computer age represents an entirely new context of mission, a new frontier that will challenge our deepest assumptions and stretch the most familiar methodologies of missiology.

The "organic" computer

Until recently, computers have been largely perceived as machines, providers of information. Increasingly they are taking on a new social significance. Sherry Turkle, a clinical psychologist and leading expert in the field of Internet sociology, writes: "A decade ago, when I first called the computer a second self, these identity-transforming relationships were almost always one-to-one, a person alone with a machine. This is no longer the case. . . . Increasingly, when we step through the looking glass [computer screen], other people are there as well" (Turkle 1995, 9).

Most people think of "information" when considering the Internet. However, the Internet is quickly filling up with real people who are making this medium their preferred means of social existence. These people live in cyber-societies, with worlds made up of interactive communication between computers. Given the existing text-based communication of on-line chatting, such as the Internet Relay Chat (IRC),[2] as well as the role-playing games of the multi-user domains (MUDs), most of these people appear as a set of faceless thoughts and ideas.

Technology already exists to allow these people to use video and voice conferencing, but it is equally probable that they will represent themselves using virtual reality in the future, or some combination of the two. Virtual reality is the ability to use computers to simulate nearly every human activity, and it is especially strong in simulating human communication (Heim 1993, vii). This means that people can appear in almost any form they wish. For many on-line users, however, it is not technology that attracts them to these virtual worlds. Rather, it is the psychological and sociological dynamics that cause them to spend many hours on-line in virtual relationships.

The missional challenge

This technology presents the missionary community with many new challenges, one of which will be our response to those who choose to exist in virtual worlds. The church will have to define its role regarding evangelism and mission in virtual contexts. In this we will face a great number of questions. Are virtual contexts psychologically or spiritually unhealthy? Are there good uses of virtual reality? Should the church attempt to bring those who spend most of their time in virtual contexts into the real world? If so, will future missiologists lament this activity and equate it to Western colonialization? Will churches exist and grow in virtual environments? How will "real" be defined in light of virtual existence?

The Internet will continue its rapid rate of growth.[3] Given the likely future of Internet communication, we can expect these virtual worlds to continue to develop. Therefore, another issue Christian missions will most likely face is whether or not to participate in virtual missionary activity.

The possibility of doing mission in virtual contexts opens up a whole new set of questions. Is it necessary to witness in person? Is mission more than communication of the gospel? Will the use of the Internet for mission practice emphasize a breach between social action and evan-gelism, because we cannot be physically involved in virtual contexts? Can holistic mission take place in a virtual context?[4]

Some predict that the 1990s will be viewed historically as the era when the Western world "got wired."[5] Cyber-sociologists see a shift from the modernist worldview characterized by linear, logical, hierarchical and concrete values, to a postmodern information age that has a worldview which is decentered, fluid, nonlinear and opaque (Turkle 1995, 17). In mission theory and practice, we are facing a context unlike any other in human history.

The virtual frontier

The once unimaginable has now become possible. Using present-day software, "[you can] create immersive virtual worlds, with sound, hypertext, 2D and 3D graphics. You can create an avatar (a 3D image of yourself), wander around a virtual space chatting with people, and click on doors to go places."[6] Although today's text-based interface of tech-nology is unentertaining in itself, the attraction is in realizing that the interface is communicating the thoughts and ideas of other people. Cur-rently, thousands of these discussion areas exist, with as many as 50 people chatting in a single area. The number of users is unknown, but it is in the order of tens of thousands.

Social behavior on the Internet

I have used the Inter-Relay Chat in order to gain a greater understand-ing of the religious beliefs of various groups. I find myself fascinated by the behavior that people exhibit in this virtual context. Frequently, some-one will join a discussion area with the intent of becoming an antagonist, swearing until a moderator kicks the person out. The more skillful of these antagonists know just enough about the beliefs of a group to make light of them.

The most striking part of this behavior, however, is how it differs from the real world. A comparable situation would take place if someone barged into a real church service and began yelling obscenities. Although possible, this would be highly unusual, due to social and cultural norms that define right and wrong.

In virtual worlds, however, these same cultural norms do not exist. People have less concern for the consequences of their actions due to their anonymity. The worst that can happen is that they will receive some electronic hate-mail that they can discard or reply to even more spitefully. This does not mean social norms do not exist on the Internet, but these norms can be quite different from the real world.

Human sexuality on the Internet

The area of human sexuality provides one example of changing social norms. It is no secret that the Internet has become a prolific means of distributing pornography. Sexual discussions on the Internet are very common. Many people join chat areas and engage in erotic conversation while exchanging pornographic photos. This is called cyber-sex or net-sex. Because this is done on the Internet, people have little concern for the consequences of their behavior.

When asked for the rationale behind choosing this behavior over human contact, those involved in cyber-sex gave the following response:

> The most obvious answer would be safety. Net sex is the ultimate safe sex, and I don't just mean safety from HIV and other transmitted diseases. Net sex leaves us safe from commitment, from entanglement, from having others witness our embarrassment. . . . If anything goes wrong, if an affair turns ugly or inconvenient, we can just switch it off (Moore 1995, 171–72).

The future will undoubtedly see an increase in virtual sexual activity. Bill Gates, chairman of Microsoft Corporation, says, "If historical patterns are a guide, a big early market for advanced virtual-reality documents will be virtual sex" (Gates 1995, 133). It will become possible for a person's primary experiences of sexual intimacy to exist solely between that person and a computer. Research efforts in this area have been underway since 1990 (Rheingold 1992, 347). In combination with existing virtual reality equipment, people will be able to use computers to engage in sexual activity with others or with pre-recorded sexual experiences. People will be lured by advertising that promotes sexual encounters with big name stars or sex symbols. It is easy to see how cyber-sex would soon become cyber-prostitution. In addition, there will most likely come a point when touch (or tactile sensory perception and response) will become a common part of the virtual experience.

We are naive if we are not theologically and missiologically prepared for a future that includes mass marketing of devices designed to stimulate human beings sexually. The moral and spiritual consequences of this type of activity could be catastrophic.

Changing perceptions of reality

Virtual sex is just one subset of computer-mediated communication that allows a person to exist in a virtual world. If this type of activity becomes normative, it could blur the distinction between "reality" and "virtuality" for those involved. Howard Rheingold, who has for the most part an optimistic outlook on virtual life, shares this concern for the future: "It's when we forget about the illusion that the trouble begins. When the technology itself grows powerful enough to make the illusions increasingly realistic, as the Net promises to do within the next ten to twenty years, the necessity for continuing to question reality grows even more acute" (1994, 299).

More critical personal issues are those dealing with self-image and relationships. Relationships in general could be perceived solely as commodities, and self-image could come largely from computer interaction. How will virtual existence affect the ways a person perceives commitment to others? How will a commodity mentality in relationships affect a personal relationship and commitment to Jesus Christ or to the church? How will the perception of reality or worldview for those who spend time in virtual communities be affected?

The virtual response

As a segment of society chooses to exist in virtual worlds, Christian mission will need to enter this context to introduce Christ to those living there. One of our first tasks will be understanding the culture and the people in it.

As missionaries we will need to see beyond the devices and into the people. We must ask questions that address the root causes that compel people to choose virtual worlds over the real world. Some simply see virtual reality as a form of entertainment and can traverse the boundaries of "real" and virtual life with little difficulty. Others may simply see this as a new tool for effective communication in education or business. For yet another group, virtual existence may be a means of escape from issues too difficult to face. When human-computer interaction becomes an unhealthy means of escaping reality, the church will need to walk into this fragile world and represent Christ and his wholeness.

The missional use of this medium does not assume endorsement of virtual living, just as Jesus was not endorsing tax extortion when staying in the house of a tax collector (Luke 19:5). It does mean that our concern for the spiritual and emotional well-being of others will need to surpass our prejudices, ethnocentrism or even fear of the medium.

The spiritual health of the missionary will be critical in this context. Non-Christians must be able to see that our self-esteem is built upon the love Jesus has for us as we share the gospel message in this medium. We should be careful not to make the mistake of leaving this mission field to Christians who are likewise dysfunctionally hiding in an unreal world. This task calls for whole people who, for the sake of the gospel, can enter virtual worlds without losing their grip on life in the real world.

A contextual approach to mission in cyber-space

Our missional approach must match the context in which we minister. This is the heart of contextualization. If we want to witness to those in an urban context, we must adopt and learn their communication systems. We will need to use virtual tools and virtual communication to witness to those in a virtual context. Quentin Schultze, professor of media and communication theory, notes that "our task as Christians, I believe, is to claim every new medium for Christ. If a new medium comes along, we should use it. Of course, all of the tough questions are in the decisions about *how* to use it" (1996).

The same technology that can be used to simulate human sexual experiences could bring some of the most powerful representations of the gospel that we have ever seen. The entire Bible could be translated as a virtual-reality experience. From a mission theory standpoint, this would most likely bring the concept of dynamic-equivalence into levels that previously could not have been imagined. Time and effort spent on some very large virtual-reality projects could produce some astounding "special effects" and virtual experiences as a means of presenting the Christian message.

Another evangelistic possibility is establishing a Christian presence in regular chat groups. Time spent interacting with people in an interest area, whether poetry, stamp collecting or the Urdu language, presents opportunities to develop relationships and witness for Christ.

The possibility of planting virtual churches must also be considered. Technically speaking, a church on the Internet could do some things real churches could only dream of. Automatic attendance records and computer checks could be performed to make sure that those absent are cared

for. In the case of someone who is sick or has undergone a personal tragedy, church members who live close by in the "real" world could be con-
tacted for help. This presumes the church can function simultaneously
in the real and virtual worlds.

The nature of computer-simulated worship would most likely be quite
different from anything we have ever seen before. Expository preaching
and storytelling would most likely take a back seat to virtual worship
experiences. Consider the traditional Palm Sunday service. Instead of
seeing palm branches brought down an aisle by church members, cyber-
worshipers could stand with a computer-generated crowd and shout,
"Hosanna! Hosanna! Hosanna in the highest!" as they look and see Jesus
entering Jerusalem. They could be in the crowd at the feeding of the
5,000. They could witness the betrayal of Judas and later stand beneath
Jesus on the cross and weep in the midst of our Savior's pain.

A word of caution

Of course, some might debate to what extent a cyber-church could actually be considered part of the church of Jesus Christ, or cyber-mission a
serious part of taking Christ's message into all the world. What might be
some pitfalls in a missiological use of the Internet?

Issues of cost, travel, culture shock and family separation could be
offered as reasons to validate virtual mission approaches over real-world
approaches. Yet missionaries will face personal challenges in determining
how virtual communication with others affects bonding with the indigenous society, government structures and their own mission agencies.

We should be careful of thinking that a virtual experience alone is
adequate to bring others to Christ. These experiences may have highly
positive effects in communicating the Christian message, but any presentation of the gospel must be coupled with relational involvement by
Christian believers.

The greatest difficulty with the use of this technology is that missions
becomes limited to communication. The ability to heal the sick, feed the
hungry and clothe the poor will never be actions we can do virtually.

In short, there is no replacement for having a physical presence in the
real world. We must not come to the point where mission is solely communication. Communication is a large part of what mission is about, but
eating meals together, assisting in crises and living in a community that
has relational integrity are also critical aspects of mission practice. Virtual mission practice will have its place in virtual contexts, but it cannot
take the place of real mission practice in real contexts.

Technology and the gospel message

While living among the Maasai, I often reflected on my training and experience as an engineer. I found myself questioning the value of Western technology in the Maasai context. We have the technology to move mountains, explore the depths of oceans and walk on the moon, but this very pursuit of technology and "advancement" has often caused us to lose sight of what the Maasai have had all the time—real human community.

The future could be a place where computer-mediated communication becomes a normative means of experiencing societal and personal relationships. This technology has the possibility to complement our lives if it is used wisely. Some may go as far as to say that the upcoming technology will reshape our society into something even better than what the Maasai have. Some even see a cyber-eschatology in this future of switches and buttons, but those who have looked behind the flashing bulbs and circuitry realize technological solutions will not solve societal problems or basic human problems caused by sin and separation from God.

Missiologists of the twenty-first century must prepare carefully to face the needs of the future. Whatever our technology, as Christian missionaries it is our job to present Jesus as the real Savior who can bring real spiritual and real societal wholeness in the various contexts of the world. As we go into all the worlds, real and virtual, we must creatively and gracefully share the message that conveys the reality of what Jesus has done on the cross for all humanity.

Notes

[1] It has been noted that the technological revolution will increase the distance between the "haves" and the "have-nots." While this distancing in itself has tremendous missiological consequences, it is not the focus of this chapter.

[2] The Internet Relay Chat is the Internet version of American On-Line's chat rooms or Compuserve's CB channels.

[3] In 1996, 30,000,000 users with 25 percent growth every three months (Dery 1996, 6).

[4] One other difficult issue lies beyond the scope of this chapter but is already taking on a technological form. This is concern over whether or not the Internet and its use will normalize much of the world's existing cultures due to Western influence of the medium and the technological epistemology behind it. Nearly every author dealing with the Internet and sociology is working on this issue. An

early book written for Christians on this subject is Emerson and Forbes (1989). Talbott (1996) also deals with this.

⁵ *Christianity Today* (April 3, 1995), 78.

⁶ For more information, see http://www.chaco.com/pueblo. The software offered at this site is free for personal use, so you may want to try it (or one of its competitors).

References

Dery, Mark. 1996. *Escape Velocity: Cyberculture at the End of the Century.* New York: Grove Press.

Emerson, Allen, and Cheryl Forbes. 1989. *The Invasion of the Computer Culture: What You Need to Know About the New World We Live in.* Downers Grove, Ill.: InterVarsity Press.

Heim, Michael. 1993. *The Metaphysics of Virtual Reality.* New York: Oxford University Press.

Gates, Bill, with Nathan Myhrvold and Peter Rinearson. 1995. *The Road Ahead.* New York: Viking.

Moore, Dinty W. 1995. *The Emperor's Virtual Clothes: The Naked Truth About Internet Culture.* Chapel Hill, N.C.: Algonquin Books.

Rheingold, Howard. 1992. *Virtual Reality.* New York: Simon & Schuster.

———. 1994. *The Virtual Community: Finding Connection in a Computerized World.* New York: HarperPerennial.

Schultze, Quentin J. 1996. *Internet for Christians: Everything You Need to Start Cruising the Net Today.* Muskegon, Mich.: Gospel Films. [Logos Electronic Version]

Talbott, Steve. 1995. *The Future Does Not Compute: Transcending the Machines in Our Midst.* Sebastopol, Calif.: O'Reilly & Associates.

Turkle, Sherry. 1995. *Life on the Screen: Identity in the Age of the Internet.* New York: Simon & Schuster.

Following the footprints of God

The contribution of narrative to mission theology

NANCY THOMAS

God is a storytelling God. Deeper than this, God is the creator of story, and it is in the context of story that God calls us into mission. God bids us follow his footprints. God asks us to realign our scripts to that of the Protagonist of God's story (mission *of* the Way), to enter deeply into the setting of the story (mission *in* the way), and to do our part in moving the plot forward to its glorious climax (mission *on* the way). These are the narrative tasks of mission theology, as we integrate being, living, working, speaking, reflecting and writing in the many contexts of the world. The hope of the authors of this book is that we have been able to model this process.

Narrative theology is one of the most exciting developments in Western theology in the last several decades, yet it has not often been considered in the domain of missiology. We want to correct that perception.

Narrative, of course, refers to story. Its crucial elements are characters who move through time and space, confronting obstacles and advancing toward resolution. Narrative theology has been called "discourse

Nancy J. Thomas served with the Friends Church in Bolivia for 18 years, where her work revolved around church planting, leadership training and encouraging Bolivian writers. A writer herself, she has published several volumes of poetry and writes regularly for magazines and devotional booklets. Nancy's Ph.D. research, completed in 1998, focuses on training writers in the Two-Thirds World to write according to their own unique styles and perceptions. She and her husband, Hal, have two children and a growing number of grandchildren.

about God in the setting of story" (Fackre 1983, 343). It combines form
(narrative) with content (theology) in a creative way that seeks to understand God and God's dealings with the human race in terms of events
that have happened, conflicts that have been resolved, people who have
been transformed—in short, in terms of stories.[1]

One of the limitations of narrative theology as it has developed in the
West is that the combination of narrative form with theological content
has often left out the area of context. The writings of some theologians
in majority-world contexts challenge this limitation.[2] A narrative
missiology would look at the storied interaction of form, content and
context—as people live out their stories of transformation in the specific
contexts of their own cultures and faith communities. Thus, missiology
has much it could add to enrich the concept of narrative theology. And
narrative as a discipline and methodology has much to offer missiology.[3]

The essays in this collection have approached mission theology narratively, integrating personal story, community story, cultural story and
biblical narrative in ways appropriate to the context and issues of each
writer. Missiological thinking is a narrative process.

The categories of a narrative missiology include canonical story, life
story (both autobiography and biography), community story (stories of
faith community and stories of culture), fiction, and the traditional myths,
legends and other folktales that interweave in the background of the cultures of the world.[4] An evangelical narrative missiology would hold canonical story as normative, letting the stories of Scripture interweave
with the stories of culture and stories of mission.

Narrative and mission

The connections between story and mission are compelling. Narrative
helps us to understand the goal, motivation, agents and means of mission.

Narrative and the goal of mission

The goal of mission is to make God's saving grace available to all the
peoples of the world. This includes opportunities for each people group
to hear the gospel message in ways it can understand, to become part of
the church as it would express itself in that culture, to see the kingdom of
God working on all levels of the culture, and to begin to participate, in
turn, with God in God's ongoing mission in the world. To follow the
footprints of God.

Communication lies at the heart of God's mission. For mission to be fulfilled, to reach its goal, it is necessary to communicate God's message in ways that make sense in each specific context. This is where narrative comes in, as perhaps the most natural and compelling form of communication.

We learn about God's missional goal through the scriptural narratives. God has communicated with us narratively, through the stories of the Creation, the calling of Abraham, the raising up of a people to be a light to the nations, the sending of God's own Son to redeem and call out a people, and the commissioning of that people to be part of God's mission in the world. The Great Commission is given to us in the setting of story. It is a narrative commission, based on the story of all that has gone before in the history of God's work in, among and through the peoples of the world. It is a mid-story commission, asking us, along with the original disciples, to become characters in the drama, to move the plot forward to the ending when all peoples, tongues and nations will gather around the throne. And the ending of that story only means the beginning of another narrative whose nature we can only guess. But we know it will be good.

It is toward this end that mission moves us. We can most clearly understand the goal of God's mission in the world when we understand it as story.

Narrative and the motivation for mission

We love because God first loved us. And, similarly, we are motivated to go out in mission as we understand the story, and know the reality of Jesus Christ, sent to be our salvation, and telling us, "So send I you. Become part of my story." This is mission of the Way. The story of God's saving work in the world through Jesus Christ, as recorded in Scripture, provides the motivation for mission. Christ's imperatives to his church— "Go; preach; baptize; make disciples"—are given in a narrative context, as part of a missional metanarrative. Really, this is the greatest story going on, overshadowing all our smaller stories, giving meaning to our stories as we offer our sufferings, struggles and sorrows to God to be redeemed for God's use.

Second, our own stories motivate us to mission, as we see how God has graciously moved in our lives, has forgiven, redeemed and transformed us. I was not raised in a Christian home, but my parents thought it good that their three children get some wholesome religion, so when I was seven years old my mom began taking us to a Quaker church. (My parents were drawn in this direction because they knew the stories of how the Quakers worked for prison reform, treated the Indians well in Pennsylvania and began the underground railroad.) In that small Quaker Sunday school I first learned the story of salvation, and when I was nine I decided it made good sense to ask Jesus into my heart, as they talked about in Sunday school. This happened one summer during brush fire season, with my intense fear of fire spurring me on. Hell did not at all sound like a cool idea. So I very simply, without telling anyone or asking for help, said the little formula one night, and Jesus became my friend. He's been my friend ever since.

As I got to college, I slowly became interested in what God was doing in other parts of the world. I loved languages, literature of other countries, anthropology. One night in prayer I simply (all the big moments in my life have somehow been simple and quiet) asked God if he would let me be a missionary. I quietly heard God tell me, "Yes."

My story is not dramatic. But it is full of grace and gentle transformations. God's ways of loving me, of working out all the details for good, of going before me, of surrounding me with loving kindness (mostly in the form of the people God brings into my life)—all of this makes me want to please God, to connect my life with God's purposes in the world, to follow God's footprints. My personal narrative motivates me for mission.

Community narrative also motivates us for mission. In that little Quaker church, and later in a Quaker college, not only did I hear the narratives of Scripture, I learned the stories of George and Margaret Fell Fox, of John Woolman, and John Joseph Gurney, of Elizabeth Fry and many others. I learned how Mary Fisher, a contemporary of George Fox in the 1600s, decided God was telling her to travel to Turkey and tell the gospel story to the sultan. I learned about Elizabeth Fry's calling in the 1700s to minister to prisoners in England and to fight for prison reform. She made a tremendous impact on the British penal system. I learned about Juan Abel, a Quaker Native American, who felt a call to go to South America and work among the Aymara peoples, thus beginning a work that today has over 250 congregations in Bolivia and Peru.

I learned I was part of an exciting story of people listening to God, obeying God, following God in a mission that integrated spiritual ministry with cleaning up prison conditions, showing justice to indigenous peoples, freeing slaves and planting better strains of corn. The story of my own faith community motivates me to mission.

Beyond denomination, stories of the greater faith community motivate us and provide models of thinking and acting theologically in mission. Mother Teresa, Karl Barth, Ernesto Cardenal, David Lim, Max Warren, Jacób Jocz and many others bid us join them in following the footprints of God.

Finally, the narratives of people around the world motivate us to mission. These are stories of brokenness and pain. Stories of people in the cities of Africa, longing for community. Stories of children on the streets of Los Angeles, of tribal peoples in the jungles of Brazil, of oppressed peoples in India and Nicaragua. Stories of people who need our Savior. The compassion of Christ must move us to listen deeply to the stories of people who need him. This leads to the next section, that of the agents of mission as people who listen to stories.

Narrative and agents of mission

Agents of mission, those people who intentionally cross boundaries (whether within or across national borders) to enable people to respond to God's saving grace, must attend to narrative. Agents of mission, first of all, must be listeners to story. Every culture has its stories, as does every person. We need to learn to listen missiologically to the myths of a people, as well as to the proverbs, animal tales and other legends that give clues to their values, longings and heritage.[5]

The Aymara, for example, have an old story about Tunupa, the son of the Creator God, sent to earth to walk among people and teach them the right way to live. He wears a long white robe, teaches, confronts and does miracles. He is persecuted by several evil shamen. Once, left bloodied in the road, he appeared in the village the next day, whole and again ready to preach. He is finally killed by a powerful shaman, his body tied to a reed boat and set loose in Lake Titicaca. As it floats away, it opens up a new river and eventually forms a new lake. This is the origin of what is today called the Desaguadero River and Lake Poopo.

The Mormons have taken this story and proclaimed that Jesus is Tunupa. Evangelicals have ignored it. But there is much to learn from the old myths. We see here a belief that God wants to communicate with people and a precedent for sending a son. Other stories and customs point out themes of reconciliation, transformation, harmony, redemption—longings and values deep within the Aymara soul.

Missionaries must also attend to the history of a people. Gustavo Gutiérrez emphasizes this, finding the source of Latin American spirituality in the history of the suffering of a people who are somehow aliens on their own.[6] As people let their story weave with the stories of Scripture, with their present daily struggles, the theology that emerges offers the hope of changing that history, of adding new chapters of redemption, transformation and participation as agents of mission in the ongoing story. Missionaries, as agents of mission, need to be sensitive listeners to all these stories of a people.

Agents of mission also need to be tellers of story. As they learn from the stories of people, they introduce the stories of Scripture, starting with stories that best connect with the people. Often this means beginning in the Old Testament or with the story of Jesus. Stories of how God has compassion on people on the margin, people who have suffered in similar ways, stories of how God loves and redeems and transforms not only individuals but cultures and societies. The whole field of narrative theology proposes that human beings learn more and learn better about God through story than through any other way. Combined with proposition, with proverb, with other ways of communication—narrative is a powerful tool for communication.

Agents of mission need to be narrative in another way, a way that goes deeper than verbal communication (as important as that is). Agents of mission need to have a narrative way of being with the people among whom they minister. This is the heart of incarnational mission. It goes beyond listening to the story of a people and empathizing with their reality of suffering. It means entering into their story, living with them, experiencing conflicts and suffering, becoming, as it were, a character in the plot. It means forming genuine relationships, walking alongside. Not just reading the story. Becoming part of it. This is mission in the way. We have the example of Jesus, who put on skin, ate bread, walked dusty roads with common laborers, held children on his lap, bled on a cross.[7]

Narrative as a means of mission

Narrative has naturally to do with means. Narrative is form. It is a way of being and a way of doing that uses story to learn about God and God's relationship with people—and to articulate that understanding in a way that makes sense to people, that allows them to enter the plot. It is a way of communication that is naturally integrative and holistic, naturally connected with life as it is lived in the kitchens and fields, conference rooms, bedrooms and church buildings of real people all over the world. Narrative allows people to translate the grace and forgiveness and transforming work of God (which could all be presented propositionally) into their own life situations. It is mission on the way.

In a sense, I have touched on narrative as a means of mission in all the above sections. It is the way we come to understand the goal of mission, the way we connect this goal to our own lives in personal motivation, and the way we come to understand the receptor culture, communicate in it and live among its people as agents of mission. Narrative provides a way of understanding and uniting the goals, motivations, agents and means of mission.

The best way to demonstrate this is to tell a story. Toyohiko Kagawa continues to inspire, amaze and humble me. He demonstrated a narrative way of being among a people, as well as a narrative way of making God's grace an option to his people as he communicated with them.

Born to a Buddhist family at the end of the nineteenth century, young Kagawa became a Christian through the influence of two Presbyterian missionaries who had opened their home to high school students wanting to learn English. Disinherited by his family following his conversion, Kagawa attended Meiji Gakiun, a Presbyterian college in Tokyo. While there his Christianity took on a strong social conscience. He often irritated school authorities by doing such things as inviting beggars into his dorm room for shelter and a meal.[8]

At the age of nineteen, Kagawa enrolled in Kobe Theological Seminary, but he soon grew restless with conventional seminary education. He had begun ministering in the notorious slums of Kobe during weekends. After a time of internal conflict, he decided to quit school, pack up his possessions and move into the slums to live out the love of Jesus among the poor.

On Christmas day, 1919, Kagawa pulled a cart with his few books, blankets, cooking utensils and clothes across the bridge that separated the "safe" part of the city from the dangers of the slums. Thus began a chapter in his life that was to eventually turn Toyohiko Kagawa into one of the most prophetic and influential Christian leaders Japan has ever known. He established Sunday schools, worship services, schools and cooperatives for people in the slums. On a national level he was influential, especially in the labor movement, helping legalize unions and working to alleviate conditions that lead to slums such as Shinkawa.

In the evenings Kagawa wrote. Over a span of 50 years of ministry, Kagawa left his country a legacy of 150 titles, works that included novels, poetry, plays, social commentary, theological exposition and children's stories. But it was his life of incarnational mission, his entering into the narrative of the people, that gave his words on paper power to change lives and institutions.

Across the Death Line, one of Kagawa's first published books and one of his all time best sellers, was, interestingly enough, a novel.[9] He deeply desired to make following Jesus Christ an option for Japanese people, and narrative writing was one of his means to reach this goal. He chose to use the most popular genre of his day, the autobiographical novel. Although the novel was fiction, it was "fiction" that told Kagawa's own story of disillusionment, conversion and subsequent dedication to living in the slums and ministering God's love in that situation. Although details differed, people knew this was Kagawa's story. It was a culturally unique and appropriate way of giving a personal Christian testimony in a land where Christians were in a decided minority. Because it was backed by Kagawa's own exemplary life, it had unusual impact and remained a best seller for several years.[10] Kagawa used a culturally accepted means to preach (without preaching!) the gospel.

Kagawa followed the aesthetic standards of his society. *Across the Death Line* demonstrates Japanese values of suggestion (showing the gospel through story rather than telling it directly), simplicity (simple structure, a simplicity in scenes and characters, for example, a focus on a flower, the smile of a child, light coming through a window), asymmetry or incompleteness (ending the story without resolution to the protagonist's court case or his romance, but simply showing him at peace, waiting to see what God will do), and perishability (scenes of death, fallen leaves, a sense of the briefness of human life). He used the communication styles and values of the people for whom he wrote.

As contextual as his writing was, Kagawa crafted his missiological narrative so it would not only value the norms and views of the culture, but also challenge them when that was appropriate. Kagawa not only adapted the value that sees perishability as beautiful, but he challenged it at the deep level of his novel. His theme is the triumph of life over death, and through the narrative he shows the protagonist's choice for life. He shows—not tells—how the life that Jesus offers transforms people, bringing laughter (as opposed to the tears of death), peace (in contrast to noise and confusion), light (in contrast to dark despair) into individual lives and relationships. He shows how the life of Jesus transforms social institutions, bringing light and laughter and hope into the slums. Without directly saying, "Here is something better, something more beautiful than death," Kagawa narratively shows how Christ's life works out in the lives of the protagonists and in the setting of the slums of Shinkawa.

Kagawa's narrative intentions were holistic and integrative, seeing salvation in Christ as applicable on both the spiritual and material levels, for individuals and for societies. Indeed, one of the results of the book was a new awareness among the Japanese middle class of the plight of lower-class laborers and people in the slums. This, along with Kagawa's political work, eventually resulted in changes in housing and labor laws.

So then, narrative becomes a means of mission—a way of learning about a culture and listening to its people and, as Toyohiko Kagawa demonstrates, a way of being in a culture and of communicating at a deep level the truths of God's saving grace to that culture. The listening, the doing, the saying and the being—all these vital parts unite in a narrative missiology.

The power of narrative

As a missionary to the Aymara peoples, I determined early to learn the Aymara language so that when I taught the women's classes I wouldn't have to use an interpreter. I met this goal and developed a series of classes on all sorts of biblical topics. Some were narrative, some were not.

When I returned recently to Bolivia to do research, woman after woman came up to me, kissed me, and said, "You were the one who told us about the little red hen." "I remember the story of the red hen." "You taught us to work hard like the little red hen." No one mentioned my lessons on the Christian family, the classes on the Holy Spirit, my admonitions on prayer. I had become known as the woman who told the little red hen story.

I remember that class well, and the attention and laughter that accompanied it as I wove the American folktale of the busy hen whose friends would not help her with biblical teaching on working together in the church. At the time I didn't realize how this story fit in with the cultural themes of reciprocity and balance, or how similar it was to their own animal folktales. The power of narrative as a communicative tool amazed and continues to amaze me.

But beyond the communicative value of narrative in mission, narrative as a methodology provides a key to missiological reflection. Mission theology calls us to approach our task as doers and as thinkers. Linking mission and theology demands servants who are deeply centered in Scripture and in the Christ of Scripture (mission *of* the Way), committed to knowing and living among the cultures of the world (mission *in* the way), able to engage in the process of bringing together the worlds of biblical, personal and cultural truth as God's kingdom manifests itself (mission *on* the way). Narrative may be key to this integrating process.

And somehow narrative adds life, joy and vitality to the process of thinking theologically in mission. It relates learning to life, connects missiology to the real-world context it belongs to. Writing narratively, speaking narratively, learning narratively, being narratively in the world— all as we're living out our part in God's story. This is what it means to follow God's footprints.

Notes

[1] For an overview of the field of narrative theology, see Goldberg (1991), McGrath (1991) and Van Engen (1996, 44–68).

[2] See, for example, Gutiérrez (1984), Koyama (1974), and Song (1984, 1986, 1991).

[3] See especially Van Engen's essay on the interaction between narrative and missiology (1996, 44–68).

[4] For biography as narrative theology, see McClendon (1974). For the intersection between theology and community story, see Goldberg (1991) and Cone (1975). Kort (1975) writes on the contribution of fiction to theology. For the interface between myth, folktale and theology see May (1991), Song (1984, 1991), Tarr (1994), and Healey and Sybertz (1996).

[5] See Koyama (1974), Song (1984, 1991), Tarr (1994), and Healey and Sybertz (1996).

[6] Gutiérrez emphasizes the importance of history to theology (1984). See also the chapters by Rodriguez and Lee in this volume.

[7] The chapters in this book on the incarnational ministries of Ernesto Cardenal (N. Thomas) and Mother Teresa (Tiersma Watson) illustrate this.

[8] Source on the life and times of Kagawa is Davey (1960).

[9] Although Kagawa wrote the novel in Japanese, it came out serially in an English language newspaper before being published as a novel in Japanese (1920).

[10] The first edition was sold out in the first month, and eight reprints were required in the first months of 1921. By 1924 Thomas Satchell, the English translator, commented that "the editions have run into hundreds and the book is still selling well. A conservative estimate gives the number of copies sold at a hundred and fifty thousand" (1924, viii). The publishers of the 1924 translation of the book into English claimed that the first English translation "met with a huge sale that approximated half a million copies in Japan and the East" (Kagawa 1924, v).

References

Cone, James H. 1975. *God of the Oppressed.* New York: Seabury Press.

Davey, Cyril J. 1960. *Kagawa of Japan.* London: Epworth Press.

Fackre, Gabriel. 1983. "Narrative Theology: An Overview." *Interpretation: A Journal of Bible and Theology* 37, no. 4: 340–51.

Goldberg, Michael. 1991. *Theology and Narrative: A Critical Introduction.* Philadelphia: Trinity Press International.

Gutiérrez, Gustavo. 1984. *We Drink from Our Own Wells: The Spiritual Journey of a People,* trans. Matthew J. O'Connell. Maryknoll, N.Y.: Orbis Books. (Originally published in Spanish in 1983.)

Healey, Joseph, and Donald Sybertz. 1996. *Towards an African Narrative Theology.* Maryknoll, N.Y.: Orbis Books.

Kagawa, Toyohiko. 1924. *Before the Dawn,* trans. Thomas Satchell and I. Fukumoto. New York: George H. Doran Company. (Originally published in Japanese in 1920. Literal translation of title: *Across the Death Line.*)

Kort, Wesley A. 1975. *Narrative Elements and Religious Meanings.* Philadelphia: Fortress Press.

Koyama, Kosuke. 1974. *Waterbuffalo Theology.* Maryknoll, N.Y.: Orbis Books.

May, Rollo. 1991. *The Cry for Myth.* New York: Delta.

McClendon, James W. 1974. *Biography as Theology: How Life Stories Can Remake Today's Theology.* Nashville, Tenn.: Abingdon Press.

McGrath, Alister E. 1991. "The Biography of God." *Christianity Today* 35, no. 8: 22–24.

Satchell, Thomas. 1924. "Preface." In Toyohiko Kagawa, *Before the Dawn.* New York: George H. Doran Company.

Song, C. S. 1984. *Tell Us Our Names: Story Theology from an Asian Perspective.* Maryknoll, N.Y.: Orbis Books.

———. 1986. *Theology from the Womb of Asia.* Maryknoll, N.Y.: Orbis Books.

———. 1991. *Third Eye Theology: Theology in Formation in Asian Settings.* Maryknoll, N.Y.: Orbis Books.

Tarr, Del. 1994. *Double Image: Biblical Insights from African Parables.* New York: Paulist Press.

Van Engen, Charles. 1996. "The Importance of Narrative Theology." In *Mission on the Way: Issues in Mission Theology.* Grand Rapids, Mich.: Baker Book House.

World Vision

Other New Titles from World Vision Publications

God of the Empty-Handed: Poverty, Power and the Kingdom of God by Jayakumar Christian.

Christian, who has worked among the poor in India for more than 30 years, explores the relationship of poverty to powerlessness, masterfully integrating anthropology, sociology, politics and theology. He avoids easy answers; instead he offers a new paradigm that can shape our responses to the poor and provide a workable framework for grassroots practitioners. 224 pp. **$21.95**

Walking With the Poor: Principles and Practices of Transformational Development by Bryant L. Myers.

The author says those who want to alleviate poverty need to walk with the poor, see their reality, and then look for solutions. He explores Christian views of poverty and looks at how it is experienced in different cultures. Draws on theological and biblical resources as well as secular development theory and practice to develop a theoretical framework for working alongside the poor. 288 pp. **$21.95**

Working With the Poor: New Insights and Learnings from Development Practitioners, Bryant L. Myers, editor.

Christian development practitioners explore how to express holistic transformational development. As they struggle to overcome the problem of dualism, they articulate a genuinely holistic approach to helping the poor. 192 pp. **$16.95**

Toll Free in the U.S.: 1-800-777-7752

Direct: (626) 301-7720

Web: www.marcpublications.com

World Vision Publications • 800 W. Chestnut Ave. • Monrovia, CA • 91016

Ask for a complete publications catalog and free missions newsletter

---